John Walsh was born in 1953 in London, and was educated at Wimbledon College, Exeter College, Oxford and University College, Dublin. He has been at various times features editor of the *Evening Standard*, literary editor of the *Sunday Times* and the editor of the *Independent Magazine*. He is currently assistant editor of the *Independent*. A prolific critic and cultural commentator, he has written for the *New Yorker*, *Vanity Fair*, *Q*, *Mojo* and *Word* magazine. He was director of the Cheltenham Festival of Literature in 1997 and 1998 and presented *Books & Company* for three years on Radio 4, where he can still be heard on the popular quiz show *The Write Stuff*. His previous book is the acclaimed memoir *The Falling Angels*. He lives in Dulwich with the journalist Carolyn Hart and their three children, Sophie, Max and Clementine.

'Walsh is spot on in recognising the enormous – if subconscious – impact films can have on the adolescent mind . . . we owe Walsh a big thank-you'
JAMES DELINGPOLE, *Daily Mail*

'Spot on in catching the mood of specific times and places . . . It's written with immense self-effacing charm, and honesty as stinging as a splash of cheap aftershave before your first dance. Nick Hornby did it for football, but Walsh's wince-making experiences exist in everyone's shared past.'
CHRISTOPHER FOWLER, *Independent on Sunday*

'As well as being an extremely funny book, it possesses an abundance of charm . . . It is well-nigh impossible to imagine it not appealing to any-one who has ever grown up, or ever been to the cinema, or ever shut their eyes and imagined their own silhouette dancing away – however briefly – at the end of a beam of light.'
JOHN PRESTON, *Sunday Telegraph*

'The great strength of *Are You Talking To Me?* is that you really do feel that Walsh is communicating with the reader . . . richly nostalgic'
HUGH MASSINGBERD, *Mail on Sunday*

'It is nice to revisit well-loved films . . . Walsh writes so well that it is a pleasure to be in [...]D, *Irish Times*

D1151254

_____

By the same author

The Falling Angels

JOHN WALSH

Are You Talking to Me?

A Life Through the Movies

HARPER PERENNIAL

Harper Perennial
An imprint of HarperCollins*Publishers*
77–85 Fulham Palace Road, Hammersmith, London W6 8JB

www.harpercollins.co.uk/harperperennial

This edition published by Harper Perennial 2004

First published by HarperCollins*Publishers* 2003

Little Boxes Words and music by Malvina Reynolds © 1962 Schroder Music
Co., (ASCAP). Renewed 1990. Used by permission. All rights reserved.

Jean Genie Words and music by David Bowie © 1973. Reproduced by permission of EMI Music Publishing Ltd/Moth Music; Chrysalis Music Ltd; and
Tintorreto Music administered by RZO Music Inc for the USA and Canada
and by RZO Music Ltd for the World excluding the USA and Canada.

There is Nothin' Like a Dame
Words Oscar Hammerstein II/music Richard Rodgers.
© 1949 Williamson Music International. Reproduced by permission of
EMI Music Publishing Ltd, London WC2H OQY.

Although we have tried to contact all copyright holders before publication,
this has not been possible in every case. If notified, the publisher will be
pleased to make any necessary arrangements to rectify errors and omissions
at the earliest opportunity.

Set in Bembo by Palimpsest Book Production Limited, Polmont, Stirlingshire
Printed and bound in Great Britain by Clays Ltd, St Ives plc

This book is dedicated, with fond affection,
to Giles Brody – nephew, godson, film buff,
crazed Tarantino fan, precociously talented script-writer
and future movie director – hoping it will demonstrate that
you don't have to be Samuel L. Jackson *all* the time . . .

CONTENTS

ACKNOWLEDGEMENTS

This book is essentially a work of dramatised memory rather than of research, and it could not have been completed without the prompting and collaboration of many friends, especially Harry Armfield, Paul Thimont, Philip Kerr, Chris Dawes and Chris ('A nation waits, dear boy . . .') Hirst. Special thanks are due to Tim and Katrin Williams, who read the manuscript, at its most inchoate and undisciplined stage, in the blazing heat of a shared Greek holiday, and were both supportive and bracingly critical. Without the initial enthusiasm and constant encouragement of Michael Fishwick from HarperCollins, it would never have got anywhere, while the late interventions of Charles Drazin – the most tactful of editors – stopped it from becoming a baggy, what-I-know-about-the-movies rant, and got it back on track. I'd like to thank my consort, Carolyn Hart, for sending me off to the coal-face of my garden shed to just get *on* with it, and my children, Sophie, Max and Clementine, for enduring, without complaint, the sight of their father slumped before a hundred videos of apparently meaningless old movies, allegedly in the throes of creativity. Lastly, a big thank you to the publishers of *Halliwell's Film Guide, Halliwell's Filmgoer's Companion* and the *Time Out Film Guide*, in whose seductive pages I have happily, serendipitously, lost myself for years.

INTRODUCTION

STRAINING YOUR EYES TO SEE

'From the movies we learn precisely how to hold a champagne flute, kiss a mistress, pull a trigger, turn a phrase . . . but the movies spoil us for life: nothing ever lives up to them'   – Edmund White

You are sitting in the three-and-nine seats at the Granada cinema, Clapham Junction in 1962, with an empty carton of Kia-Ora crushed in your hand, and you are gazing into the horizon of a hazy, golden desert. Your eyes are straining to see what you think you see – what you might be able to see if you craned forward just a bit.

You are oblivious to the other people around you in this cut-price Alhambra Palace in south London. But even if you could register that 300 other people are sitting beside you, staring at the screen, you couldn't believe they can see what you're seeing. The experience you're going through is wholly individual. Your eyes are – surely? – the only eyes capable of picking out the tiny dot on the horizon.

The film is David Lean's *Lawrence of Arabia*. It's not ideal entertainment for an eight-year-old. It's full of men in military uniforms telling each other what's what in the First World War, and talking about the Turks and a prince called

Faisal. The hero is a pale, blue-eyed, extremely odd fellow called Lawrence whose party trick is to extinguish matches with his bare fingers without squealing with pain. He is cheeky to everyone, even to murderous-looking Arabs in black robes. He rides a camel like a ninny, though, stretching forward over the camel's neck, waving a stick like someone trying to conduct an orchestra.

At this point in the film, he and fifty men in long skirts and head-shawls have crossed a huge desert called 'The Sun's Anvil'. Suddenly, Lawrence notices a riderless camel loping along the boiling sands, and decides they must go back for the fallen rider. The skirt-and-shawl brethren argue that the guy is probably dead by now, but Lawrence doesn't listen. He sets off, bravely, suicidally, to rescue the man, while the others continue their journey to a nearby oasis. Watching them go is Lawrence's young servant, who sticks around on the edge of the desert, waiting for his return. You are with him. You are waiting and watching beside him. Together you inspect the desert horizon, flat and shimmering and empty. The waiting servant, on the edge of nowhere, snoozes in the heat – but suddenly he is awake and alert, and can apparently see something. You look at the horizon again, flat and shimmering and – is that a fleck of something? What is he looking at? What are *you* looking at? Is that a tiny interruption in the hazy nothingness, a speck like a single grain of pepper in the soup of earth and sky? As you look at the horizon, you start to become the boy on the camel, you widen your eyes so they can see more clearly, willing the speck to become a man coming out of the desert, you sit forward in your seat as if bidding the seat to move. As the servant rides forward, picking up speed until the camel is racing along, your heart races alongside him, until you are running with him into the middle of nowhere, racing the kid to get there first, to see the unimaginable sight before he does.

The tiny speck in the distance gets larger, more defined, more vertical, until it's a small wobbling figure – and the camera cuts away, to disclose a triumphant full view of Lawrence on his camel. They're running at full tilt, the saintly rider waving his camel-urging stick like a magic baton, and the Arab guy he has rescued (hurrah!) has his arms round his saviour's waist, clinging on, the way a nervous passenger might embrace a speed-crazed biker manipulating a Harley-Davidson down the New Jersey Turnpike.

It's a brilliant rescue sequence, and one of the most visually involving scenes in film history because it makes you stretch your eyes to the horizon. It plays games with your assumptions about what exactly you can see on the screen when you think you're being shown everything. It's also a big moral schoolboy lesson – that going back for your fallen mates is the only right and decent thing to do, even when logic dictates that you might die as a result. But there is more to come.

Not long after the rescue, Lawrence and his Bedouin brothers are camped outside Akaba, which they plan to invade the next morning. Akaba is a distant necklace glow of light on the horizon. Lawrence and his swarthy pals discuss tactics until interrupted by a single gunshot. One Arab has just killed another Arab from a rival tribe, just at the moment when the tribes are meant to be pulling together for the attack. He must be punished, publicly, by death. But (we quickly learn) if a fellow Arab kills him, it will be the start of a terrible internecine vendetta. He must, therefore, be killed by someone from outside the tribes.

Lawrence proposes himself as the executioner and, as he adjusts his huge revolver, the camera closes in on the bowed head of the doomed prisoner. He lifts his face, and – as the camera itself seems shocked to discover – it's the man Lawrence rescued in the desert.

He can't – can he? – possibly shoot a man whose life he saved. You admire Lawrence for diplomatically offering his services, but you know he can't possibly kill the guy. Something will happen, you just know – some kindly intervention at the last moment will . . .

But then Lawrence's eyes take on a cruel gleam, and you can almost see his heart hardening. He fires six times, and kills his former friend, for whom he braved certain death the day before; kills him with single-minded efficiency. And you never get over the shock that he could do such a thing.

Here were two scenes of entrancement: one a classic bit of *Boy's Own Paper* derring-do, the hero going back to rescue a stricken comrade in the teeth of warnings and mockery and the threat of the Desert of Death; the other, a moment of grown-up horror, as the hero summarily kills the man he saved. For the eight-year-old viewer, these two scenes – just five minutes apart – offered fantastically conflicting signals. One said simply: you look after your mates when they're in trouble, no matter what the odds. The other said: you may have to kill your mates if it's strategically necessary, because of some bewildering higher good called 'Akaba'.

Picture, if you will, the palpitating kid in the stalls. I remember being shocked by these contrasting moral lessons, exhilarated by the former and outraged by the latter. The five minutes of film-time that separated them represented, in hindsight, the transition from a schoolboy's to a grown-up's view of the world. I didn't care for what I saw of the latter, but I now knew it existed – Grown-up Land, a place full of stern logic and chilly compromise. And these two scenes got under my skin because they were presented in a way I'd never experienced before, on stage, book or screen. It was the use of the camera lens – one moment stretching my eyes to the horizon, the next closing in on the doomed man as if asking, 'What are you going to do about this?' – stretching, then closing in on, my awakening consciousness.

Do we learn useful lessons from the cinema? When we're young and impressionable, do we become better or worse people, less moral or more so, more civilised or more brutalised, by being exposed to two hours of celluloid dreams every couple of weeks? Crime psychologists speculate that because a murderer watched a violent film the day before a murder, it may have been a 'spur' or 'spark' that precipitated his actions – as if murder were the result of terrible how-to knowledge or dumb bovine imitation, rather than terrible will. Other people will insist that film (like poetry, according to W.H. Auden) makes nothing at all happen, apart from changing the way some people buy clothes after seeing *Annie Hall* or *The Matrix*. I've always been convinced that the cinema is a universe of mostly benign influences, and that it educates us by the simple act of showing us other lives in spectacular close-up.

Here's another example. When I was twelve, I went to see *His Finest Hour*, a glowing hagiography of Winston Churchill, made to coincide with his ninetieth birthday. I was impressed with the historical stuff, the massing of troops and the making of speeches, but it didn't make me understand about love of country, or whatever that thing is that made men go off and die for England, home and beauty. You could attend a three-hour lecture on the wonderfulness of England and Englishness, about honey for tea and pints of beer on cricket greens, about vicars and seaside vulgarity, and you might be charmed by it all, but what did it have to do with dying for your country, with that fantastic, logical, voluntary swapping of everything the world brought you every day – the sunshine on the houses in your street, the procession of raindrops down a window, the lazy collapse of a log in the living-room fire – for some dimly-imagined ideal of patriotism?

But then you'd see *Casablanca* and understand it perfectly. It's the scene everyone remembers: the Germans in neutral

Casablanca have taken to hanging out at Rick's 'Bar Americain', drinking beer and flirting with the local girls. One evening, Victor Laszlo (Paul Heinreid) is in the bar, surveying the officers of the Wehrmacht with contempt. Relaxed and laughing, the Germans start to sing an awful barrel-organy marching song, waving their steins to the rhythm. Laszlo strides over to the dormant orchestra, picks up the conductor's baton and says, 'Play the Marseillaise!'

After a nod from Rick, they do. Some barfly, a Spanish dame with a guitar, starts to sing the words. Others join in. The Germans sing their oompah marching song louder. Laszlo's baton becomes more agitated. The French national anthem gets louder still. The Germans give up and return to their beers with gestures of contempt.

Then the Marseillaise hits the chorus (*'Aux armes, citoyens!'*) and glory breaks out. The beautiful prostitute, who has shamed herself for so long by fraternising with the German generals, jumps to her feet, eyes shining with tears, because of the glory of the singing. When the anthem ends, she suddenly cries *'Vive la France!'* with a kind of instinctive passion. Oh *yes*, you think, and you shout with her, though patriotic love of France is something wholly foreign to you. She is finding something to be proud of. After selling her soul and her body, she is rediscovering the concept of pride, and is on the way to re-finding pride in herself.

And there you find the essence of patriotism. That it isn't a simple love of your native land. It's a love of, or a pride in, yourself, only blown up to a huge, sentimental, national scale.

The irresistible martial swing of the 'Marseillaise' helps, of course, but the scene works because of the faces that the camera cuts between, aglow with longing and desperation and a gleam of resistance. You suddenly realise how the soul of a country might be seen in the faces of its people.

Even in the epic movies that you saw, it was the tiny details, the intimate human scale amid the panoramic action, that made the deepest impression on you. Take that gross, baggy, unstructured, triple-director, hundred-stars monster, *The Longest Day*, which I saw in 1962, when I was just nine. It was a three-hour attempt to make sense of the Normandy landings, but I emerged from the cinema with no clear understanding of how D-Day was meant to have worked, nor whether it had been a success or a terrible tragedy (more the latter, as far as I could see). But some key images stuck in my head.

One was the cake with which the German high command celebrated a general's birthday – the way the Germans sliced it right across the centre, bisecting the whole thing, this way and that, rather than cutting elegant wedges, as one did at English children's birthday parties. It struck me at the time as a typical example of Hunnish perversity.

More potent was the scene in which the lone German soldier discovers the invasion has started. Played by Gert Froebe, the fat militiaman is on lonely sentry duty somewhere above, say, Omaha beach. He is bored, sleepy, looking forward to his breakfast, and soporifically riding a mule up a gentle incline of Normandy cliff, when he turns and looks out to sea. Stretched across the horizon, a vast flotilla of invading landing-craft is cruising straight towards him. Instantly he is a-flurry with activity, falling off his mule, grabbing for his gun, wondering whom to call, worrying about what correct procedure you should adopt when the odds are approximately 500,000 to one against you. While the audience laughed at his panic, I felt for him. Forgetting, for a moment, that I was supposed to be rooting for the Allied forces in the boats, I sympathised with the poor schmuck on the other side, with his limited response materials and his ridiculous donkey.

I think it was this personal connection with an individual

that explains why the parachute-drop scene also haunted me. As the paratroopers fall out of the sky into a French village where the German army is waiting for them, most are killed in mid-air or shortly after landing. Some of the descending parachutists found themselves in farcical circumstances, landing in a tree, or crashing through the roof of a greenhouse. One man went straight down a well, his parachute imploding above him as it disappeared. I remember the yell of laughter that went up in the audience at this bit of slapstick – and then how the laugh changed to a pitying 'Ohhhh'. Soon my eyes were misting up at the fate of another victim. A soldier played by the American comedian Red Buttons came to land on the side of a church, his parachute speared by the steeple. He hung there, hardly daring to breathe, watching the killing going on below him, while the church bell donged and clanged just a few feet away from his ear. Against the odds he survives, but when we meet him later in the film, he is completely deaf.

I could just about cope with the massacre of men falling out of the sky – but this poor man whom the bell had made deaf went straight to my tear ducts. As in the case of Gert Froebe on his stumbling mule, his situation posed the question how *you* would have got on in wartime, how you would have fared. In a departure from the triumphalist, us-against-them glorification of war that I encountered in just about every other war movie I saw, it was a key to understanding the sorrow and the pity.

I grew up mesmerised by the movies. My relationship with the Big Screen was more heady, more intense, more hungrily passionate than my civilised involvement with books, my light flirtations with theatre, my patronising kiss on the forehead of television. Watching films in the dark never seemed to me a passive activity. It was more like visiting a shrine,★ going to a great dark church for prolonged communion and prayer – even if the only prayers were that Clint Eastwood should waste the bad guys in *A Fistful of Dollars*, or that Julie Christie should find true love with Alan Bates in *Far from the Madding Crowd*, or that Kim Novak should, at some point, take her clothes off in *Vertigo*.

Cinematic shrines were everywhere when I was young. I was surrounded by them. On St John's Hill, Battersea, down the road from our house, there were no fewer than three cinemas: the Imperial, the Essoldo and the Granada. The Imperial, despite its grand name, was a fag-reeking little flea-pit where uncouth kids ran about the stalls and there were constant rumours of mice underfoot. The Essoldo was rather grand, a rococo palace of varieties, the kind of place where Robert Donat might have seen Mr Memory in Hitchcock's *The 39 Steps*. The Granada looked boringly municipal, like a bank only with more dramatic lighting, but it had the largest screen and showed the best new films.

Between them, the three picture-houses showed hundreds of movies every year – not just first-run features, but re-runs of old Bogart movies, James Bond double-bills, classic Westerns, Japanese Godzilla movies, cartoon extravaganzas, war films, Biblical epics and slightly moth-eaten romances starring Rock Hudson and Doris Day. The double-bills could yoke together some very odd bedfellows. Who, for instance, would have been the ideal consumer to appreciate both *The Wizard of Oz* and the new Elvis movie,

---

★ J.G. Ballard, speculating about Hollywood's influence on American attitudes to war, came up with a startling theory about movie-worship. 'Any dream that so endures,' he wrote, 'must draw its strength from the deepest survival instincts. The potent spectacle of bright light playing against a high wall taps into something hard-wired in our brains – memories, perhaps, of the first dawn.'

Roustabout, back-to-back on the same afternoon in 1964?

In the pitch-black cinema, you received occasional glimpses of the grown-up, X-rated world that seemed to lie ahead of you. The Granada was where, aged eleven, I watched a trailer for *A Study in Terror*, James Hill's energetically nasty conflation of Sherlock Holmes and Jack the Ripper. As trailers go (I've always loved trailers), it was a humdinger, a howling farrago of blood, screams, swollen bosoms, knives, gurning costermongers, dirt-streaked Victorian tarts in shadowy alleyways and massive close-ups of John Neville's pinched Sherlockian physiognomy. Minatory banner headlines unwrapped themselves across the screen like a series of flung-down Biblical warning – 'A MANIAC IS ON THE LOOSE!'; 'TERROR STALKS THE STREETS' – and left me badly shaken, as my trembling fingers searched for another orange cream.

My Battersea friends, my sister and I haunted the cinemas at weekends and in the school holidays. Sometimes we'd sit in the stalls without caring much what film was showing. We'd go into a double-bill of second-rate spy movies, half an hour after the first one started, blithely uncaring that we'd missed the premise of the whole movie and would have to work out the plot by ourselves. We were content in the knowledge that, in three hours' time, the programme would have rolled round to the point where we'd started. 'This is where we came in,' we would whisper, although we might perhaps stick around for another hour for the exciting bit where somebody blew up a helicopter, or the master spy got to fondle a Swedish cutie in abbreviated swimwear.

We didn't care about narrative coherence. We just liked being shown wonders, and spectacular sights, things we'd never seen before, like the plains of Africa or the lunar bluffs of Monument Valley. We enjoyed the darkness, the crepuscular excitement of the long funnel of smoky light stretching out its fat, tapering glow above our heads. We liked the

Pearl & Dean advertisements, especially the stunningly tacky ones for local restaurants with their still photographs of wanly deserted curry houses: 'After the show, why not visit . . .'

My world in the Sixties remained stuck in a time before the metropolis began to swing – a place of grey streets and rainy puddles and soul-destroyingly dull bus rides to Nowheresville and Loser's Lane. I travelled between school in Wimbledon and my home in the blank, unfriendly back streets of Battersea, where the biggest excitement that stealth or enterprise could buy was to visit Arding & Hobbs department store and travel up in the lift to the third-floor carpet department to ogle the gorgeous, hopelessly unattainable local beauty, Mary McCarthy, as she saucily advised the newly-married about their urgent need for Berber shagpile.

The cinema became our cultural porthole, our window on a Zeitgeist that never seemed to make its way to Battersea, our palace of shadows, our University of Life. It was there we saw Cleopatra float into Rome and El Cid ride out to battle one last time, strapped dead but upright on his horse; it was there we saw the innocent hayseed James Stewart shoot the bullying villain, Lee Marvin, in *The Man Who Shot Liberty Valance*, and the downfall of the enormous German howitzers in *The Guns of Navarone* . . . We spent weeks, months, years watching people completely unlike us emoting and punching, going on safari, carrying out elaborate jewel heists, riding a rickety horse-and-trap through the flames of a burning Atlanta, and falling in love with each other in the middle of a war. How could we have expected to emerge from all that and not be profoundly affected?

You could regard these early movie experiences as just fleeting memories from your childhood, like Desperate Dan or Dan Dare; but some of them made a nagging, intrusive, almost pernicious claim on your consciousness long after they should have been wiped away by the stern blue pencil of time. For years I couldn't work out why, if things were going badly at work, or a threatening Final Demand arrived from the taxman, I would find the words 'Mother of mercy, is this the end of Ricco?' forming, unbidden, in my head. Nor why, as I walked to some job interview or some appearance on a radio show, my hands would twitch involuntarily, and mime the cocking of an imaginary rifle.

What was going on in my mind that hijacked the real world at these moments, and substituted some vivid otherworld in its place?

It required only a little thought to realise that it was the movies I'd seen years before bobbing up to the surface as bits of a counter-life in my mind at moments of crisis, telling me how I should feel, or think, or talk or act. They offered an alternative to the life I was living and tried to persuade me I was someone else. It was a strange form of substitution because it made no sense. I've never known anyone called Ricco, and stopped invoking the name of the mother of God when I was fifteen. I've never owned a firearm and never cocked a real rifle, but when I tried to nail down what was going on in my head at these moments, I discovered I was a) quoting James Cagney in a forgotten gangster film, possibly *The Roaring Twenties*, and b) imitating the final walk-to-glory of William Holden and the last of his gang at the end of *The Wild Bunch*.

The fact that I could still display these behavioural tics many years after seeing the films made me wonder. Were they essentially nostalgic memories of movies I had once enjoyed? Or was something more profound going on – namely, that all my life I had been storing up images and dialogue and epiphanies from the movies that had come to mean more to me than my own true-life experiences?

Much of the time, we don't realise the effect that films have on us. As we emerge from the cinema blinking into the lights of Soho, we are dragged back into the real world.

Lots of movies slide off us, like mercury off a plate, leaving no trace behind. But sometimes, when it's all worked out as the director planned, when we've seen everything we were supposed to see, have been strung out by the drama, dinned into submission by the galloping soundtrack, carpet-bombed by the special effects, made to laugh aloud or weep real tears, we make a connection with the screen that's life-changingly powerful. Sometimes we find a narrative in which we unconsciously lose ourselves, mingling with the furniture, the props, the wide-shot landscape, the medium-shot high street, the close-up faces . . . It's a quality of involvement of which only the cinema is capable, when, for a while, we borrow a life from somebody else. And from the array of on-screen characters and attitudes, small gestures, behaviour patterns, bits of dialogue, revelations of personality, we unconsciously select things that will affect our lives outside the cinema.

When we are young and silly and have no distinct person-ality with which to confront the world, we sometimes take a screen *alter-ego* home with us. The moment, for instance, in *The Magnificent Seven* when James Coburn is harassed by a bullying loudmouth into a gun-versus-knife duel was too good not to replicate in my bedroom the following day, where I confronted myself in the mirror of a chest of drawers, and flung my puny Boy Scout knife at the woodwork a couple of dozen times, replaying the scene until the blade started to become unhinged – not unlike Travis Bickle, the eponymous Taxi Driver in the Scorsese film, whose chal-lenging monologue in front of his own bedroom mirror* gives this book its title and sums up many years of day-

---

* Which goes, in its entirety: Yeah. Huh? (Pulls out gun.) Huh? Huh? Faster 'n you. Go fuck yourself. (Puts gun back in holster.) I saw you comin', you fuck, shitheel. I'm standing here. You make

dreamy adolescent mimetics. But there's a deeper form of identification that (no matter what your age) summons from your lower depths a more heroic form of the self that dumbly takes out the rubbish on Saturday morning and submits to insultingly brusque demands from the Inland Revenue. It's the alternative counter-self that's ridden along with Steve McQueen, smooched with Greta Garbo, been harangued by Jack Lemmon, spied on Janet Leigh in the shower, chased a small red PVC coat with Donald Sutherland or drowned alongside Holly Hunter at the end of *The Piano*. Sometimes, as we shall see, the shadow cast by this dim *doppelganger* can go on and on down the years . . .

The immediate spur to writing this book was a discovery one night in January 2001. It was 4 a.m. My consort, Carolyn, was away, staying with friends. The children were asleep at the top of the house. I woke up for no obvious reason – beyond the standard, middle-aged panic about money, mortgages, school fees, dwindling talent, thinning hair, dyspeptic twinges and terror of death – and lay on my back gazing at the ceiling. I couldn't get back to sleep. But as time ticked by and the room gradually lightened, I slid into a state of semi-consciousness and, looking at the end of my ancient bed, saw a great black shape looming over me. But it wasn't the figure of death, cowled, scythe-bearing and melancholy. It was just a solid black mass, a neutral rectangular object standing where no monolithic block had stood before, both alarming and obscurely comforting. As I lay half awake wondering what it could be, for some inex-

---

the move. You make the move. It's your move. (Pulls out gun again.) Huh. Try it, you . . . (Puts the gun away.) You talkin' to me? You talkin' to me? You talkin' to me? Well who the hell else are you talkin' . . . ? You talkin' to me? Well, I'm the only one here . . .

plicable reason the words 'Where are we going now?' ran through my head.

Then I switched on the light and and all became clear. The thing at the end of the bed was the doorway of my bedroom, backlit by the sleepy dawn light from the landing window. It was new to me because we had recently taken on a cleaner, and the usual collection of discarded shirts, trousers and manly impedimenta that had habitually hung over the brass struts at the end of the bed had been tidied away. I was seeing my own doorway for the first time in ages. Ridiculous, really. But in that sleepy disarray, I had conjured up something else.

It was, of course, the climactic scene of *2001: A Space Odyssey*, in which Keir Dullea, playing Dave, the only surviving astronaut on the mission to Jupiter, wakes to find himself in what seems to be the bedroom of an eighteenth-century hotel. Kubrick fans will remember Dullea's alarmed eyes inside his futuristic space helmet, his widened stare that reflected our own wild surmise of where-in-the-universe-have-we ended-up? In the film, Dave/Dullea walks about the elegant suite, discovers an older version of himself eating dinner at a spindly table, and ends up lying on an elegant bed. As he does, the black monolith, which has turned up throughout the movie as a cosmic emblem of progress and education, appears like a warning, or a threat, or a portal of discovery, whereupon the astronaut dies and is re-born as the Star Child, the master of the world.

I'd been stunned by Kubrick's masterpiece when I saw it on a huge screen in 1968. Now, thirty-three years later, lying on a bed fretting about mortality in the dark watches of the night, I had conjured the film's ambiguously alarming monolith to come and loom over me and take me some-where ('Where are we going now?') more interesting.

I sat up and looked, as though for the first time, at the bed in which I was lying, an antique divan I'd picked up in the Eighties. It was, I realised, not a million miles from the one in the film. I looked around the room. An antique gentleman's wardrobe that I'd bought in 1995 gaped open, self-consciously mimicking the one in the movie. I thought of the armchairs in yellow-gold brocade that I'd bought (I couldn't have told you why) years ago for the sitting-room downstairs. And the threadbare Ottoman sofa. And the spindly-legged occasional tables that Carolyn had often tried to throw out because she couldn't see any beauty in their false antiquity. And those heavy old hotel curtains I'd insisted on . . .

Could it be true? I went downstairs, switched on the light in the living-room and stared. Yes, it bloody well could. For years, I had unconsciously been furnishing my home to look like a simulacrum of the room in *2001: A Space Odyssey* where an astronaut had fetched up thirty-odd years before, the room in which he was re-born into something infinitely grander than a mere Earthling. For years, it appeared, I had been patiently, unconsciously, nagging away at an image of transcendence in my head, one that had steered my taste in something as banal as furniture, and all to create a scene – actually *in* 2001 – where, at the end of your long journey, you don't die after all.

It was such a shock that I began to wonder what other movies had sowed a corresponding seed, or how they had altered the course of my life when young. And gradually I began to isolate the films that had had a specifically moral, physical or psychological effect on me or had made me behave in peculiarly uncharacteristic ways.

Only a fool would admit that he or she has become a better person through their exposure to the cinema. It's never been the natural home of great moralists. Sentimental film buffs still go to see D.W. Griffiths's *Birth of a Nation* and emerge stunned by its casual racism, its black baddies and Ku Klux Klan heroes. But the cinema screen works an insidious magic on the emergent consciousness, and leaves us *charged with feeling* in ways that we only dimly understand. Unlike books or plays or TV programmes, the movies make you do weird stuff. And it's this egregiously personal response to the key movies in your life that I try to explore in the ensuing chapters. I've included nothing I saw after I was twenty-one because it's before that age that films imprint themselves on you most deeply; after twenty-one, your life is too hijacked by work, drink, sex, family demands and all the compromises you make with the Real World to be awestruck to the same degree by the plush curtains and the massive screen.

Perhaps my youth was mis-spent in darkened cinemas, when I might have been better employed reading Hegel or Gibbon or Proust, climbing Snowdon or Helvellyn with the Venture Scouts, travelling in the Sudan or the South China Seas, helping the sick with Mother Teresa. But the movies changed my life in the Sixties and early Seventies, and this is a celebration of that heady metamorphosis. And I cordially invite the reader to raid his or her own filmic image-bank and consider what flickering presences, what seductive scenes and passionate epiphanies, made them into the people they've become.

1

THE CAT IN THE CRIMSON SOCK

Mutiny on the Bounty (1962)

It was a fabulous wedding. At least they all told me it was. I hadn't a clue. I'd never been to a wedding before.

The lady coming towards us was an apparition in rolling breakers of white shiny stuff, surmounted in her upper reaches by wavy clouds of white net that hid her face like tumbling cumuli obscuring a pale, autumnal moon. Everybody in the crammed pews had turned to look, as she drifted down the aisle on the arm of a teary-eyed old geezer with a moustache – what was he, her granddad? – processing slowly down the whole length of the church. I gazed at her too, this ghostly bride, but I was shocked by the sight of the whole congregation brazenly turning their backs on the altar and the tabernacle and the priest who stood beside me.

It seemed, to my prim, eight-year-old eyes, jolly rude to behave that way. You didn't turn round and look behind you in church. Even if a platoon of Protestant militia were (as seemed likely, in those doctrinaire days) suddenly to burst in, blasting assault rifles in the air, you always faced the altar when the priest was on it, doing his priestly business. It was a rule of Catholic church-going, like not fidgeting during a sermon, not remaining seated when you were supposed to kneel, or not playing with your wodge of Potty Putty during the dead quarter-hour when everyone joined the queue for Communion.

I'd been an altar server for a year or two, and I knew the rules. I was a strict little Papist gauleiter, a stickler for correct form. Any junior acolyte who rang the gold three-dome shamrock of bells in the wrong place during the Mass would get a vicious ticking-off from me or from Thimont, my friend and co-adjutant in the altar-server army, just as he had once abused my stupidity when I'd been a bungling starter on the altar steps.

Now he and I stood on either side of the priest in his white-and-gold chasuble, waiting in our off-white vestments for the dame in the pristine cloud to arrive before us. As she drew level, she was joined by a sweating chap from the front pew who had got up to stand beside her, nervously pulling his fingers as if trying to make his knuckles crack, along with an identically-dressed other chap by his side, the pair of them quaking slightly.

The priest asked the bride and groom some simple questions at dictation speed and they repeated everything he said like parrots. I wasn't impressed. They seemed so nervous. Would the priest speak harshly to the lady if she got a word out of place? Would he say, 'No, that's wrong, you stupid boy,' to the man, as the Religious Education teacher at school ticked you off if you got a bit of the catechism wrong? Would they both wind up in detention?

It was a pivotal year, 1962. The Kennedy assassination, the Profumo scandal and Beatlemania were just months off. The old world of the Fifties, had I realised it, was about to change for ever. But at home in Balham, south London, life was still shrouded in Fifties gloom. It was a mono-chrome time. The smell of beef sausages lingered in the hallway where I drove my Dinky Toy Bentleys at reckless speed down the banisters, and constructed Airfix models of Fokker triplanes and Sherman tanks, and supervised pitched battles of tiny plastic soldiers – British Tommies and German desert rats – with their feet disablingly clamped onto tiny skateboards.

My mother read *The Lady*, a shiny magazine of unimpeachably correct, upper-class rectitude, which featured small-ads for nannies and cook-housekeepers in its latter pages. I was devoted to a comic called *Valiant*, full of the exploits of adventurous misfits in jungles, war zones and minor-league football clubs. My father came home from the surgery in Latchmere Road for his supper at 8 p.m., drank gin-and-orange cocktails that smelt of clinics and tut-tutted over pretentious arty documentaries (like Ken Russell's film of Elgar) on a TV show called *Monitor*.

Sunday family outings in our Renault Dauphine took us to wasp-infested picnics in Cannizaro Gardens in Wimbledon, the suburb where my sister and I went to school during the week. We went to church twice on Saturdays, morning and evening, as well as the be-there-or-die mandatory Catholic attendance on Sunday mornings. It was a grey, craven, mind-your-manners time, with no hint of the rebellion to come.

Back in church that day, everyone seemed to be in uniform: long grey suits with graceful tailcoats, black-and-white suits with shiny lapels, ladies' hats with farcically wide brims and fussy arrangements of flowers that could not possibly – not in a million years, I sternly and silently informed them – keep the rain off in the event of a June cloudburst.

I was impressed to see that everyone had made an effort. The uniform at Donhead, the prep school which Thimont and I attended, was a pale blue blazer and shorts with a white shirt and white socks, and the photographs of my first day there show a boy beaming, fit to burst with pride at having joined the army of normal boys at last, after spending too long in the mixed-infants hell of the girly Ursuline Convent one road away.

At the age of eight I was an unusually conservative kid, anxious to do right, keen to conform, one of nature's milk monitors and junior prefects. I was probably insufferable, but I knew that I knew right from wrong. The son of sternly moral, right-thinking Irish Catholic parents, I was as straight as a poker and as square as a boxing ring. I served mass in the school chapel and once a year (a head-spinning privilege) I'd be called on to make the bleary-eyed, late-evening journey to Farm Street, the London headquarters of the Jesuit brotherhood, to serve with my mentor, Thimont, at the Easter Saturday vigil Mass in front of the country's most seraphic Catholic top brass.

My eyes were fixed on the glory of service. I had no ambitions beyond being good and perhaps one day, if I kept away from bad company, graduating to the rank of Master of Ceremonies on the high altar in Westminster Cathedral.

While the choir, at the wedding, were singing the 'Ave Maria', and the bride and groom were signing the register somewhere out of sight, I leaned over to Thimont, my co-server, and said, 'Teapot, who's the bloke in the grey suit who was at the altar but wasn't marrying the woman?'

'He's the best man,' said my friend, who knew such things.

The Best Man? I'd never heard the phrase before. Gosh. Had there been a competition?

Thimont (his name was Paul, but we were very formal kids in grammar school) explained, in his worldly way, that the best man was the bridegroom's best friend, that he was keeper of the Wedding Ring and the life and soul of the Reception festivities, and would have to make a speech in front of all the wedding guests. He and the groom had been friends with one of the teachers at Donhead, and that was why we were there at all, serving Mass at this wedding, and that was why the school choir was currently up in the music loft, singing the 'Ave Maria' with a terrible, grinding slowness. We'd all been hired for the day, like a job-lot of farm labourers, by a sentimental fan of our school.

As I listened to the singing, with its listless and drooping cadences, a martinet frown creased my brow. Buck up, you chaps, I thought, put some life into it. The honour of the school may be at stake here. You cannot sing so boringly in front of someone who's been deemed a Best Man (though he was still backstage at the time, doing his register duties). I wanted him to be impressed by us. I wanted him to admire our cadet rigour, our parade-ground smartness, our polish and swagger. But in the event, it was he who subverted all our lives. Because, in gratitude for our labours that day, he bought the choir and the altar servers tickets to see *Mutiny on the Bounty*.

It was my first-ever movie. I was, at eight, a virgin of the picture house. Other boys in my class had been to Disney cartoons in local picture houses, or to Saturday-morning cinema club, or even to school-holiday first-run features: they could discuss the wonders of *In Search of the Castaways*, and its star, the wide-eyed, beautiful Hayley Mills, every eight-year-old boy's dream companion. I knew nothing of all this. My Saturday mornings were spent in church. My parents didn't disapprove of the cinema as a temple of sin, they simply ignored it as an irrelevance in their children's education. Going to the movies was something grown-ups did, by themselves as a foolish bit of time-wasting, or else as a couple at the start of a long, chaste and protracted courtship.

But it was my first time, and I was tremendously excited. Not just by the prospect of seeing a movie, but a grown-up movie at that; not just an adventure film, but one lasting three hours. Not just an evening out that would go on well beyond the bedtime hour of 8 p.m., but an evening in the West End of London, where there were pubs and ritzy neon signs – the last word in glamour in 1962 – and restaurants with dressed-up couples you could see through the windows, eating steak and drinking wine, and all the rackety bustle and hum of the capital I'd only ever seen through the windows of the family Renault, when we were taken, as a colossal treat, to see the Christmas lights of Oxford Street and Piccadilly.

The day dawned. My mother insisted I take a scarf in case the evening grew cold – a needless precaution in June. My father gave me a stiff, brand-new pound note to spend on ice-cream. At school, the form teacher Mr Breen announced there would be a special class at 3 p.m. for those attending the evening screening. What could it be? A lecture on cinema etiquette? No, it was an extra lesson on maritime history. For an hour we looked at maps of eighteenth-century exploration, we heard about colonial expansion in the Americas, we learned about the importance of bread-fruit as the staple diet of South Pacific tribes and how it used to be imported to feed the slaves in the British sugar plantations of the West Indies . . .

Rigid with disappointment, we suddenly realised that this whole, supposedly exciting movie venture was a con. We had hoped for pirates and grog and swordfights. We'd have settled for sailing ships and people shouting 'Splice the main-brace' and maybe a shark attack. But instead we were going to get a dramatisation of the historical significance of bread-fruit. Three hours of it. Some of us wondered aloud if it was worth the bother of going. But, we conceded, a trip to the West End *en charabanc* with your mates was still a better prospect than staying in, doing your homework and (in my case) saying the rosary before going to bed. So we set off with mixed feelings. We sang little songs in the coach, and pulled faces at passing motorists, the hard cases in the choir swigging bottles of Corona Cherryade and belching exuberantly.

In Leicester Square, the trees were full of chattering jackdaws, flying in and departing on black wings against the still-bright, school-uniform-blue sky. Huddled together by our coach, we suddenly became aware, for all our bravado, that this was grown-up land – a territory of strange, obscurely alarming, adult to-and-froing. It was not a place to get lost. We milled about Mr Breen, fourteen anxious acolytes around this trustworthy figure with his slicked-down, Brylcreemed hair (how his name suited him) and his youthful, big-brotherly authority.

Accompanying him on the trip was Miss Stacey, class mistress of the fourth form. She was a handsome, meringue-haired, statuesque termagant with a bosom like a sack of concrete, and a face liberally basted with orange foundation. She stood no nonsense. Her sharp blue eyes sought out tiny displays of rebellion like a searchlight. My friend Palmer swore he'd once found her and Mr Breen locked in a passionate kiss on a piano stool in the Music Room; but there were some things in life that were completely beyond comprehension or likelihood, and the idea of Miss Stacey kissing anyone was right up there with Abominable Snowmen and the Holy Trinity.

The Odeon loomed above us like an enormous temple. It took up as much space as our local church and seemed to bulge with light, eclipsing all the other buildings on one side of the square. We walked towards it in a hushed gaggle, impressed beyond words, and stopped to consider its immense beauty. Up the wall, above the huge ODEON sign, the film's title shouted across the square in a blaze of million-watt illuminations: MUTINY ON THE BOUNTY. Each of the letters was about two feet high. Presumably they'd been manipulated into place earlier that day by a master sign-writer with superior spelling skills. He must (I reasoned) have a box containing the whole alphabet in red, light-up signs, but since the title contained two Os, two Ys, two Us, and – blimey – three Ts and three Ns, it occurred to me he'd need two or three different boxes to rummage in. And were there any films which had three Xs or Ys or Qs . . . ?

I broke off this absorbing line of enquiry to register that we were standing in a great big cave that was the Odeon's lobby. Everything about it was plush – the carpets felt four inches thick, the white walls featured a thick anaglypta, frieze-like wedding-cake-decoration motif and even the staircase in the distance seemed to lie back luxuriantly on soft pillows. It was like the soft furnishings department of Arding & Hobbs, grown to colossal size but with no merchandise in sight. Instead there was a manager in a formal tuxedo and bow-tie, and two ladies in strict red-and-white stripey uniforms selling things. One had a tray that hung around her neck on long ribbons, full of tubs of ice-cream.

'No ice-creams until the interval,' Mr Breen sternly informed us. 'And everyone must spend a penny before we go in.'

The other lady sold big, glossy magazines with pictures of actors on the front. 'Don't bother with the programmes,' Mr Breen warned us. 'They're a waste of money. You can't be too careful in these places.' Instinctively he had become our intrepid native scout guiding us through the jungle of the modern commercial cinema. The foyer of the Odeon didn't look much like a jungle, though. It was more like a big sofa. The atmosphere was almost creepily tactile, like velvet or suede, something you could run your finger along, something you could almost fondle.

We shuffled upstairs, marvelling at the airy splendour of this secular cathedral, were dispatched to the Gents, were reassembled like a lost platoon, ticked off for talking and shoving, then, in a fourteen-strong group, went through the door into a profound darkness.

It was like going over the top in a war. I could see nothing but a massive sheet of screen on our left, on which a giant young woman in a gingham frock was accepting a light for her cigarette from a laughing man about Mr Breen's age. They were enjoying a picnic beside a river. I kept my eyes on the girl, who was pretty and seemed very easily amused, and, moving forward blindly, I crashed into Armfield, who'd stopped in front of me.

'For Christ's sake, Walsh . . .' he said crossly.

'Sh!' whispered Mr Breen, as our troop of choirboys and servers milled awkwardly around the Dress Circle. A grown-up woman flashed a torch at an empty patch in the third row and we filed into it like automatons.

'Consulate,' intoned an adenoidal voice from the screen in seductive tones. 'Cool as a mountain stream . . .'

While the others took their seats around me, I stood looking at the gigantic plaque of light, transfixed, turned to stone by my first encounter with the big screen, oblivious to my co-scholars and the rest of the audience, gazing at the bright cloudless day in front of me, feeling a strange longing to get up on-stage and walk straight into it.

'Sit down, will you?' asked a stroppy voice from behind.

Beside me, Armfield yanked the sleeve of my school blazer. I subsided, and sat on a surface approximately one foot wide. It was amazingly uncomfortable. How, I thought, can I sit on this for three hours? Without undue fuss, Armfield reached behind my back and pushed, so that I flew forward as my first-ever tip-up seat subsided beneath me with a bump.

It had a strong spring, this seat. It was far from certain that my puny weight would keep the thing down under me. Could it, I wondered, tip right back up again, folding me in half and leaving me helplessly mewling with only my legs and school socks showing? This was a whole new territory of alarm – the total darkness, the usherette's stabbing light, the fearsome jaws of the seat I was perched on, the huge, brightly-lit, wall-sized rectangle I'd never encountered before – that screen that drew your eye, whatever was on it, and made you forget everything else. It was fantastically exciting, all of it, better than any funfair ride. Best of all it was in colour, whereas our tiny Rediffusion TV back home showed things only in monochrome greys. I felt simultaneously lost, elated and completely at home with the enormous new world unfolding in front of me.

The words 'Preview of Forthcoming Attractions' appeared on the screen. They meant nothing to me, but I watched like an urchin with his nose pressed against a sweet-shop window as the faces of Leslie Caron and Tom Bell appeared – emoting, argumentative, flushed, agonised, rapturous – in a series of bleak domestic scenes and dismal black-and-white views of London parks. It was the first trailer I'd ever seen (advertising *The L-Shaped Room*), and although the story looked fantastically depressing, the voice-over dramatically promised that it was shocking and challenging and 'a film for today', so that you felt duty-bound to see it as soon as possible, despite being eight years too young (it carried an X certificate) to do any such thing.

The preview ended. Two mile-high curtains swished shut. The lights came on. Was that the end? Had we come to the wrong cinema? I could see the bright auditorium at last, and looked around. We sat, all fourteen of us plus two teachers, line-abreast across a whole row, chattering and gazing at the Odeon's mile-high ceiling, the complicated sculptures on the facing walls, the great proscenium arch. I wondered if people – real people – came out and acted on this massive stage in front of the film while it was showing. If not, it seemed a shocking waste of the dramatic expanse before us – it was a sort of epic altar, far bigger than the stage on which I'd witnessed *Puss in Boots* at the Wimbledon Theatre's panto season the previous Christmas.

Then the lights went out again, and the great curtains swished back to reveal a snarling lion. The unseen speakers took the snarl and fed it through some abysmal sonic filter so that it reverberated until the sound went down underneath where you were sitting, and made your seat vibrate. A pause, and the lion slothfully disgorged a second, basso profundo growl that was like the post-lunchtime belch with which my friend Grzedzicki could thrill his classmates, but magnified 4,000 times.

Then the title came on screen and remained there for ages, while an overture of orchestral savagery thundered behind it. Kettledrums bonged, cellos sawed like neighing horses, violins ran about shrieking 'ding-didaling-didaling', brass trumpets went 'dum-da-dah!' and, in an abrupt mood-swing, breathy woodwinds came quietly into the mix, conjuring up a moody Tahitian sunset before we were returned to rolling waves of splashy brass and chaotic surges of strings. It was tremendously exciting.

The film began. A botanical expert from Kew was strolling along the quay at Portsmouth in a tricorn hat, with a cylinder under his arm and what seemed a pitifully small sack of clothing for a long sea voyage. (My mother would never have let me bundle up my shirts and trousers in a horrible sack like that.) He encountered a gaggle of sailors, some with elaborate beards, some with rolling eyes, all destined for the HMS *Bounty*. They laughingly upbraided him for calling a ship a 'boat' and talked in unfriendly, joshing tones about the ordeal that lay ahead. The man from Kew Gardens was earnest and slightly lost, a nice guy fallen among rough, know-it-all companions. As he signed on for the voyage, leaning on a slanting desk, something about the opening scenes began to strike a chord – but I didn't yet know what it was. The rough-diamond sailors pulled the cylinder from under his armpit.

'Careful with that,' he said. 'Those are scientific documents.'

But they were merely pictures of breadfruit, which he laid out on a convenient barrel and used as part of a lecture about West Indian eating habits, not unlike the lesson we'd endured two hours earlier.

We'd been right. This was going to be an educational bore after all. Then Captain Bligh, played by Trevor Howard, appeared. He had a lined, rather cruel face and small piggy eyes, and something about his old-maidish mouth suggested he was always chewing something nasty without ever spitting it out. Dressed in white stockings, a dark blue uniform and a Duke of Wellington hat, he cut a comical but faintly sinister figure. He instantly reminded me of Mr King the sports master, whose appearance on the rugby pitch in his navy blue tracksuit was always the prelude to random acts of violence.

Fletcher Christian wafted on board. I had heard about Marlon Brando, the American actor with the cissy name. He was a real hero, my friends said, a brilliant actor, an exotic figure who probably lived in New York and knew other famous actors, and went round to the houses of famous people all the time and, you know, *had lunch* with them. It was important that he was American because we were in love with American things – the cars with the sharky fins, the Western guns, the tough-guy fist-fights, the space suits, the fact that, according to 77 *Sunset Strip*, American policemen chewed gum all the time and actually got to shoot people. Most of all we liked their accents, and sometimes tried to imitate them. They sounded like English accents on a slide, a drawling, don't-care voice, far more appealing than the stuck-up, sit-up-and-beg accents of British people who read the news and appeared in quiz shows.

But was this really Brando, the famous actor-hero of whom I'd heard so much from my clued-up, movie-going friends? He wore a light-blue fancy-dress outfit, a comical hat and a red cloak like Superman's, and my first reaction was of distaste: he seemed a bit of a *garçon de Nancy* as we called cissy actors on television. His hair was pulled back off his forehead and worn in a greasy ponytail, and his face was pulled back with it, so that his eyes were oddly slitty and Chinese – and he talked in a weird, affected, fastidious neigh of British distaste, as if he could hardy bear to say anything at all through his clenched teeth. He seemed about as heroic as the adjustable mannequin that posed in the window of Arding & Hobbs. He came aboard flanked by two ladies of fashion, one English, one French, who flapped and dimpled like flamingoes among the creaking sheets and elderly timbers of the merchantman, until they were shooed ashore by the captain.

He and Captain Bligh were soon having a row about why Brando had bothered going into the Navy.

'The Army didn't seem quite right,' he told the captain, 'and affairs of state are rather a bore . . .'

Ratha a *bawww* . . .

Captain Bligh pursed his skinny mouth with distaste. Well, I thought, this is going to be fun: one nasty, face-chewing man in long white socks, and one Chinky-faced, oily-haired clot with a foolish accent and a cloak, who was happier with silly women in ringlets and picture hats than with daggers and swords and stuff.

But once Mr Fryer, the dependable first mate, said, 'Set topsails and headsails,' we were away on a voyage and I was happily away too. There was an unstoppable swing to the voyage, and the narrative on which we'd embarked, a feeling of being swept up in it all as if you'd been press-ganged aboard and you wouldn't be able to get off, even if you wanted to. It was like being on a ride at Battersea funfair – a place I haunted for weeks every summer – when you'd ridden the long train to the top of the Water Splash and were turning into the long slide down to where the water lurked, and there was nothing you could do but sit there amid a lot of screaming strangers, and scream along with them.

The *Bounty* hit the open sea, to the strains of 'Rule Britannia'. The sailors swarmed up the rigging, spread themselves out on the crossbars like slivers of marmalade along a thin slice of toast, dropped the sails and watched them fill with wind. There was surge. There was heft and swell. There were creaking timbers and sailors doing baffling things with ropes. But things soon took a turn for the worse at deck level.

Seaman Mills, played by Richard Harris, the devil-may-care Irish troublemaker among the roistering matelots, was accused of stealing some ship's cheeses.

Fletcher Christian listened to the complainant with a superior smile and dismissed the whinger condescendingly. 'Was there something further you wished to discuss? Early Renaissance sketching, perhaps?'

Below stairs, surrounded by his mates, Mills blamed the captain, who, he said, had asked him take the cheeses to his home. Suddenly we were involved in a hurricane-lamp-lit subversion, as Harris recklessly urged his fellow rank-and-file scum to believe their captain guilty of pilfering. Unluckily, Bligh chose just that moment to descend the gangway, where he stopped to listen to Mills's accusations. The thuggish sailors fell silent, but Mills was unstoppable: 'It was the captain helping himself to the ship's stores,' he shouted into a mortified silence. 'The captain's the thief, not me!'

Behind him, Bligh and Mr Christian took stock of what

had been said. For us schoolboys, it was a terribly familiar scene, familiar from a dozen classroom encounters when we'd performed a hilarious impersonation of the Maths master while the Maths master watched unnoticed, from the doorway.

A nasty smile twitched across Bligh's razor mouth.

Christian recommended cancelling the mouthy Irishman's grog for a month.

'Two dozen of the lash will teach him better still,' grated Trevor Howard. 'All hands on deck to witness punishment, Mr Christian, if you please.'

Along the row of seats, Mr Breen leaned forward, looked to right and left, and said, 'Boys? This man is going to be flogged. It may get rather nasty. If any boy wants to sit on my lap, now is the time . . .'

Film and reality suddenly merged. We were all, choir and altar servers and teachers and actors alike, suddenly complicit in an act of collective sadism. We schoolboys were suddenly hands on deck, forced to gaze at a punishment ritual, whether we liked it or not. Nobody took Mr Breen up on his kind offer, for fear of seeming a wimp. We sat there, entranced by our first exposure to the delights of sadomasochistic teasing.

For minutes that were like hours, the hapless Mills was filmed sitting on a bunk, wondering how savage his punishment was going to be. We were obliged to look very closely at Richard Harris's handsome, sunburnt face. He appeared half in love with his distress, while a dangling rope behind him suggested a death that might soon overwhelm him. One of the sailors offered him a cup of grog, but he waved it away. All his brave buddies fell silent. And then Quintal, the second mate, dragged something out of a storage cupboard and brought it down to the floor, there to ferret out, from its rummagy depths, a long red crimson sock with a draw-string neck. We watched its retrieval with collective foreboding, as if we were all, individually, the miscreant sailor looking at the thing that was about to lacerate his flesh.

But of course, we knew all about this stuff already. In the early Sixties, it was a matter of no great consequence that schoolboys could be flogged with a ferule, a short rod made from a whalebone encased in leather. If you forgot your sports kit twice in a row, or were caught fighting in class or throwing paper darts or cheeking the bovine Geography master, you might be sentenced to four or six ferulas, or (if you were really evil) nine or (for unimaginable depravity) twelve. At 4 p.m., when the lessons were over, you presented yourself outside the headmaster's study, where pipe tobacco smells mingled with the sweat from your fear. You joined the queue of chastened youths, who all, in those days, simply accepted that they were about to be whacked and brutalised as a normal part of the school routine.

When it was your turn, you knocked on the door and, at the words 'Come in!', turned the handle. Inside the room, everything looked posh and stately, the living room of a successful gentleman-scholar, with a humidor smelling of cigars on the antique desk and a gramophone softly playing some sobbing Italian operatic tenor.

You had to say, 'Six ferulas, please, sir,' in a polite, Oliver-Twist-asking-for-more voice that was the second-worst thing about the experience.

The head would write something in a little book ('Walsh – 22 May 1961 – running in crrdr – 6f') and stand before you, with one hand behind his back. He would beckon with his fingers for you to extend your arm, palm upwards, and from its hiding place the whalebone would suddenly appear, soaring up then crashing down on your innocent flesh in a vivid trajectory of blurred malevolence, and a noise like 'Whop!' that didn't seem to suit the astounding, metallic pain that shot up your arm. You would put the bruised limb somewhere behind you and extend the other arm, with a kind of stunned fatalism, and that hand would be whopped in turn. Then the first hand again, rising from the depths of wherever it had sunk, like an animal returning to a vicious master out of some sad, vestigial loyalty, then the second, the first, the second . . .

The headmaster never, ever, looked at you. He stood with eyes cast down at the glum brown carpet, waiting for you to say, 'Thank you, sir,' like a good little victim and take yourself off to the lavatories where you anointed your stinging hands with soap and running water.

The worst bit, though, was the waiting. From sentence to execution, hours would pass when nothing entered your mind but the prospect of what was to come. Bluebirds could circle the playing fields, grocer's boys could whistle on their bicycles in a sonic emblem of the freedom beyond the school gates, but none of it would alleviate the pain of your imminent tryst with The Lash in the headmaster's study.

So we watched with lively professional interest as Mills, stripped to the waist, was tied to a trellis and Quintal hissed in his ear, 'Now just remember this, mate, it ain't me that's whipping yer.' I've never forgotten those words. The crimson sock from the teak chest yielded up its baleful cargo of a cat-o'-nine-tails, Quintal shook it out and, before the ship's crew's incurious gaze, proceeded to lash Mills's remarkably white flesh.

Counting off the lashes, we took in with our young eyes the blooding and flaying of Mills's back, the wincing of the more sensitive crew-members, the gloating interventions of Captain Bligh ('You're going too soft, Quintal – lay on with a will or you'll take his place' – a classic piece of schoolmasterly brinkmanship) and the gradual sinking down of the victim.

Bligh's mouth twisted in a smile. God I hated him. He reminded me so much of Mr King, the sports master, who always had me in his sadistic sights. Once, when I had weedily underperformed at some football practice, he actually picked me up by the ears and held me dangling in agony. But you didn't fight back or argue with Mr King. You accepted that he had every right to do horrible things to you, because you were a nasty little boy who was probably in the wrong. All you would say was 'Flippin' heck, sir,' like a Cockney droll, and take your punishment in good heart and not complain. You weren't allowed to make a fuss, even to answer back, when you were eight, in Wimbledon, in 1962.

When Quintal had delivered the final lash and his shipmates had thrown a bucket of water over the flayed and knackered Mills, we breathed a collective sigh, we innocent choirboys and altar servers – half relief that it was all over and half a perverse satisfaction in cruelty that would live in our impressionable hearts for years. But something more important happened in those five moments, something that was to change us all. It was the first time we'd been confronted *en masse* by the grotesque unfairness of corporal punishment, a system that had changed little since the days of Tom Brown and Dr Arnold. At school, we sympathised with the boys who were on their way to the punishment room, and afterwards noted their tears, the weals on their flayed hands. But we'd never all witnessed it taking place in front of us before, never watched it as a hostile, wounded, grumbling, collective unit. You could almost hear a mutinous sigh from the fourteen schoolboys in the cinema stalls. We'd all experienced it as individuals. Seeing it portrayed on screen as an example of capricious revenge by an autocratic authority figure was something new.

It was shocking. No, it was outrageous. Why was Mills being subjected to such treatment? Because the Captain said so. Whose rules allowed the Captain to say so? Some naval statute, thousands of miles away in London. For the first time, we considered the possibility that the rules might be wrong – that it shouldn't be possible to flog someone half to death because of some gubernatorial whim. And that it shouldn't be possible to find oneself beaten in a book-lined study because some ancient ruling dictated that it should be so, because you had forgotten to bring your sports kit on a particular day. A shock-wave of rebellion passed through us. Mr Breen looked down the line of boys, checking to see that we had all come through the trauma of the flog-ging scene and nobody was weeping with distress. We weren't. We were thinking how we'd all put up with it for so long. And how we might change the system so that we wouldn't have to go through it any more. But where did you start?

In the captain's cabin that evening, Bligh and Christian discussed punishment. Christian advocated leniency and charm to win over a crew and make them sail a happy ship. Bligh rejected such piffling liberalism. He was an advocate of 'cruelty with purpose', the efficiency brought about by pain. When a sailor has to be ordered aloft in freezing weather, Bligh maintained, it was better that he feared the retribution of his captain for being a bad sailor more than he feared death itself. 'When a man has seen his mate's backbone laid bare, he'll remember the white ribs staring at him, he'll see the flesh jump and hear the whistle of the lash for the rest of his life.' Against which, all Christian had to say, with a glass of port in his hand, was, 'I'd steer clear of this *cheese*, sir – I think it's a bit tainted.'

I'd never heard the like of it before. Christian was subtly alluding to the cheese-stealing incident, criticising the captain in his own study and getting away with it. This would have been described by our parents as cheek. It was a smart remark on the lips of an inferior, directed at a figure of authority, its implied condemnation of the man and his attitudes sleekly concealed behind a veil of polite warning.

It was cool. I was beginning to like Fletcher Christian.

There was another significant row, when Bligh announced his intention of sailing round Cape Horn. Rather than declare him an outright madman for steering them into a Force 12 inferno of crashing waves, 200 m.p.h. tempests and certain death, Christian said, 'Well, we shall have ourselves quite a little adventure . . . Of course, Admiral Anson did it, but not in a 91-foot chamberpot.'

Bligh lost his temper at last and told Christian that he possessed only one emotion, namely contempt.

And Marlon Brando said this marvellous thing. He didn't deny the accusation, but replied: 'I assure you, sir, the execution of my duties is in no way affected by my private opinion of you.' And he left the captain silent and fuming, unable to out-sleek his hated rival, glaring uselessly at the sea with his lower lip petulantly stuck out like a drawer in a Regency dresser.

You have by now, I'm sure, realised what was going on, though we hardly knew it ourselves, in the Odeon, Leicester Square, in 1962. We were watching the world about to collapse. We were watching a film about school, in which the whole system of masters and students, bound together in ancient protocols of supposedly common ideals, was about to founder. It was the moment with the crimson sock that did it – that collective shudder about a punishment we couldn't evade – that made us realise the *Bounty* was a huge floating metaphor of school. Everything on board had its counterpart in the inky purlieus of Wimbledon College.

Captain Bligh was a classic headmaster – Mr Quelch from the Bunter books, Jimmy Edwards from the *Whacko!* television series, and Father Egan from our prep school. The sailors on the quay were second-year rude boys, joshingly welcoming the new bug, Wilson; they'd even watched him sign on for the voyage at a stained and pock-marked old desk. They'd told him to beware of the head's frightful temper. The uniformed midshipmen were prefects, boys you couldn't be friends with because of their little tin badges of authority and their direct line to the caning room. The three miscreant sailors, played by Richard Harris, Chips Rafferty and Gordon Jackson, were the anarchic naughty boys in class, always getting into trouble with the beaks as if they longed for punishment

And there, right there on screen, was a blueprint about how you could deal with the beaks, if you had the nerve. You could be cool. You could be sleek and inscrutable. You could fight back with words which couldn't get you into trouble, either because they seemed to be about something else (like saying the cheese was tainted) or because they were simply too polite. We suddenly learned, at eight years old, the vital weapon of irony.

The rest of the film passed in a blur. I came out of the cinema with my head full of sea water, Pacific sunsets, rolling barrels, Tahiti dances, half-naked native girls holding nets in the sea, and disjointed images of the mutiny itself. After three hours of sadism, storms, death, topless women, breadfruit, romance, attempted escape and the final drama of the *Bounty* in flames, I was overwhelmed by sensation, jaded by extreme emotions, exhausted by proxy passion, and ready for bed. But all the action stuff was superfluous to the two crucial events, the flogging and the shipboard spats between Bligh and Christian. We had all, I think, learned collective outrage, although the actual chances of organising a decent mutiny at school seemed desperately slim.★ More important was the

★ When Lindsay Anderson's *If . . .* came out, six years later, its satiric portrait of a public school peopled by mad masters and machine-gun-smuggling Upper Fifth desperadoes was welcomed as a subversive metaphor for the Establishment under threat. 'It's something like

personal lesson I'd learned – about the power of words to help you stand up for yourself.

A week later, at Saturday morning rugby practice, Mr King, the sadistic sports master, stopped our listless passing and tackling and delivered a pep-talk about our lack of energy and attack. We'd heard it all before. We knew he'd pick on someone to hurt, as he always did. He called out Paul Gorham, a small fat boy upon whose prodigious folds of warm flesh we used innocently to rub our freezing hands when nothing much was happening at our end of the pitch.

'Gorham,' he said, 'you're useless. Why are you not trying harder? Mmm? Mmmmmm?'

'I don't know, sir.'

'So it's just ignorance, is it, Gorham, rather than just indolence, mmmm?'

'No, sir. I'm a defender, sir. I thought I'd better wait at this end, sir, in case they tried to break through, sir. And,' he concluded pathetically, 'it's very boring, sir.'

'Well,' said Mr King nastily, 'we must try and make life more exciting for you, mustn't we?' And, as he'd done a dozen times to a dozen other boys, he ran his hands over poor Gorham's face, circled them around the boy's cold-reddened ears and began to hoist him up off the ground.

'Aaargh,' said Gorham. His portly frame dangled agonisingly, four stone of small fat boy held up in the air by two straining lumps of cartilage and flesh.

'Don't do that, sir,' I said, out of nowhere. 'You'll hurt his ears, sir.'

Mr King put Gorham down and ambled over to me.

'What did you say, Walsh?'

---

the Writing on the Wall,' Anderson told the press. I dare say he was right, but some of us felt we had been there already, watching a film in 1962 about a floating school whose headmaster simply had to go.

'You'll hurt his ears, sir, picking him up like that. My father's a doctor and he says it damages the ear-drums.' It all came out as a rush. It must have sounded a little too prepared, but I'd been thinking about Mr King's casual savagery, and I was fed up with it.

'Do not tell me what to do, boy,' said Mr King. He sounded momentarily puzzled. Had the parents, urged on by my father, been talking about him? 'This team is a disgrace to the rugby pitch, and you, Walsh, are one of the worst offenders.'

'Yes sir,' I said.

'You run about aimlessly, you can't tackle for toffee, you're positively lily-livered in the scrum. You don't even try to play rugby. And to cap it all – to cap it all – you are cheeky to my face. I don't like your attitude, Walsh.'

I looked into his eyes. They were a milky shade of blue. I'd never looked him in the eyes before. You didn't look a teacher in the eyes. You looked at the ground. You muttered 'Flippin' heck, sir' while he punched you in the stomach or hoisted you aloft by your ears. But for the first time, I looked straight into his blue eyes.

The words came into my head, unbidden, perfect: 'I assure you, sir, that the execution of my duties on the pitch is in no way affected by my private opinion of you.'

Did I say it? Of course I didn't. What was I, asking for trouble? But my cheeks burned with the unsaid rejoinder and I knew, for the first time, that such words were there at my disposal. Had I the balls, the cheek, I could have said it, and taken the consequences. He might have slapped me across the face. He might have recoiled, as if stung. As it was, twenty seconds passed like an eon between us. In the distance a dog barked in the peculiar silence.

'You will come and see me after the game,' he said at last, loudly enough for the others to hear. 'I'll deal with you then.' And he blew his pathetic whistle and we all ran off towards the second half of the afternoon's cold misery.

But after the game he wasn't waiting for me outside the changing rooms, even though my sporting pals confidently predicted that a terrible fate lay in store for me. I hung around for half an hour, waiting to be summoned, desperately trying to think of other useful Fletcher Christian lines I might (but probably wouldn't) say, and finding none that would stop a furious sports master baying for blood. But he'd gone, and I snuck off home at 3.30 wondering if I'd got away with it.

In the next rugby class, and the next, he ignored me completely. But I noticed that, although his verbal assaults grew, if anything, more contemptuous, he didn't do the ear-yanking routine on boys again.

It wasn't much of a victory. But in its mild, unspoken way, it was a giant leap forward, into the Technicolor dawn of the Sixties.

2

FACES AT THE WINDOW

The Innocents (1961)

It was a Saturday night in 1963 and it was bathtime. It was one of the worst nights of my life.

I was nine and my sister, Madelyn, was ten, and we did what we always did on Saturday nights. We accompanied our parents to the knobbly-Gothic church of St Mary's, Clapham Common, for a service called the Novena. It was a form of Catholic insurance policy. You were supposed to attend this downbeat vaudeville show of hymns and prayers for nine weeks in a row (hence novena), in order to rack up moral credits that would, in theory, reduce your final sentence in Purgatory. It was not unlike accumulating supermarket air-miles over several years in the hope of eventually claiming a flight to Rome; but it lacked any sense of collector's achievement, since we just did it week after week without claiming any reward or enjoying any respite.

The only excitement the trip offered was the place where my father parked the family Renault in St Alfonsus Road, SW4, round the corner from the church. He always took the same spot, under a streetlamp beside a shop. On the wall to the right of the shop window was a film hoarding.

It was a matter of vivid excitement to me, each Saturday, to see what new film was being advertised. I had no idea which cinema was displaying its wares; I still don't know its exact location; I never went there. But the hoarding had a magic of its own, like an endlessly-shifting art gallery of startling images. It never advertised children's movies, cartoons, musicals or comedies. It was always a horror movie. *The Kiss of the Vampire*, *The Evil of Frankenstein*, *The Gorgon*, *Dr Terror's House of Horrors* . . . The titles, in the early 1960s, became interchangeable: *The Curse of This*, *The Tomb of That*, *The Masque of The Other*, *The Black What-Have-You*. Hammer film studios seemed to have a grip, as determined as Peter Cushing's thin, professorial lips, on the imagination of Clapham Common audiences.

Sometimes, in a sinister variant, the movie on offer would depart from the Gothic hysteria – the haunted houses and screaming faces, the blood dripping off the title – and deal in something worse, something modern. I gazed at the picture of *Devil Doll*, with its hideous smiley-faced, ventriloquist's dummy mask, a midget killer in a sensible black suit with a gingham tie and a hankie peeping from its breast pocket, and had to avert my eyes because its promise of playroom homicide was too close to home to be borne. *Whatever Happened to Baby Jane?* also featured a doll's head with its forehead bashed in, and sickly pictures of two old ladies with huge staring eyes. One was stern and vindictive (Bette Davis), clearly Snow White's wicked stepmother grown old and mad; the other (Joan Crawford) was fretful, nail-chewing and demented in a different way, but I couldn't then register the iconography of paranoia. I just knew they both spelt trouble.★

★ Sex films occasionally featured in this weekly induction to the Real World, but they too hinted at bad times: *Bitter Harvest*, with its back

·I would pause every Saturday evening and explore every corner of the new frights on display, like a connoisseur inspecting the brushwork at a Monet exhibition. I took in the disarrayed limbs, the torn clothing, the suggestion of devoured flesh, the craggy lettering, the open mouths, the torrid reds and decadent greens of the colour palette, even the subtle placing of the 'X' to indicate that this was an adults-only treat, until I was ordered back to reality by a parental shout, and dragged away to the church, there to kneel in silent contemplation of a naked man on a cross, with a gaping spear-wound in his side, dying slowly of asphyxiation, and an audience of middle-aged loners and crumbling old ladies with whiskery chins and parchment cheeks.

The images on the film posters became my weekly dose of fright, a bracing insight into a world of cruelty and dementia, a nasty newsreel bringing fresh information about terrible goings-on in Gothic castles and gloomy mansions. They would stay with me during the Novena service, bound up with the gloomy shadows of the Lady chapel and the imagery of religion. So many movies featured crucifixes, Satanic faces and sacrificial victims that it was easy to confuse the church-stuff and the cinema-stuff. They were both alarmingly keen on death and darkness. For ages I was convinced that horror films were shot in the dark, and that the whole movie would be swathed in blackness from start to finish. It seemed an odd form of enjoyment, to sit in a dark cinema watching mad people with staring eyes making

view of the naked Janet Munn, seemed to promise that some poor girl would suffer undreamt-of agonies simply because she went around showing too much flesh. *Love With the Proper Stranger* had Natalie Wood lying in disarray, apparently in the street, in the arms of Steve McQueen – the victim, I innocently assumed, of some traffic accident.

each other bleed in dark rooms and spooky exteriors, but no odder than to kneel for half a hour in a crepuscular church, listening to tales of crucifixion with a moaning organ accompaniment.

Some nights, the advertisement featured double-bills, an extra-strength dose of horror. One night it was *Maniac*, Michael Carreras's psychological chiller about an oxyacetylene-torch killer on the loose in France, and *The Damned*, Joseph Losey's early classic about leathery bike-boys and radioactive children. *Maniac* and *The Damned*. Two in one evening! The poster for *Maniac* urged interested punters, 'Don't go alone – take a brave, nerveless friend with you!' Its imagery was simple and effective: two eyes looking at you, wide and deranged, with spooky concentric rings around them, to indicate they were the eyes of an Unbalanced Person.

I had some experience of the type. I'd seen patients in my father's surgery at our home in Battersea with a similar stare, as I came through the waiting room to tell him, *sotto voce*, that his supper was ready. I'd watched Dad, one Saturday morning, negotiating with a very disturbed man who was dressed in his pyjamas under his shabby macintosh, and who talked a stream of gibberish and brandished a portfolio of medical records as thick as a phone book, while my father encouraged him to calm down, sit down and 'wait, like a good man' for the ambulance to arrive. I hung around in fascination, as the man's long face twisted this way and that, like someone looking for a wasp buzzing in the air, and his disturbed eyes occasionally locked in panic on mine.

Another morning, while the surgery was in full swing, someone had an epileptic fit on the No. 37 bus, and was carried off at the stop across the road from our front door. He was brought into the house and lain, twitching horribly, on the carpet, with his head rolling on the Welcome mat. My mother, a former nursing sister, had taken charge and was kneeling on top of him, pinning down his shoulders, when I arrived to see what the commotion was. It looked like the aftermath of a one-sided wrestling match. Flecks of white spit lined the corners of his mouth. There was a noise of grinding teeth. The man's legs pounded on the swirly, heavy-duty Berber carpet. My mother grunted with the exertion of keeping the spasming patient from writhing across the hall. I stood watching it all, transfixed.

Finally she looked up. 'John,' she panted, 'run up to the bathroom and grab a toothbrush and bring it down here.'

'But you can't clean his teeth *now*,' I wailed. 'He's having a *fit*.'

She explained that the toothbrush was to stop the guy biting his own tongue off and I fled to retrieve a dental scour, mentally noting that, whichever one I chose, it sure as hell wasn't going to be mine.

I had, in other words, seen apparitions, victims, nutters, every class of Gothic weirdo staring and twitching before me, right there on the home turf. I was used to it. Just as I'd seen emblems of torture and death nailed to the wall of the murky church every Saturday. The combination of a medical father and mother, and an enforced regimen of Catholic iconography, had made me an early connoisseur of the grotesque.

And in the early Sixties there seemed to be a lot of dark around. The drive to church was dark, the Clapham streets were dark, people moved around swathed in uniformly grey overcoats, and the shadows of St Mary's church found a domestic echo in the gloomy upstairs rooms of our new house, to which we'd moved in 1962, when I was eight.

We lived, it seemed, in a 40-watt zone. Nobody ever left a room without turning off the light, so the house stayed in semi-total darkness, except for the first-floor living-room, where we gathered on Saturday evenings, like well-off refugees. The Clean Air Act was yet to be introduced to

London, and smog could still descend in a grey blanket on the streets of Battersea and make the outside world through the windows seem clouded and sinister, as if seen through gauze or tissue paper. My mother drew the heavy brocade curtains firmly shut at 7.45 every Saturday evening, on returning from church, and switched on the tiny lamps on the mantelpiece and the big standard-lamp in the corner. We didn't have an open fire, but a newly-trendy, coal-effect, three-bar heater threw unconvincing wiggly shadows over the white rug where Madelyn and I always sat to watch television. My parents ranged themselves on cushioned thrones on either side of the fire, Dad nursing a gin and orange, Mother a newspaper or a copy of *The Lady*. We were a family group straight out of Norman Rockwell, cosy and warm, the long red curtains keeping out the cold night, the fog, the heaving swell of the big lorries on the road, the drunken shouts from sloshed revellers stamping home-ward from the Northcote pub down by the market.

I was allowed to stay up till 9 p.m. but was expected to put myself in the bath when I was told, get soaped and rinsed, towel myself dry and emerge, in pyjamas and dressing-gown, to warm up by the fire before bedtime.

On this hellish night, before bathtime, I was eating cheese and onion crisps and reading one of the Molesworth books, *How to Be Topp* – a favourite, full of spidery drawings of oikish schoolboys and hopeless elderly masters – when the Saturday-night film came on at 8 p.m. I was engrossed in the fictional cricket match at St Custard's, but the dark spidery fingers of the film's credit sequence gradually stole my attention away.

'I did it for the children,' a woman kept saying in a tight, guilty whisper. The whisper gradually crawled inside me while I was reading. I would look up now and again, see that this was grown-up stuff, go back to the book, look up again . . . On screen, the lady was twisting her hands. You could see only her hands and a dark side-view of her troubled, whispering face, as she said it over and over: 'I did it for the children.' On the screen I read the words superimposed over her hands: 'Screenplay: William Archibald, Truman Capote', 'Based on *The Turn of the Screw* by Henry James', 'Produced and directed by Jack Clayton'. The words came and melted away like a series of threats. I tried to continue with my book, but couldn't. The tiny TV set in the corner contained something intriguing with which even a favourite funny book couldn't compete: an early inkling of how fascinating the human heart finds things that will scare it to death.

The movie got under way. A Victorian governess called Miss Giddens, played by the buttoned-up Deborah Kerr, was being interviewed by a business-like character in an old-fashioned coat (Michael Redgrave) who was talking about his children. Ms Kerr was pretty but formal, a very correct sort of schoolmistress in a black dress, her fair hair drawn back from her forehead and clamped in a matronly helmet over her tiny ears. The man was brisk and slightly bullying, but he hired Miss Giddens anyway, and she was soon riding in a horse-drawn trap on a sunny morning towards a country house to take up her new position.

The children, Miles and Flora, were cute but rather stiff, unlike any children I'd ever met. The housekeeper (Megs Jenkins) wore a starched white head-dress and a pleated apron and was obviously a pushover, keen to be liked by the new arrival.

Everybody was getting on fine. Nice house, nice children, nice servant, all of them glad to see the nice nanny. My crisps were a nice treat, the fire was warming, the room breathed family togetherness. Maybe I'd been wrong to be worried by the credit sequence. The Saturday-evening world inside the curtained windows was as nice as could be, and so was the posh-kids drama on the television screen.

Then it started to go wrong. There was a scene in which

Deborah Kerr was talking to Megs Jenkins and Flora, the little girl, out in the garden – and the governess suddenly saw, on the battlements of the house, a man looking down at them. She gazed up at the figure, trying to make out who it could be, but was blinded by sunlight, as the music emphasised her sudden panic. Tiny hairs prickled on my arm. Assuming the man to be an intruder, Deborah Kerr rushed inside the house, up the stairs, up to the flat roof – and discovered only the brilliantined Miles, sitting there playing with some pigeons. The governess asked if anyone else has been standing there. No, said Miles, there'd been nobody around but himself. But the scene intimated some evil and dread about to take over the ordinary world.*

'This is awful boring grown-up stuff for you to be watching,' said my mother. 'I think it's time you had your bath and got in your pyjamas.' How shrewd of her to sense that the film wasn't going to be a joyful experience for a highly-strung kid.

I looked at Madelyn. She was eating a Kit-Kat, unconcerned, her eyes fixed on the TV. 'Tell me what happens, Mad, OK?' I said.

'Sure, yeah. Don't take too long or you'll miss the plot.'

Outside, on the landing, the bathroom door yawned open on the right. It seemed like a dark cave, the invitation to some frightful ambush. I looked up at the 40-watt bulb. The figure of the man in the film, standing in blinding sunlight, seemed to lurk there. On the wall outside my

---

* Children are famously conservative readers, but there was something positively neurotic about the way I preferred cosy set-ups to narrative complication. When reading Enid Blyton, I used to wish the Secret Seven could just stay having meetings and drinking ginger beer for ever, and not worry about the Mysterious Foreigner, the conveniently discovered Puzzling Clue, and the Light Out At Sea in Chapter 6 . . .

parents' bedroom, the pictured face of Christ the Saviour regarded me calmly, his opened-up heart (that classic piece of bad-taste Catholic iconography) streaming light.

I rushed into the bathroom, closed the door and locked it firmly. There's nothing wrong, I told myself, it's only a silly film from a hundred years ago. The long bathroom window had a venetian blind which threw slatted shadows from the streetlamp onto the vinyl floor. I switched on the light over the sink and peered out the window while the bath was running. Nobody was around on Battersea Rise. No walkers, no dogs, no drunks. Maybe they were all indoors, watching two Victorian children explaining away their ghostly visitations.

Ten minutes later, bathed, towelled, pyjamaed, tooth-brushed and ready for bed, I stood in the bathroom doorway. The living-room door was three steps away, but it seemed like half a mile through a graveyard. A nagging alarm was dinging in my head, because I had to turn out the bathroom light, and I couldn't bear to. I wanted the whole house to be lit up like a pantomime stage. I wanted to be un-frightened. Eventually I took a deep breath, yanked the light switch, crossed the big hallway and opened the living-room door.

My family's eyes were fixed on the TV screen. I reclaimed my position on the white rug.

'What's happened?' I asked, as airily as I could.

'Shhhh,' they all said, in chorus.

'Mad? What's happening now?'

'It's nothing,' said my sister. 'They're just playing Hide and Seek.'

That sounded OK. How frightening could that be? Back beside the fire, I saw that Miss Giddens was looking for her young charges in the dark upstairs rooms of the old house. As she moved along a spooky corridor, the wraith-like figure of a young woman suddenly glided across it and disappeared into the wall.

'Who was that?' I said. There was no answer.

'Who was that lady?' I asked, more loudly.

'It's obviously a ghost,' said my sister. 'She's haunting the little girl.'

Icicles prickled up my back. My mother looked at my father, possibly imploring him to send me to bed before something awful happened, but he was engrossed in the TV. Minutes later, Miss Giddens found both Flora and the little boy, Miles. The children leapt upon her with jolly shouts and playful embraces. I breathed more easily. Then Miles, shouting with glee, put his arm around the governess's neck and started playfully to strangle her. 'Miles,' she said. 'I can't breathe . . .'

I didn't like this film one bit. I picked up my funny book again and tried to read, but the words wouldn't connect. My eyes seemed magnetised by the television screen. I couldn't stop myself watching. Soon it was Deborah Kerr's turn to hide in this horrible game. She found a hiding-place behind one of the curtains in the old house's dining-room, and stood in the moonlit darkness, looking worried and awfully vulnerable.

And when I next trusted myself to look, something terrible was happening. We were looking more and more closely at Miss Giddens's worried, handsome face and – Oh no, oh no! – just behind her, and through the window, a man suddenly appeared, out in the garden. He was gliding towards the window, was creeping up on her with fright-ening intent as she stood there, in hiding, oblivious to the danger. His face was looming up out of the darkness, coming to see, coming to look in, coming to get her, coming to . . .

I froze, as if I'd been immersed in icy water. Sensing some awful presence behind her, Miss Giddens turned round – and there, filling the screen, was the face of the awful man glaring at her. He was swarthy, black-haired, and he looked at her with eyes of pure hatred. His face was dark, his eyes the eyes of the Maniac in the film hoarding beside St Mary's church, as mad as the patient I'd seen in my father's waiting-room. He was the worst person in the world – the embodiment of everything evil – and only the glass in the window separated him from the innocent governess.

I shrieked with terror. Seconds later, I was lying on the rug, panicked out of my wits.

'John, for God's sake, will you calm down?' demanded my mother. ''Tis just an old fillum.'

'Ahhhhhhhrrrrggghhh,' I shouted, my face pressed against the ticklish carpet.

'The children shouldn't be stayin' up watchin' this awful stuff,' my father muttered, to no one in particular.

'Blimey,' said my sister, coolly, 'that made me jump.'

I groaned, tears squeezing through my tight-shut eyes.

'John, come here and sit on my lap,' said my mother, 'and stop that awful noise. Look, the horrible man has gone away.'

I couldn't look. Nothing would make me look at the television ever again. I was some way beyond any dispassionate connection with the narrative on the 20-inch Pandora's box in the corner of the room. I keened, banshee-like, unstoppably.

'It's not a real ghost,' said Madelyn diplomatically. 'Just some bloke out in the garden looking through the window. Don't make such a silly fuss.'

'I saw a ghost once,' said my father, stubbing out his cigarette in his marble ashtray. 'In a big old hotel, over in Galway. It was an old feller from another century, gliding about in a long grey cloak. And believe me, John, 'twas nothing like that feller at all.'

'Uhhhhhhhhgggg . . .'

'Martin,' said my mother sharply. 'I don't really think that's helping.'

My mother picked me up in a quivering heap and hugged me. 'Where's your dressing-gown?' she said. 'You're going to bed right this minute.'

'No!' I shouted. 'I'm not going upstairs. Don't make me go upstairs.'

'It's your bedtime,' said my mother, 'and you're not staying here a minute longer.'

So I was led weeping off to bed. I could hardly get up the stairs, where there were doorways and shadows and too much dark to be borne. All the cosiness of home – the warmth and comfort inside the drawn curtains of the living-room – was obliterated now, because of the man with the horrible eyes outside the windows.

I made it to my room at the top of the house and was tucked up in bed and kissed goodnight, but I couldn't sleep. I looked at the wall on my right, where giant shadows from the traffic outside the curtains sent bars of light marching up the flocked wallpaper. They were like demons, cunningly abseiling upwards to the ceiling to hang over me all night. I twisted round in the bed. To my left was a glooming darkness, irradiated by a clock with greenly phosphorescent hands that ticked the seconds away, loudly, relentlessly, tockingly-torturously, like the grandfather clock in *Dombey and Son* that I'd tried to read earlier that year, the one which tocks out the words 'How. Is. My. Lit-tle. Friend?' while Dombey Junior is gradually dying. The face of the devilish Peter Quint – the former gardener, I later discovered, who used to bully and sexually abuse Miss Jessel, the poor former governess, and who had now come back, in the person of the innocent Miles, to brutalise the poor Miss Giddens – kept looming towards me.★

★ Discovering, much later, that this ghastly revenant was played by Peter Wyngarde, the actor who was to play the insufferably camp

53

My mother came up later, to find me whimpering uncontrollably.

'John,' she said, 'you mustn't upset yourself about a stupid thing on the telly. It's only a story.'

'I can't stop thinking about the horrible man,' I said into the pillow. 'He won't go away.'

'You mustn't get so upset about things in stories,' she said, sitting down on the bed. 'The people who make these silly fillums are just playing on your fears. You have to learn not to take them seriously, like learning not to be scared of the dark. You'll find that goodness always wins out at the end. Everything turns out all right, in these silly movies, provided you stick it out for long enough.'

'I can't sleep,' I moaned. 'He's there all the time, outside the window.'

'For heaven's sake,' said my mother. 'The thing is almost over now. Any minute, the police or somebody will arrive and the man'll be carted off to prison, and the children will be all happy and playful again.'

I ceased whimpering. 'Are you sure?'

'Why wouldn't I? I've seen a hundred of these stupid ghost stories.'

'So, can I come down and watch them being all right again?'

'Well . . .'

So somehow we decided I should come back downstairs and watch the end of the film sitting on her lap in front of the fire.

---

crime-fighter Jason King in the ATV series *Department S*, and enjoyed his own spin-off show, *Jason King*, deploying his twin affectations of rolled-back jacket sleeves and long coffee-coloured cheroots, until his career was sunk by revelations of gay cottaging, did nothing to assuage the memory of this most-frightening-ever movie moment.

Had I been familiar with *The Turn of the Screw*, I'd have known that things weren't going to end happily. I sat on my mother's matronly skirts to watch the final unfolding of the tragedy. It was pitiless. The death of Miles, the possessed and malevolent little boy, in the governess's arms was pretty bad. The whirling camera that disclosed the appalling Quint, standing on a plinth like a statue presiding over the kid's death, wasn't a barrel of laughs either. But neither was as bad as the final shot of Miss Jessel. She was seen standing in the rain among the reeds beside a lake, a vision of utter misery in her black governess threads, her arms hanging dejectedly by her side, her long black hair drenched and clinging to her white face. Nobody in history ever looked so desolate. And to emphasise her lonesomeness, this poor, wretched, rained-on, loveless ghost was seen in the middle distance, far from any comfort that we or Miss Giddens might be able to offer. And she was seen through a window.*

God knows how I got to sleep at all that night, but it left me with a scar. For years, I had a fetish about windows. I learned not to look at them when approaching a friend's house, especially when it was night-time, lest I should see something I'd rather not see. When I entered my bedroom each night, I used to play a foolish game of Scare Yourself. I'd stick out my left hand and, walking over the threshold, I'd sweep it down the wall to switch the light on. If my hand connected with the switch, the light would come on and all would be well, and I'd walk to the windows and draw the curtains without a care. But if, in that downward swipe, I missed the switch, and walked into the darkness, I somehow convinced myself that there, right before me, the worst person

---

* Jack Clayton, the director, claimed he'd actually had a vision of this sorry image in his own garden, a few days before filming it. 'Just the sadness of it was what I think I saw,' he later remarked.

in the world would be staring in at me through the glass . . .

It was a masochistic little game, the kind of challenge you set yourself when you're young, but it was a paradigm of the impulse that takes us to scary movies. We dare ourselves not to be scared by the demons lurking on screen. We test, in some perverse way, our capacity to become, voluntarily, gibbering wrecks when confronted by our own paranoia.

Windows, for me, became emblems of seeing the world all wrong. There is a long pedigree of minatory casements in English literature to legitimise my personal dread about the things. Poets from Chaucer to Wordsworth have presented windows as the eyes of houses, and, by extension, the eyes of the beloved figure within, who has turned her face away from the poet, leaving the house shuttered and forever blind to him.

Louis MacNeice in 'Corner Seat' identifies a moment of paranoia we've all felt on the 11.58 p.m. ride home from the fleshpots of the West End:

Windows between you and the world
Keep out the cold, keep out the fright –
So why does your reflection seem
So lonely in the moving night?

It may be a universal emotion to be upset by seeing your reflected face, not as a reflection in a mirror but as a face beyond the glass – as if some alter ego had come a-calling through the window from another world, full of worry and pain; the face of someone who is not the real you, but a subconscious stranger who surfaces only in dreams.

When I was older, and saw *The Innocents* again at fifteen, and was still petrified by it, I wondered about my neurotic dread of windows. It seemed there must have been some earlier image that lay deep inside me, a fundamental dread summoned back by the horrible face of Peter Wyngarde. Eventually, I worked out what it was: *The Snow Queen*, an animated version of the Charles Perrault fairy tale about a cold-hearted monarch who steals away a little boy and takes him to her kingdom, where he is eventually rescued by his sister.

I was about three or four, at my first home, in Balham, South London. We'd had a television only a short time (this would have been 1957 or 1958) and Madelyn and I watched it obsessively. She and I had a cunning strategy for the moments when anything scary or unpleasant appeared on screen. One of us would pretend to go to the loo, crying out 'Tell me what happens next!' as we fled upstairs, returning only when the frightening scene was safely out of the way. We never bothered asking each other about the intervening scariness. We knew it was just an excuse.

When a cartoon of *The Snow Queen* was broadcast one Sunday afternoon, Madelyn and I were by ourselves in the living-room. On the TV, a boy and a girl, slightly older than us, were playing in a Scandanavian homestead when, suddenly, the Snow Queen came whistling through the air and gazed in through the window at them. She envied their innocence, their purity. She wanted to make the boy her slave. . . .

Madelyn had seen what was coming and legged it upstairs, crying 'Tell me what happens' in time-honoured style. I was left behind. Because of our you-must-watch-it protocol, I had to see the story unfold. So when the Snow Queen inspected the children and stared in at the doomed little boy, I had to watch it alone. Her cartoon eyes were enormous, lit with a cruel, unearthly brightness. They stared through the glass, her great green pupils mad and comfortless. There was no escape for poor Hans, nor for me. She was out to get both of us. A missile of ice sprang from her eyes and hurtled through the glass and flew into the small boy's spindly chest. He turned instantly into a zomboid slave of the frigid queen, unable to speak to his sister or anybody else, utterly in the power of a woman who lived in an awful cold white land impossibly far from the comfort of home . . .

It was appalling. I let out a four-year-old shriek that brought my parents running. I could not be consoled, even with hot milk and marshmallows. My parents were up half the night, reading me stories and trying to reassure me that the Snow Queen wasn't lurking outside the windows of the nursery, ready to steal me away. Forty-odd years later, I still shudder at the mention of her name.

Most horror films in the Sixties were dreadfully anti-climactic after *The Innocents*: all those tiresome bits of Hammer Guignol, with Peter Cushing playing his pinch-faced Man in the Library With a Skull On His Desk, and Christopher Lee sweeping about in a cloak, baring his ridiculous teeth in a blood-curdling Count Dracula leer that looked more like the smile on the Joker in the *Batman* comics. Even the old horror movie classics seemed pretty small beer. I watched the first Dracula and Frankenstein movies with interest but no great concern: I watched *The Mummy* and *The Wolf Man* and found them about as scary as a trigonometry exam. I sat through that bewildering expressionist farrago *The Black Cat*. without raising so much as a shiver. Nothing got to me as directly, as viscerally, as *The Innocents* and Peter Quint's elderly, frozen, window-haunting predecessor from the Arctic wastes.

The windows stayed in my head because of that night in 1963, when I was nine. All the components of the night came together as random images that suddenly cohered: the movie posters, the dripping blood, the staring eyes, the Gothic church with its congregation of grotesque old folks, the great wooden crucifix with its hanging man, the mad patient in his pyjamas standing in our hallway glaring at me, the man having an epileptic fit on the Welcome mat, that business with the teeth – they all were part of being a God-fearing, church-visiting, cinema-loving doctor's son. And among these troubling Saturday-night images I could now introduce the Dark Face at the Window as an emblem of fright.

This stream of images, spooling through my subconscious, got to me in the real world eventually. One episode demonstrated their hold over my imagination. It was the summer I worked, aged seventeen, as a ward porter in Queen Mary's Hospital, Roehampton. It was a holiday job and I loved it. The other porters were impossibly worldly and blokish twenty-somethings who read the *Sun* during their tea-breaks, smoked roll-ups and talked about West Ham and Queen's Park Rangers with a kind of sulky enthusiasm as though somebody was forcing them to support their favourite football teams. They ruthlessly itemised the charms of every single nurse they came into contact with, and bragged shamelessly about the ones they'd managed to sleep with.

The majority of the nurses were barely older than I was. I conceived a passion for the staff nurses, whose little tiaras of starched lace struck me as fantastically chic and sexy. A plump blonde radiographer called Linda ran the X-ray department. She was soon to be married but was obviously going off the whole idea. She would explain to me, in the brief moments of chat after I'd slid a patient off his trolley and on to an X-ray couch, how sick she was of everyone telling her it was normal to have 'doubts', that it was a natural response to your imminent nuptials, that her Bernard was a fine bloke and she didn't want to let everyone down now, now did she? I murmured sympathetically. I told her that her friends seemed foolishly unsupportive, that her fiancé was shockingly insensitive. Each time, Linda said, 'Oh, you understand, don't you,' and folded me in a wobbling embrace, thus ensuring I would treble my efforts to sympathise with her next time I had a patient on a trolley, whether he needed an X-ray or not.

I enjoyed the camaraderie of the porters, the romance of the nurses, the swishy 'Don't speak to me, I'm too important' heroism of the doctors, the little brothers and sisters in the kids' ward, the coolly insouciant technicians, the lovelorn not-quite-girlfriend among the X-rays. It was like living in a village, or more precisely, in a village-based TV soap opera. Everywhere you looked, there was gossip and romance. Roger Moore, the actor, had been spotted in F Ward, allegedly there to have the bags under his eyes removed. A little girl in J ward was due for surgery to have her bat-ears pinned back, and when I went to pick her up from the Recovery Room and said, 'Come on, Natasha, time to get back to your friends in the ward,' she leaned over, fast asleep, and plonked a big kiss on my cheek. There was just so much going on. For a newly socialised seventeen-year-old, it was Hog Heaven.

The only drawback was G Ward.

The hospital was famous across the nation for two things: burns and plastics. At a time (1971) when plastic surgery was still considered a wayward course of action for the terminally rich and achingly vain, Queen Mary's specialised in it. Actresses came for face-lifts, little girls like Natasha came to have tiny disfigurements adjusted or concealed, a whole department specialised in prosthetic limbs for amputees. It was known as the Spare Parts Unit. (A sign outside the main door read, a little insensitively, 'Out-Patients Must Assemble Before 10 a.m.') And it also did burns. If a particularly bad motorway car crash or domestic fire was reported on the News, Queen Mary's was where the burns victims would be taken. They had all the top technology of skin-grafts and maxillo-facial surgery. They could do anything – except stop some people looking absolutely terrible.

Sometimes, burns patients recovering from long-term treatments would find their way back to one of the ordinary-patient wards, which I visited with my porter's trolley every day. Sometimes a screen would go back in C Ward, revealing the wrecked features of a poor man who had poured paraffin onto a Guy Fawkes bonfire and had the whole can explode in his face. Months of treatment later, he still looked, above the neck, like the Creature from the Black Lagoon. When he tried to arrange his ravaged complexion into a smile, you felt like your heart would break. When he moved his lips – which were no longer lips but white horizontal smears below his nose and above his chin – and tried to talk to me, I would grip the cool metal rail of my trolley, look away and tell myself sternly, 'You. Must. Not. Faint. You *must* not faint. It will only upset the patient.'

I could be weepingly sensitive and casually heartless about these patients at the same time, but I couldn't help the way I responded to extreme disfigurement. I found myself wondering: if this is the way the poor man looks now, after months of ameliorative surgery, what in God's name did he look like on the day they brought him in?

But I didn't know, because new arrivals with severe burns went to G Ward, and I never went there. It was the only ward from which ordinary porters like me were excused duty. It had a dedicated porter of its own, a guy called Geoff. He was something of a legend for his bovine insensitivity. He was allowed, or invited, to do the G Ward runs because he didn't seem to mind the awful conditions. He didn't notice, or worry about, people whose faces and limbs had melted in a furnace. Once, they said, Geoff had been present at an operation where a patient's burnt skin was being removed with a metal device like a spokeshave. He was standing too close to the operating table and a lump of charred skin, accompanied by globules of pus and blood, came flying off the patient and whacked him in the face.

Geoff (other porters told me in awestruck tones) had registered no emotion whatsoever. He had simply removed his now-opaque spectacles, wiped the greeny-red gunk off the lenses, replaced them equably on his splattered countenance and gone back to the operation. He was the G Ward man. He presided over its mysteries. It was a mysterious place. You heard things about it, unsettling things. That, for instance, it smelt really bad – the authentic smell of human flesh which, according to rumour, smelt uncommonly like roast pork. I heard that it was uncomfortably, tropically, freakishly warm in there because the thermostat had to be turned right up, or the patients' burnt skin would contract in the cool air. I heard that patients lay on their backs all the time, with a thin cotton sheet suspended above their recumbent frames, because if their flesh touched the sheet it would stick to the fabric and would have to be yanked off in screaming agony. I learned that this was why Geoff's trolleys had to be lined with antiseptic paper, for the lumps of charred human being. . . .

Thank God for Geoff, we used to agree. He was welcome to the battlefield of burns victims. Rather him than me, everyone used to say. I'd as soon shoot myself in the head as go near the burns patients . . .

G Ward stood by itself, a whole corridor's width of Burns Hell. The entrance was at the far end of a side-corridor, up a long incline. The letter 'G' stuck out from the wall, like the sign over a concentration camp. Walking past (no, accelerating past) when one of its doors was being opened, you would occasionally get a stray whiff of roasted meat. You imagined the nursing sisters inside the swing doors, speaking in urgent whispers, a sisterhood of suffering, girls who had seen terrible sights, who'd become inured to human torches and Roman candles and people set on fire by their neighbours or co-religionists because of a minor difference of opinion. You imagined all the staff in G Ward moving about in tropical darkness because it was more restful that way, just as I used to think that horror films must be conducted all the way through in Stygian gloom.

One evening in July I was on late shift. I wasn't due to knock off until 10 p.m. Things were quiet and I was sitting in the Porters' Room at 9 o'clock, reading Kafka and waiting for the last hour to while itself away.

The phone rang. 'Is Geoff there?' said a voice.

'I think he's gone to the canteen,' I said.

'Tell him to ring G Ward, would you?' drawled the voice. 'Emergency theatre, fifteen minutes. OK?'

I promised I'd tell him, and went back to *The Castle*.

Three minutes went by. An anxious woman, a junior houseman, put her head round the door. 'Where's the porter, what's his name, Geoffrey? They're yelling for a porter in G Ward right now. Some patient has to go for surgery, pronto.'

'Geoff's in the canteen,' I said. 'I'm sure he'll be back soon.'

'We need him now, for God's sake,' said the woman. 'We can't have the operating theatre staff waiting around for a porter to finish drinking his tea.'

'But I'm sure –' I began.

'You'll have to do it,' she said. 'You'll need to wear a mask. Do you know where Geoffrey keeps the disinfectant masks?'

'I can't do that,' I said, a panicky tremor entering my voice. 'I'm not going to G Ward.'

'What do you mean, not going?' asked the woman. 'This is an emergency. You will go up there right now, collect the patient and transfer him to the operating theatre on the first floor for immediate surgery. And you'll need a disinfectant sheet on the trolley, I hope you realise.'

'I'm not trained,' I said, having a sudden brainwave. 'I'm not a burns porter because I haven't had any training. I wouldn't know how to do it. I'm sure Geoff will be back any moment and –'

'Oh, *training*,' she said nastily. 'Is that it? Oh, I see, you feel you need some kind of degree in – what? – Advanced Portering Skills and Trolley Management before you can do a simple thing and help to save somebody's life. Is that it?'

She all but said, 'You stupid boy,' and smacked me round the head.

'You have been to school, I take it,' she continued. 'And you have got half a brain? And I know you can walk and talk, because I've seen you do both. Now get a trolley up to G Ward this minute, before I lose my temper.'

So I found some sheets of special skin-soothing paper and put it all over the trolley. I couldn't find a mask anywhere. And I set off with a heavy heart on the nastiest journey I'd ever known.

I was going to have to go inside G Ward, into the fuggy, tropical, pork-smelling hell of the burned and damned, and I knew that, as I walked through the ward, the burnt patients would lift up their *Night of the Living Dead* faces and their *Souls in Purgatory* blackened limbs and I knew the minute I saw the special, just-arrived Emergency Case for which my trolley was meant, I would pass out with the horror of it, and everyone would get really upset.

I came out of the lift, pushing my paper-coated trolley before me. My legs were like lead. Though I was supposed to be helping out at an emergency, my reluctance and cowardice (though I liked to think it was a stubborn refusal to be pushed around) meant that I was walking slower and slower. There was nobody around, just the blankness of the horrible, custard-yellow NHS walls and the glaring, recessed lights overhead. Here was the corner of the corridor. Up a long incline, perhaps sixty yards away, the big, black-on-green sign read 'G WARD' like a ghastly threat.

I pushed the trolley into the side corridor. Fifty yards

ahead, the great black 'G' wiggled and danced about in front of my vision. I had become a *cinema-verité*, hand-held camera and all the shots were jiggled and out of focus, as I blinked back tears of alarm and struggled to see clearly. But my destination was all too clear. I was going to the worst place in the world.

And it was because of the blasted windows that I felt so appalled. The doors of G Ward were always shut because of the need to keep the air temperature consistent and un-wavering. Every other ward had its door open to visitors and passing medics and droppers-by; but not the ward from hell. I'd noticed, when furtively passing the doors, there were two little porthole windows at which you were supposed to present your face, to be identified before you'd be allowed in.

In thirty seconds, I told myself, I will have to present my face at the window and wait to see what unspeakable appari-tion gazes out at me . . .

I can't do this, I said silently.

I am walking, I told myself, into the biggest horror film I've ever seen, and it's all going to be real.

Something had changed about my relationship with windows. At home when I was small, they'd been the glass shelter that kept the outside world at bay. Then they were the screen through which awful people could come and look in at you, like Quint and the Snow Queen, as though inspecting your tortured soul. Now there were these round porthole windows, where I was the outsider looking in, but the people on the inside would have gargoyle faces. Everything had got all topsy-turvy. A crucifix on the wall brought back memories of St Mary's, and the staring-eyed Maniac, my father's crackpot patient, the asphyxiating Christ, the blood-boltered posters, the red-rimmed eyes of Dracula just before he pounces – all my most dreaded images.

The big G loomed nearer. It began to take on a three-dimensional quality, like those monumental slabs of brick wall that spelt out the letters of *Ben-Hur*. I was about to be engulfed in heat, and the smell of cooked people, and the noisy whimperings of the dying and the muted groans of the ones whose skin had only recently started to tighten up and blacken.

Oh no, I kept whispering to myself. Please no. Let me not have to do this. I will be good and virtuous and behave myself for ever and ever (I seemed to be praying to some Higher Being, halfway between God and my mother). I could hear a foolish mewing noise, a pathetic whimpering, issuing from the corridor. Was it the noise of some unfortunate patient . . . ? No, Goddammit, it was me. I was in the final throes of panic. 'Eeeennnmmm,' the little mewing noise went, 'Eeeeeennnnnnmmmmm . . .'

Suddenly I was there, G Ward. My Nemesis. My Golgotha. My Destination of No Return. The double doors were as firmly shut as if everybody inside were having a day off work. (If only.) The circular porthole windows lay before me, like two eyes looking at me.

I tapped on one of them. I waited, a palpitating wreck, for something resembling Quint's saturnine visage or the Snow Queen's glacial physiognomy to stare back at me. Then a curtain twitched and a senior orderly looked out, the lower half of his face covered with a green mask.

He opened the door and came out to where I was standing, gibbering with apprehension.

'Ah, John,' he said. 'Good of you to do this. Geoff would normally have done it, but he's in theatre at the moment, so I thought you wouldn't mind . . .'

'It's OK,' I said in a teeny-tiny voice, like Piglet in the Winnie the Pooh stories. 'Where is the man with the terrible —'

'No, no, the patient's already been taken to theatre,' he

said, as though to a half-wit. 'We rang down for another porter because we need to get a machine, a new respirator adapted for burns patients, to the operating theatre. It's a bit heavy so we thought we'd send it by trolley, but you'll have to take it along right now. Would you mind?'

'I'd –' I was almost incoherent with relief.

'What?' said the orderly.

'I'd *love* to,' I said with pathetic gratitude. 'I'd absolutely love to.'

'Well, it's only a machine, old boy,' said the orderly. 'Of course we appreciate your enthusiasm for these, ah, menial tasks . . .'

'Where is it?' I asked, suddenly raring to go.

'Just inside here on the floor in Sister's office,' he said, opening the door a couple of inches. 'But I wouldn't come too far into the ward itself, if I were you. It can seem a little, er, stifling if you're not used to it.'

'Doesn't bother me,' I said with airy confidence, and I pushed the trolley in through the awful doors of what was no longer necessarily Hell.

I picked up the machine, and plonked it on the trolley, and set off to the operating theatre with a spring in my step. Peter Quint and the Snow Queen never showed up at any point. They stayed somewhere at the back of the ward, having their macaroni cheese supper, apparently uninterested in ruining my life any more.

3

JOHN WAYNE'S
FILTHY TEMPER

Red River (1947)

'Thanks to the movies, real gunfire has always sounded
unreal to me, even when being fired at'

— Peter Ustinov

The first time I was ambushed by the Baxter Gang, I was
ten years old, walking home from choir practice at the local
church of St Vincent de Paul. It was a dusty, sun-bleached
London Saturday afternoon in high summer, so hot that the
granite pavement winked at you until your eyes hurt, your
black school brogues felt like twin ovens around your baking
feet, and the only solace for your raging thirst was to spend
two shillings on a pyramid-shaped lump of frozen orange
squash called a Jubbly. It was not an elegant form of water-
ice — you had to strip back the slimy, orange-silted bits of
cardboard from the apex and plunge your mouth over it,
grinding away with all your teeth at once, like a horse, to
loosen some icy shards of squash and hold them, melting,
in your mouth until you couldn't stand the pain any longer.
Satisfying, yes, but strangely headache-inducing.

I was walking home along Lavender Sweep, a road whose name (though once presumably thought charming) always put me in mind of a loo-brush, when the Gang appeared in front of me. There were two of them, about my age, and they meant business. One was a skinny oik with a crew-cut and a green Ben Sherman shirt, the kind with the button-down collar. His sidekick was a classic School Fat Boy, a roly-poly, broken-winded gobshite with a spotty chin and a greasy Prince Valiant haircut. They stopped as I drew level.

'Give us a suck of yer lolly, then,' said the skinny one.

'Who are you?' I countered.

'We run this place,' said the oik. 'Don't we, Jeff?'

Jeff said nothing, but looked at me with a scowl.

'What, all of it?' I said, looking round. 'You mean, you own this whole street?'

'Where d'you live?' asked the oik, with an attempt at truculence.

'Round here,' I said neutrally.

'That your dad's motor?' he said, indicating what was indeed my father's Rover 2000.

'Might be,' I said.

'Rich ponce, are you?'

'Where do *you* live, then?' I asked in return. 'I 'aven't seen you round 'ere before.' I had slipped, cautiously, into the Battersea vernacular.

'His dad,' said the skinny one, indicating the fat Jeff, 'he's been in the nick. Got no time for rich ponces.'

'Oh, really?' I said. Our encounter was proceeding in meaningless, small steps, but there was no doubting the threat that lay beneath our trading of questions and answers. The back door of my house was precisely ten yards away, but I could hardly flourish my key and let myself in, leaving them to trash my father's car and run away laughing.

'I got to go,' I said. 'Got a karate lesson in fifteen minutes.'

The blatant lie hung in the air, an unmistakable counter-threat.

At last the fat boy spoke. Like an old tape-recorder switched on and slowly whirring into life, Jeff gathered his great brain and said: 'D'you want a fight?'

'No,' I said. 'I got to be somewhere else. 'Bye now.'

'You startin' somethin', mate?' Jeff persisted – an absurd question, since I was clearly trying to signal my departure. 'Cos if you are, I'm going to finish it.'

It was obviously a speech he'd been practising for a while, part of a preamble to violence he'd learned from a cooler kid, and was desperate to try out on somebody, no matter how unpromising the circumstances.

'No, no, honestly not,' I said. Whereupon he hit me with his fist, surprisingly gently, on the chin.

I couldn't believe it. Nobody had ever hit me there before. At school in Wimbledon, surrounded by the cream of the Catholic middle-classes, we didn't do such things. We wrestled, we inflicted arm-locks and head-locks on each other, we dealt in Chinese Burns and Dead Legs and agonising Half-Nelsons, but we never took a swing at another chap's face. That was the stuff of gangster movies and cowboy films.

The blow in my own backyard, didn't actually hurt, but it was incontrovertibly a punch in the face, and demanded some form of response. Though it didn't hurt, it was extremely *annoying*. So I did what any bourgeois movie-going kid would have done. I balled my fists, narrowed my eyes and bore down on the fat pillock with the words 'Why, you . . .' grating from my ten-year-old lips.

Amazingly, he and his skinny friend hastened away down the street. It was enough that they'd laid a featherweight blow on a local boy (especially a rich ponce). They had no more interest in a full-scale fight than I had. The gesture was, it seemed, enough.

In the badlands around Clapham Junction in 1963, you had to watch yourself. I was a well-educated doctor's son, living in a working-class neighbourhood populated by criminals, toughs, tearaways, blag-artists, shoplifters, dodgy market traders, the weasel-faced sons of whippet-thin men who worked in the motor business.

Most of my days were spent at school five miles away in Wimbledon, where the streets were leafy, the shops were full of new pastel fashions, and the houses on the Ridgeway and the Downs sported glamorous, off-street driveways. Around my home in Battersea, everything was terraced, shuttered, council-owned, bleakly functional. I wish I could say I became street-wise from growing up in a tough neighbourhood, but the only streets I knew were the long shopping thoroughfares of Battersea Rise and Lavender Hill, places down which I tramped aimlessly on Saturday mornings without picking up any proletarian *savoir-faire* at all. Most of the time, I longed to get home, where I could read my comics and make my Airfix models in peace, away from the noisome reek of Northcote Road market and the hopeless furniture shops on Rise and Hill; full of leatherette-and-draylon three-piece suites.

When I encountered the tough kids in the neighbourhood, I had no idea how to behave − what to say, how to initiate or conclude a fight, how to handle the endlessly protracted, preambular exchange of insults. But what struck me about the encounter in Lavender Sweep was that we were all − all three of us − going through the motions of a fight rather than actually fighting; and that everything we said and did came from movie Westerns.

Take that moment when the skinny one affected to 'run this place' and I scoffed at his presumption. God knows what he meant by saying it, but he and I were mimicking a scene from *Red River*, a classic John Wayne movie. In an early scene, an exotic Mexican dude rides up just as Wayne is explaining to his toothless sidekick Groot (Walter Brennan) and his adoptive son Matthew (Montgomery Clift) that the patch of land on which they're standing is an ideal place to start a homestead ('There's good water and grass – plenty of it') and that he will establish the Red River D cattle company on this very spot. The Mexican explains that all the land is, in fact, owned by a shadowy megalomaniac called Diego, and that Wayne has a bit of a nerve to claim ownership of it on a whim.

'Go to Diego,' grunts Wayne, 'and tell him all the land north of the river is mine. Tell him to stay off it.'

'Others have come here and tried to take this land,' says the smiling Mexican. 'Others have thought like you . . .'

'And you've always been good enough to stop them?' says Wayne, employing a sophisticated play on the words 'good' and 'enough'.

'Señor,' says the Mexican, smiling fit to bust, 'eet ees my job.'

'Pretty unhealthy work,' says Wayne, waving his *compadres* away from the imminent shoot-out.

'I'm sorry,' says the Mexican, and pulls his gun, but Wayne shoots him, right there on his horse, and that, it seemed, was the way you ended any tiresome disputes over who owned the territory with the good water and the plentiful grass.

If only we could all be like John Wayne. The thought filled the heads of several million Americans (and several million English schoolkids) for decades. If only we could bully our way into acquiring land and telling people what to do, if only we knew, like him, when to pull a gun and do the right thing about territory, or justice, or cattle, how much simpler life would be. Whatever character he played, Wayne seemed to make up the rules of the Old West as he went along, and everyone just agreed with him. It saved time and meant you didn't have to get shot. He was the Man, the

Chief, the natural leader – a gun-slinging Moses who knew the way to the Promised Land and who assumed personal charge of the Ten Commandments. He had a gruff authority nobody could argue with. He showed you how things were done around these parts, and you just had to go along with it.

Perversely *Red River* was the key Western of my young days precisely because it presented John Wayne, for once, as wholly *un*-admirable. But before we get into that, a word about the stranglehold that Western movies exerted on the impressionable youth in the Granada stalls.

Being ten years old, in 1963, wasn't much fun. You were still a kid, but you weren't a child any more. You lived in a worrying interregnum between childish toys and pubertal exhibitionism. Your life took a sudden turn into intense physicality. Your friends suddenly turned into football fans, and their conversation degenerated into a recital of goal statistics or players' names. Two of my closest pals became Boy Scouts and went around with flashes of green ribbon on their school socks as an insignia of their new identity as expert knot-fashioners and the like. (I was once invited to join their hearty freemasonry, to go on marches with them, attend a jamboree, and spend a weekend climbing a mountain called Snowdon in Wales. 'No thanks,' I said, 'I just can't stand all the baked beans.' It wasn't just a smart remark. The Scout movement had been hijacked by a Heinz sponsorship and were expected to turn out *en masse* in a beans-fuelled, march-and-sing advertisement. Both the prospect, and the sponsor, turned my stomach. I was happier being a non-competitive school swot.)

If you were neither a Chelsea supporter nor a Scout, there were other opportunities to test your physical robustness in public. Like being casually whacked around the head by the school bullies, Lemmon and McGuire, as they passed you in the playground. Or being winded in the solar plexus by your friend Mick Hewitt, as you walked together to rugby practice in Coombe Lane – a moment that left me gasping, 'Why did you do that?', to which there was no answer, except, 'Because you were there.' Casual violence was in the air in those days, the first whiffs of national testosterone, perhaps, in the first generation to have survived both the war and the exhausting regimen of rationing.

It seemed that you were always a heart-beat away from being punished by masters, duffed up in the locker rooms, chased across the playground by a *Lord of the Flies* posse of thugs who didn't appreciate your smart-alec interventions in the classroom. And that was just at school in Wimbledon. At home in Battersea, where I hung out with the boys at the church, I watched with incredulity as, one by one, the members of the choir transferred their allegiance to rival street gangs. The sight of my one-time pal Gerard Kelly, a weedy falsetto who used to hit the high notes of 'Faith of Our Fathers' better than anyone else, newly kitted out in skinhead braces and steel-toed boots, swaggering down Battersea Rise arm in arm with a little girlfriend (both of them aged eleven) in her rat-tail hairdo, *en route* to a gang rumble in the Station Approach outside Clapham Junction, was both laughable and alarming. These guys meant business. Unlike the pretendy hard-cases at school, my angelic former choristers were looking to do some serious damage. Anybody was fair game. Even me.

The Baxter Gang started to appear all over the place. (I never knew their real names, but the skinny oik in Lavender Sweep had borne a faint resemblance to Chris Baxter, a nice, inoffensive kid in my class at school, so Baxter became the generic name for everybody who was out to whack you in the face for no reason.) The worst time was in February 1964. It was another Saturday afternoon, and I was walking up St John's Hill to the Granada cinema when someone behind me said, 'Got the time, John?' Thinking it must be a friend, I stopped, turned round, and found myself sandwiched between two teenagers. One was about fifteen, a standard-issue Battersea thicko, but his friend was older and nastier – maybe eighteen or nineteen – and clad in a skinny macintosh through which he was clearly freezing. He was unshaven and undernourished.

'What?' I said.

'Just keep walking, John,' said the thicko. 'We just want a little chat.'

What could I do? Since we were walking up the hill, it would be hard to run away up the steepening gradient. I didn't fancy hurling myself into the traffic. As for turning round and running away down the hill, it never even occurred to me. You just don't run away down a hill. We walked along, line abreast, in an awkward silence. Nobody tried to make conversation. Then one of them said, 'How much money you got? Gimme all the money you got.'

I actually laughed, rather bravely, at that point. 'I'm only ten,' I said. 'I don't have any money. How much money do you expect a ten-year-old schoolboy to have on a Saturday afternoon?'

They didn't argue the point, even though I was (they'd spotted) a future Rich Ponce. Instead: 'Take off yer watch,' said the unshaven one. 'No I won't,' I said firmly.

It was a good watch, with an electric-blue face. My mum had bought it for me. I'd picked it out myself from the window of Laucher's Jewellery and Clocks emporium on the Queenstown Road, and accessorised it with a thick, metal-studded leather strap. It was a prized possession.

'Take it off, or I'll –'

'No I bloody won't,' I said, astonished to hear myself swear. 'Just push off.'

The tall freezing youth brought up the pocket of his raincoat, through which poked something long and thin. It pointed at my stomach.

'See that?' he said. 'That's a knife, that is –'

I looked at the pathetic coat and its equally puny protuberance. It was so obviously a finger. How could anyone fall for such a pathetic deception?

'Oh sure,' I said.

'You want me to prove it then, do yer?'

'Gow on, stab 'im,' said the thicko, gleefully.

I looked at the unshaven chap's face. He really was in a state. He looked as if he hadn't eaten for weeks, months. But he was capable of a lot of things, done casually, done offhandedly, done without a thought of the consequences, just to get some money or something that could be turned into money. His face was dead. His eyes were incurious, wanting this unpromising encounter to be over soon, one way or the other.

I couldn't take the chance. Appalled at myself, I took off my watch and handed it over.

'Now just keep on walking, mate, OK,' said the thicko, 'up the hill and don't look round, because we'll be just behind you for a while, and if you so much as look round, we will kick the shit out of you, OK? Just remember – keep walking, no looking. OK?'

In the days that followed, the response of my family and dearest buddies to my tragic loss was, frankly, unsupportive. 'How *could* you lose your lovely watch,' wept my mother, 'when I thought it meant so much to you? How could you let them awful boys take it off you?'

'But Mum,' I said, 'I didn't *offer* it to them. I had no choice. They were going to duff me up or stab me or something . . .'

'God, what a weed you are,' said my sister. 'You should just stand up to people like that and be firm.'

'But Madelyn,' I said, 'there were two of them. Horrible, nasty big guys with scars, probably just out of prison.'

'So *you* say. We've only got your word for it. There was

probably just one boy. I bet he just asked for your watch, and you gave it to him and ran away crying.'

'I did *not*.'

'Tis an awful pity,' said my father, 'that you didn't take a swing at them. If I'd been there . . .' He punched the air lightly with both his fists.

How could my whole family be so intensely, unhelpfully irritating?

At school, my spot of bother soon leaked out. All my classmates asked for minute details of what had happened. They pretended kindly concern and interest while I revealed all the salient facts, and then they started in. How I should have grabbed the knife, stamped on the first one's foot, gouged out the other one's eyes, chopped the side of my hand into someone's Adam's apple, kneed someone else in the bollocks, kick-boxed my way out of trouble . . . It went on and on. It was like being mugged all over again, belaboured with idiotic advice, threatened with accusations of cowardice and relieved, none too gently, of my dignity.

The boys' brave assurances of how one should behave with tough guys all came from Western movies, of course. A hundred saloon-bar brawls had made them worldly connoisseurs of how to throw a haymaker punch, how to smash a pub chair to smithereens over somebody's back, how to dodge out of the way as a villain's head connected with the gilt-framed mirror over the bar . . . Snake-eyed filmic encounters on the walkway outside the sheriff's office, gruff exchanges of threat and counter-threat outside barn and homestead and railway depot had given them a feel for the dialogue of manly confrontation. All they were doing was passing on what we all knew already – if somebody tries to attack you, this is how you retaliate.

There, once again, was the shadowy space between what movies teach us and how incapable we are of reproducing it in real life. And as I passed through a post-mugging trauma, it seemed to me that we all lived in a daydream of *retaliation*. It was the semi-permanent condition of the pre-adolescent. You spent much of your waking hours anticipating trouble – from the priests and teachers, the bullies in the playground, the hard nuts in the rugby team, the bastard who stole the sandwiches from your locker while you were at Double Chemistry, and the Baxter gang at home – and wondering how you were going to retaliate when it struck. And if ever it *did* strike, as it struck with me, you then spent feverish weeks of hindsight rearrangement, of *l'esprit de l'escalier*, your tongue razor-sharp as you gazed in the mirror, your fists and elbows flailing in an empty room, even if your passionate, murderous imaginings left you in tears of frustration at the end.

It's axiomatic to say that the old-style Western is, or was, the most moralistic of movie genres. The classic Westerns constantly harped on the need for duty, self-reliance, hard work, husbandry, god-fearingness and learning to stick up for yourself. The films were about self-sufficiency, appropriate behaviour, personal skills, doing the right thing. They were about Being Yourself, only a cooler, braver, smarter, more quick-thinking, more ambitious self than you realised you were capable of. To be a Western hero was to have an identity outside the serious world of trades and professions. The cast might feature doctors, lawyers, bankers, politicians, preachers and so forth, but the real men were people outside the ordinary world of jobs, starter-homes and civilised values.

And they were centrally concerned with retaliation – defending the weak against the bullying, settling the hash of whoever killed your dad or abducted your niece, setting out on a journey which would show everyone (including yourself) how brave you were. They were impulses to action, legitimate spurs to violence.

The cowboy (though we probably didn't notice at the

time) thus resembled the schoolboy, the pre-employment free spirit who lives in a world of constant intimidation and fear, and is keen to prove himself among his peers, doing things faster and (you hoped) more skilfully than anyone else, always on the lookout for villainy and betrayal. If you misunderstood the codes of behaviour that operated in the school or the streets, you could get bullied or bashed up. If the cowboy got the signals wrong, the chances were he'd end up spatchcocked against the saloon hitching post, with his life blood soaking into the dust and the townspeople shaking their heads and saying, 'I guess he had it comin' . . .'

I saw a whole lifetime's worth of old Westerns in the Sixties, on TV and in the cinema. Some were first-run epics (*How the West Was Won*, 1962) or recent box-office smashes (*The Magnificent Seven*, 1960). Some were frankly ancient. South London picture-houses routinely showed limited, two-day re-runs of classic sagebrush epics like *She Wore a Yellow Ribbon* (1949), *Winchester '73* (1950), *High Noon* (1952) and *Shane* (1953), to which I was taken by the kindly *au pair* at eight, nine and ten. Sometimes I'd be dismayed to discover the film was in black and white, when you were by now used to glorious movie colour. Sometimes it was disconcerting to hear a stentorious male-voice choir well up on the soundtrack, at the climax of the action.

From such movies, and their like, you could draw up a simple list of behavioural rules and conventions – lessons taught in the schoolrooms of John Ford, Howard Hawks and William Wyler:

You did your best. You did the right thing. You tried to be virtuous, resourceful, self-reliant and cool. You kept your own counsel. You didn't blab or gossip, or tell strangers too much (or indeed anything) about yourself. You knew in advance the territory through which you rode. You knew the reputations of certain alarming figures and approached them with caution. You rarely carried any money, but ate and drank on credit. At the bar of any saloon, you ordered whisky, the bartender poured a tiny glassful from a bottle half-full of a red liquid, which you knocked back in one, before slamming the glass on the bar and demanding a refill (no bartender in film history ever said, 'That'll be $2.50 and *don't* bang the glasses, you'll break them.'). You worked as a hired gunslinger for farcically small sums of money, because honour and justice meant more to you than cash. You rarely owned a house in town because you were always travelling, restlessly onwards, across the wide Missouri or the Rio Grande, in search of a homestead where a man could settle down . . . But sometimes you put up in a hotel for several days and were visited by a variety of hysterical women.*

You wore a neckerchief, to keep the sweat from dripping down your neck and ruining your shirt. Sometimes you wore a waistcoat, occasionally a pair of ridiculous leather outer-trousers called 'chaps', which flapped about as you walked and called attention to your crotch. You could ride for days through scrubland, bluffs and plains, through Monument Valley and Painted Desert, without any apparent need for sustenance, snacks, water or bathroom tissue. You talked as little as possible, except to exchange information about railroads, ranches and the reputations of charismatic gunslingers.

You minded your Ps and Qs. It was OK for you to get drunk, provided you expressed your exuberance by singing,

---

* Women fell into two categories. Either they were schoolteachers with short curly hair and tightly-buttoned white tunics, who didn't like the rude manners and sweaty demeanour of cowboys but learned to respect them and later accept their rough proposals of marriage; or they were lipsticked and flashing-eyed houris who danced in the saloon, snogged the hero in his hotel room or entertained men in a garishly-decorated house run by a blowsy dame called Kitty.

rather than shooting up the saloon, as the bad guys did.★

You did not laugh at a fellow cowboy's mule, nor at his ludi-crous hat, nor his fading eyesight, for fear of getting a baptism of lead. You could take part in ferocious shoot-outs for twenty minutes without having to reload your six-guns. You were allowed to kill, although the exact protocol involved was hard to grasp. When approaching your rival down a deserted street, for instance, did you *always* stop exactly twenty yards apart? What if one of you kept on going? If you drew first and shot the other chap, would you be guilty of murder? Since it was invariably the guy who drew first who got killed, what would happen if neither of you made the first move? Would you both stand there until it got dark? What was the correct form of words for calling somebody to take part in a duel, and what did you do if they simply ignored your overtures? The Western – so elementally, mythologically simple, a test of Good pitted against swarthy, fly-buzzing-on-the-face Evil – sometimes left you puzzling about a hundred details of How to Live a Decent Life.

In the meantime, you bought the paraphernalia, and lived to the full the shadowy counter-existence of a Texan gunslinger. By ten, I had an impressive arsenal of toy guns: the long Winchester rifle clamped to its cardboard pack-aging by twisty wire restraints; the matched Colt .45s in their trashy holsters with plastic fake-mother-of-pearl gun butts; I even had a toy version of the Buntline Special favoured by Wyatt Earp, with its infeasibly long 12-inch barrel. I was a wild devotee of gun-barrel fetishism. But at

★ Bad guys also tended to molest the womenfolk. When a painted floozie on stage in the saloon was doing her sassy, petticoat-lifting, hoedown routine, there was always one drunken prat who made a lustful grab at her skirts to be rewarded with a kick in the chest from her laced-up prairie boots. You told yourself, However sloshed I get in a bar in the future, I will *never* make a grab for the good-time girl while she's doing her high-kickin' routine. A useful lesson in life.

least I never went as far as buying the Stetson, the leather chaps or the spurs that were available for the terminally naff in Harrods toy department.

I longed for a horse. I'd actually ridden on real horses in Ireland on summer holidays among my Galway cousins when I was small, and tried to imagine myself on a cattle trail, eyes squinting into the fiery sunlight (fat chance in Galway), scanning the bluffs for signs of Indian smoke, wishing I had the kind of saddle on which you could hang a lasso, a sleeping-bag, a long rifle, a few crucial kitchen implements (metal tray for cooking beans, knife, fork and spoon, shovel for burying the corpses of inept shootout victims) and the rest of the burdensome impedimenta that fashionable cowboys always seemed to carry with them. But the living, breathing horses, though they smelt fantastic, and swished their tails around their dignified arses with magnificent insouciance, were never quite the real thing. The couldn't compare with the horse I had at home.

In the spare room of our house was a big, discarded dresser, with two narrow chests of drawers and a huge vanity mirror in between them. I used to sit on the right-hand chest, six-guns holstered around my waist, long ropes of reins tied around the mirror supports, my juvenile bottom posting up and down on the glass top, my weedy heels spurring the frisky walnut sides as I rode into Dodge City (How the locals came out of the saloon to stare and mutter, 'Whoa – who's *this* guy?') or galloped away from hordes of yelping Cheyenne savages, or hid in a handy fissure in the rocks while the posse of crooked Santa Fe deputies cursed and swore in frustration and finally called off their pursuit of Johnny Battersea, the Lonesome Kid.*

---

* I was appalled, much later, when a rival to this title appeared at the start of Arthur Penn's Brando and Nicholson farrago *The Missouri*

82

Day after day in the school holidays, I could be found astride this haemorrhoid-inducing bit of furniture, riding to God knows where, running the risk of terrible injury by sitting at an angle of 45 degrees sideways, the better to see my heroic features in the big central mirror. And the face I thought I saw was John Wayne's. He was the moral fulcrum of all the rules of Western conduct. He was the final arbiter of right and wrong. He knew how things worked and why things failed. He was the mentor to whom you went for advice.

He was a dinosaur from the Forties' golden age of Westerns, but he was still around in the Sixties – in *El Dorado* and *McLintock* and *The Sons of Katie Elder*, the fag-end of his career. He was a connection with the past, but he still kicked ass. With his strange, pigeon-toed walk, his worn face, his tired, seen-it-all eyes and his twisted mouth (he spoke at a permanent *angle*, just as we thought of the American accent as a twisted, sideways version of English), his raggedy neckerchief and his uhhh-*slow but emphatic* delivery, Wayne was an elderly role model, but we took his moral authority at face value. In Sixties Westerns, he was the King Lear-like essence of the Old West, emerging from his bedroll-beside-the-river to dish out orders, give advice, say 'Now look, mister . . .' or go all dreamy-eyed about some unclaimed bit of prairie. If the Western was a kind of township, he ran the joint, no question. He was old, grumpy and wise, and he was always right.

What most struck me, though, was that he seemed to exist in a permanent state of irritation. John Wayne was

---

Breaks (1976). In the film, the youth in question, about to be sentenced to hang for his 'devil-may-care gunplay', tells the assembled ranchers that the Lonesome Kid is the name by which he'd like to be remembered, and they just laugh at him.

always pissed-off about something. He was always arguing with people. He was always ordering them around. He was terribly rude, to young and old, male and female, posh and low-life alike. His natural discourse was confrontation. He existed to tick you off, like a superior, fault-finding ancient prefect, because he was always right and everybody else was a misguided loser. In *El Dorado*, when Robert Mitchum, playing the town's chronically inebriated marshal, points at his sheriff's badge and asks, 'Whaddya think that is?', Wayne replies, 'I'm looking at a' – pause – 'tin star with a' – *really* contemptuous pause – 'drunk pinned on it.' Crush-*ing*. In the great classroom of Western movies, he was always the top beak.

But then one day I saw him in *Red River* and the whole moral universe shook beneath my feet. It was in Ireland on a rainy afternoon in the autumn of 1963, when my father and I were visiting relations during half-term. The back pages of Ireland's west-coast newspaper, the *Connacht Tribune*, were full of cinema advertisements for films on release in Ballinasloe, Loughrea and other towns, most of them films that hadn't been seen in years. The choice in the town where we were staying was an old Bogart movie called *Key Largo*, and *Red River*. I chose the latter because, at ten, I could never quite take Bogart seriously as a real hero. My father and I came in out of the Irish rain, and sat in a mostly deserted cinema and watched John Wayne slowly falling apart.

Wayne plays Tom Dunson, an ambitious cattle rancher who builds up a homestead and a huge herd (the Red River D) over fourteen years only to find, after the American Civil War, there's no market in which to sell them. He is forced to drive the entire herd of 9,000 steers to Missouri in search of buyers. The core of the film, chronicled by handwritten inter-titles, is the epic hundred-day cattle-drive. At its outset, Dunson warns his small army of cowpokes that 'Every man who signs for this drive agrees to finish it. There'll be no quitting along the way – not by me and not by you,' and explains the dangers and terrors that lie before them – Indians, border ambushes, the abysmal weather conditions. But it soon becomes clear that the thing most to be feared is John Wayne's filthy temper.

Heading the drive is his faithful lieutenant and adoptive son, Matt Garth (Montgomery Clift). Their relationship is fond but argumentative. Their characters are sharply contrasted. Dunson is a classic old-fashioned, shoot-first, make-your-own-morality frontiersman who (as we have seen) makes up the rules as he goes along. Garth is a more sensitive soul, a manager rather than a leader, a cautious, diplomatic man, who none the less can stand up to his adoptive, tough-guy dad. Even at their first meeting, when Dunson removes the teenage Matt's revolver, the kid is infuriated. '*Never* take my gun away from me again,' he says, 'or I'll kill you.'

The cattle drive starts, amid a lot of whooping optimism. But soon the cowboys turn to discussing whether they're travelling the best route, and whether they'd be better off heading for Kansas, where there is rumoured to be a railroad. Dunson comes up behind the chattering cowpokes. 'We're going to Missouri,' he grates.

'If you ask me –' says Groot (Walter Brennan), his oldest friend and trusted sidekick.

'I *didn't*,' says Dunson, brusquely silencing the man who is easily identifiable throughout the film as Dunson's guilty conscience.

After grinding along the trail for days, Garth stops the cattle drive beside a water-hole. Dunson rides up and demands to know why they've stopped. 'The men are beat,' says Garth. 'They've had a pretty tough day. I thought –'

'*I'll* do the thinking,' snaps the ever-more-unpleasant trail boss.

Dunson's growing tyranny turns to sadism in two key scenes. One is the aftermath to the great stampede that kills Dan Latimer, one of the more charismatic cowboys. The stampede was started, albeit accidentally, by a simple-minded but enormous lummox called Bunk Canelli who has a raging obsession for sugar, which he was pilfering when he knocked over the kitchen-irons, the noise of which sent the cattle into a frenzy. He is, understandably, a little nervous about his immediate future. After the trail-riders have buried Dan, and Dunson has read from the Bible over the grave, he comes back to his wagon. The cowboys are sitting around, waiting for some form of reprisal.

With hard-to-miss symbolism, Dunson tosses his Bible into the wagon, as his eye falls on a bullwhip hanging there. He calls out Bunk Canelli. '*You* started all this,' he tells him. 'We lost three hundred head of cattle. And you killed Dan Latimer . . .'

Bunk is too thick to do anything but agree wholeheartedly. 'Sure, sure, I know it, I know I did, and I'd do anything to – I'd give my right arm to . . .'

'Stealin' sugar like a kid,' says Dunson contemptuously. 'Well, they whip kids to teach them better, don't they?' And he advances on Bunk, shaking out the bullwhip meaningfully.

I couldn't believe my eyes. This was *John Wayne*, defender of the weak, scourge of the bullying cattle baron, Nemesis of the cruel baddie, behaving remarkably like a cruel baddie himself. I wondered if the scene was meant to be funny, as the pathetic Bunk cringed before the advancing whip.

'Tie him to that wagon wheel,' orders Dunson.

'Oh no,' says Bunk. 'No one's gonna tie me to no wheel.'

'Then you'll have to be whipped without a wheel to support ya,' says Dunson, displaying a slightly creepy familiarity with the subtleties of flaying, an expertise that would probably be admired by Captain Bligh. 'Turn around,' he keeps saying.

'No, no, *oh* no,' says Bunk, determined to avoid the pain and the humiliation.

'Turn around or you'll get it in the eye,' says Dunson.

'I was wrong, awful wrong, Mr Dunson,' wails Bunk, 'but no one's gonna whip me' – whereupon he draws his gun. So does Dunson – but Matt Garth gets there first and shoots Bunk in the shoulder. He's hurt, but not as dead as he might be if Dunson had shot him.

Matt looks his adoptive father in the face. 'You'd have shot him right between the eyes, wouldn't you?' he asks, marvelling at the older man's sudden loss of human feeling.

'Just as sure as I'm standing here,' grates Dunson.

Everyone is sent off to round up steers. But beside his wagon, Dunson finds Groot – his ancient conscience – regarding him with astonishment. 'Go ahead, say it,' says Wayne.

'You was *wrong*, Mr Dunson,' says Groot, not for the first time.

The idea that John Wayne might somehow be *wrong* about things was piquant. But more was to follow. Short of money, Dunson cuts the men's rations and a small mutiny breaks out, once it's been noticed that Dunson isn't, for once, wearing his gun. Three men refuse to go any further, on what they're convinced is the wrong trail, with too little proper food and drink. It wasn't just that Dunson shot all three of them (helped by Garth and Groot, his faithful retainers) that bothered me. It was the way he'd yelled at his most trusted *compadres* while making his I'm-a-tough-bastard speech warning the assembled cowboys against any more desertion.

When Garth makes a move to sit down, Dunson says, 'Where you going?' When a trusted cowpoke called Buster goes to get a drink of water, Dunson challenges him too. He has become a man who no longer trusts his friends, who will point a rifle at anybody now, such is his paranoia. Walter

Brennan looks on incredulously as his heroic old friend starts to alienate his own high command. Dunson orders that somebody should bury the 'quitters', drawing an eloquent response from one of the odder rank-and-filers. 'Plantin' and readin', plantin' an' readin' . . . You fill a man full o' lead, stick him in the ground, and then read words at him. Why, when you've killed a man, do you try to reel the Lord in as a partner on the job?' It's an echo of the moment when Dunson swapped a Bible for a horsewhip with the same casual authoritarianism. Matt Garth and Dunson have high words, and Matt, when he leaves, kicks over the half-bottle of whiskey that Dunson has lately started drinking from.

John Wayne as drunken tyrant and sadist? Bloody hell. My eyes were out on stalks. Could things get any worse? Amazingly, things did get worse. By the time the men have taken the herd across the Red River, Dunson is in a terrible state. His gaunt face is caked in white dust like a corpse, his cheek is scarred, he has picked up a bad limp from somewhere, and his speech is slurred from excessive shots of red-eye whisky. The central scene of cowboy mutiny follows, when two deserters are brought back to camp. Dunson is lying back on a chair like a disintegrating sultan, unkempt and shagged-out, swigging moonshine, reeking vindictiveness. He regards the deserters with hatred. 'Get down off them horses,' he says. 'I don't favour looking up to the likes of you. You should be crawling.' He accuses them of theft and desertion.

One of the men tries to defend himself. 'The law might see it diff—'

'*I am the law,*' Dunson shouts.

The man makes a passionate speech about Dunson's bullying ways and, incidentally, what a wreck of a man he has become. 'I just wanna say one thing. You're crazy. You been drinking and you ain't bin sleeping, and if you're not crazy, you're skin-close to it . . . This herd don't belong to you. It belongs to every poor cattle-man in the whole state. Now get your Bible,' he concludes with (under the circumstances) great dignity, 'and read it over us after you shoot us.'

The camera closes in on Dunson's pitiless physiognomy for the four words that changed my whole attitude to Westerns for ever. John Wayne's face is a placid picture of smug, Caligulan cruelty. His hair is awry, his eyes are like slits and there's a trace of glee about the way he trumps the man's final words. 'I'm gonna *hang* you,' he says, with appalling decisiveness.

The two men are shocked to silence by this casual refinement of their death sentence. And from nowhere comes the word, 'Naw.'

In the audience, I wondered, Did I hear that right? Did somebody say something? Nobody on screen has spoken. It's a brilliant moment of overhearing a one-word mutiny, just as Dunson himself half-heard it, and wondered if he was dreaming. But somebody did say 'Naw', and it was Matthew Garth.

'You're not going to hang anybody,' he says, now in full view.

Dunson cannot believe his ears. 'Who's gonna stop me?' he asks, perhaps genuinely interested in such a suicidal proposition.

'I am,' says Garth.

The other cowboys melt back a step as Dunson struggles to his feet and grabs a gun, but it's shot out of his hand by Cherry Valance, the hired gunslinger who has just brought back the deserters. Dunson tries to draw his own gun, but his bloodied hand cannot hold it. He reaches down to pick it up with his other hand, but it's shot away by Buster, another trusted trail-hand. And that's how the mutiny happens, with all the cowboys taking a hand in it, like the murder on Agatha Christie's Orient Express.

The rest of the film follows the herd to its triumphant

arrival through the main street of Abilene, intercut with Dunson's vengeful pursuit of Garth, and the two men's climactic confrontation, in which – a little absurdly – Garth refuses to draw his gun and they fist-fight until stopped by the irate Tess Millay, who has fallen in love with Garth and been propositioned by Dunson. They end up laughing together and agreeing to share the Red River company in the future, and append Garth's initial (but 'M' for some reason, not 'G') to the brand logo. It's a happy ending of fabulous implausibility – like seeing Captain Bligh and Fletcher Christian settling their differences and going out for some wine and cheese together – but it didn't matter a hoot to me.

What mattered, and had me walking out of the cinema in emotional disarray, was the memory of John Wayne, in what was probably his finest piece of acting, acting a complete bastard, a coldly unemotional and inventive sadist. It was, of course, only acting, and in terms of film narrative Dunson's vileness could be considered just a glitch of excessive behaviour in an otherwise heroic character, but its effect on a ten-year-old went beyond such subtleties. The scene with the bullwhip, the way he threatened his best buddies, most of all the close-up of his face as he said 'I'm gonna hang you' stayed in my head like a liberation. Never again need I – or could I – think of John Wayne as a god-like figure who knew all the answers, who reminded you of where your duty lay, who made up the Western rules that must be followed. Even his drinking had shocked me. I had never seen my father drunk – flushed and hilarious, yes, musically inclined and excessively gallant to young women, certainly, 'euphoric and fatuous' as he liked to call himself after ten gin-and-oranges, perhaps – but never sourly and nastily pissed. Seeing John Wayne drunk was a life-changing event. In one scene, it took away two or three years of incrementally built-up respect and grudging admiration.

And one more thing – it changed the whole universe of *retaliation*, that low hum of concern that used to buzz in my head in those days, when so many hours and minutes at school and at home in Battersea were filled with thoughts of danger and how you should go about redressing some imminent wrong. I don't believe I decided that I was going to be like Matthew Garth from then onwards – saintly non-combatant, refusing to fight, accepting his fate. But I think that a lightness of spirit settled on me thereafter, and took away the sense of requirement that you had to right every wrong, confront every wrong-doer and live in a state of chronic defensiveness.

My post-mugging daydreams took on a different complexion. Instead of imagining myself dealing with the Clapham Junction Two in a flurry of karate chops and concealed weapons, I now affected a languid insouciance. 'Sorry, guys,' I would say to them now (in my imagination) as we walked up St John's Hill in that awful, awkward silence, 'but I don't think this is going to work out,' and I would step to the roadside, wave my arms and shout 'Police!' and generally make a nuisance of myself, rather than a victim. Or if anyone ever raised the pocket of their grubby macintosh at me again, I would say, 'I'm sorry, but I'm just too old to be worried about being stabbed by a finger.' Or I would say to the skinny, unshaven one, 'Are you OK? You look terrible. Have you eaten anything today? Don't you think you should be at a hospital?' These weren't very heroic daydreams, I know, but I'd come a long way from dreaming of fights I could never win.

The Sixties, did I but know it, were going to bury the classic Western for good under a heap of new identities – the kill-'em-all spaghetti Western (*A Fistful of Dollars*), the charming-buddy Western (*Butch Cassidy and the Sundance Kid*), the comic-spoof Western (*Blazing Saddles*) and the anti-Western (*McCabe and Mrs Miller*). I sat in the garden at home in Battersea Rise, in the summer of 1964, reading the first reviews of *A Fistful of Dollars*, tremendously excited by the prospect of the first X-rated Western, and all the details of Clint Eastwood's Man With No Name – how he wore a poncho (where could I get one?) and smoked cheroots in the corner of his mouth, and rode on a mule and killed anybody who got in his way on the smallest pretext (like laughing at his choice of steed). The nameless gunslinger, I read, was a disgraceful innovation in the Western genre because he was a wholly amoral figure – a man who owed allegiance to nothing but money, who played off two warring families against each other by killing everyone in sight and pocketing two salaries. Were we (harrumph) supposed to regard this man as a hero?

You bet. It sounded like another spectacular liberation: the Western freed from every impulse of decency and correct behaviour and the noble tug of retaliation, leaving only action, drama and style. After a bellyful of John Ford's massed choirs, and Howard Hawks's epic moral adventures that were finally resolved through a woman's *lurve*, Sergio Leone's omnicompetent mercenary promised a new world of clear, stripped-down, blackly comic heroism. I was pushing eleven when the film came out. I'd have to wait five whole years to see Clint Eastwood waste four swarthy, nasty, laughing, Clapham Junction-style scumbags in the opening minutes. I couldn't wait. But then again, I wasn't too bothered. I was beginning to go off Westerns, and all their troublesome freight of decency, duty, self-improvement and communal responsibility. To hell with all that. Once I'd witnessed John Wayne, on a provincial Irish cinema screen, drunkenly deciding how lingeringly he was going to kill two men who'd transgressed his own stupid rules, I was over my long love-affair with the saloon and the sage-brush. *A Fistful of Dollars* was the revolution; but *Red River* had been the manifesto.

As to my domestic obsession with cowboy stuff – my gun collection, the chest-of-drawers horse, the mirror which was my own private OK Corral – most of it had gone up in flames a few months before.

It was Boxing Day, 1963. I'd been given, for Christmas, a perfect new shooter, so fat and chrome-shiny I could see my eager little face distended in the barrel. Even after the shock of seeing *Red River*, two months before, I retained an atavistic liking for the things. You could break it open by pressing a lever with your thumb and the revolving chambers had genuine, heavy plastic bullets in them. You could tip these six leaden suppositories into your hand, imagine each one to be the ghastly fate of some enemy at school, slot them back in their moorings, spin the chamber, snap it shut and brandish the gun at the wall, the bathroom basin, the neighbour's cat, confidently homicidal, transported to that Valhalla where nobody can defeat you.

Unfortunately, it came without a holster, and was too big to fit into any plastic Woolworth's holster I possessed, so I had to draw it from my trouser pocket. This was disablingly anti-heroic – you would never find Gary Cooper pulling a gun from his Army & Navy Stores trouser pocket. But I persevered, shredding the lining and then the pockets themselves with my impetuous fast-draw technique. The plastic bullets remained where they were, but you could fire caps with it – a whole roll of the little exploding micro-dots wound around a metal stalk inside the gun, the residue of their tiny explosions gradually emerging, with a satisfying smell of cordite, on a raggedy paper printout, rising through the place where the hammer met the blackened metal flange.

I spent Christmas Day bang-banging happily around the house, bringing down successive waves of charging Apaches and Cheyennes, standing in front of mirrors calling out red-handed card cheats and panicky-eyed losers who had roused my fictional ire by killing distant family members, laying waste to the Walsh homestead in Denver, Colorado, or just pissing me off in the saloon bar while I was pitching woo at their slatternly womenfolk.

It was fantastic. Nobody ever shot back. I was still – though less whole-heartedly now – the kid with right on his side. Part of me was still enslaved by the conventions of the Old West. I would go snake-eyed before the mirror and say, 'You've had it comin' a long time,' or 'Seems to me you oughta 'pologise.' A swift flurry, as the miscreant tried to rise to his feet and fumbled for his gun, his mind befuddled by age and whiskey, and I'd whip out the shiny Colt .45 from my trouser pocket and blast away at the mirror until the room stank with cap-smoke like a Kansas saloon. That would teach people not to muck about with the Lonesome Kid.

Eventually my mother got sick of it. 'You are *not* to fire that thing around the house, John,' she said. 'It's dangerous. I'd be terrified that a sudden spark might jump out and there'd be a terrible fire and then you'd be crying.'

On this Boxing Day, my parents had invited friends round – Nuala and Eddie Shelock and their pretty daughters, Siobhan and Aiofe, old friends of the family, familiar faces. I wasn't in any position, at ten, to entertain romantic thoughts about the girls but I was glad of an audience for my dead-eyed-gunslinger ways.

We had lunch. Eddie was large and bearded, a librarian with a restless magisterial streak, who liked to introduce the impressionable young to whole subject-areas – linguistics, gastronomy, chess – in the course of a single evening. Nuala was sweet-faced and chuckling, a doctor chum of my father's from years before. The two girls, my sister and I snuck away as early as possible from lunch and the paper-hat rituals, and I showed them my new gun, oblivious of the Freudian symbolism involved, and blazed away at them until my mother appeared once more. 'John,' she said, 'I've told you before. *Not* in the house. If you must shoot that bloomin' thing, go outside in the garden.'

But outside was freezing. The winter of 1963 was parky beyond belief, the robins falling dead from their perches on the lime trees. Besides, I was not pleased to be upbraided like some stupid kid in front of the Shelock babes, and I went off to my bedroom to sulk. And there, the spirit of Montgomery Clift entered my soul. Was I to be pushed around by my Maw? The hell I was. I looked at the mirror. A swarthy rebel looked back at me. 'Don't,' I told her severely, 'ever take my gun away from me again.'

I can't remember what fantasy narrative took me over. It may have been a memory of the end of *Stagecoach*, when John Wayne confronts Luke Plummer and his two side-kicks in the main street of Lordsberg and – in possibly the only recorded instance of a Western hero shooting first – flings himself on the ground and blazes away at his enemies.

I dived on to the carpet, fired three times at an invisible assailant, rolled over theatrically and, finding myself suddenly lodged against the edge of my bed, reached under it, and loosed off a final shot at Luke Plummer's most vicious associate who was hiding just beyond the pile of *Beano* comics under my bed.

Instantly, a spark from the caps caught on to the under-hanging bits of feathery thread that dangled from the mattress like Spanish moss. I got up, conscious that I might have done something a little foolish, and put the gun back in its pathetic trouser-pocket holster. When I looked under the bed, I discovered an awful thing. The spark had run around the whole perimeter of dangling material. Even as I watched, it resolved itself into a horrible plaque of heat, bang in the centre. It glowed bright red, a menacing unarguable vermilion. It was fire. The flipping bed was on fire.

Jesus. What would Matthew Garth have done? He'd have

put it out, *pronto*. So I lay on the carpet and kicked and *kicked* my not-long-enough legs to kill the awful will-o'-the-wisp of flame. It only made things worse. A couple of burning caterpillars of fire fell on the carpet, while the upper jungle of hanging tendrils burned more glowingly, more heart-achingly, red.

Oh my God, I thought. I've just ruined Christmas.

Wild thoughts whizzed through my head. Could I leave this tiny conflagration, as if nothing had happened, and try to explain later, around bedtime, why there was smoke billowing from under my mattress? No, not really. When you're ten, you know the limits of concealment. This was serious. This was beyond me.

I rushed downstairs, where my family and their guests were gathered around the piano. Madelyn, my sister, was playing 'I Saw Three Ships' and everyone was singing lustily, the men flushed by a surfeit of Côte du Rhone: 'On *Chriss*-masday, on *Chriss*masday . . .' they were going, with awful enthusiasm. How could I interrupt this jolly gathering with the news that the, as it were, bunkhouse was ablaze?

I pulled my mother's arm.

'You must come with me,' I said.

'Don't pull me, John,' she said, laughing.

'Come with me, God damn it,' I grated. 'I'm *serious*.'

She realised something was wrong, if only because I'd never dream of taking the Lord's name in vain (a hanging offence in a Catholic household) in front of her.

'My bed's on fire,' I said. 'Upstairs. I was just . . . playing and it sort of caught fire.'

She searched my face for clues as to what was really bothering me.

'What are you talking about, John? Is this some joke?'

'You have to come and look *now*, Ma,' I shouted.

I pulled her arm hard. I half dragged her out of the room.

I did everything, in fact, except pull the gun out and threaten her with it.

We went up the stairs together.

In the doorway, we regarded the smoke that was now curling in a menacing way from under the bed. It looked bad, but kind of spectacular.

'Sacred Heart of Jesus,' she breathed. 'What have you been doing?'

'I was just sort of lying down, and I musta fired the gun somewhere, and accidentally, some sorta spark . . .' Even in the panic of the moment, I still clung to the idiolect of the Old West.

'Go and get your father,' she hissed. This time I wasn't in any mood to pussyfoot around with the piano singers. I leaned over the banisters and yelled to the company, 'COME UP HERE QUICK. MY BED'S ON FIRE.'

There was a gratifying moment of consternation as they bundled into the hallway like sheep, regarded my sweaty little face – and then Dad and Eddie, two burly, overdressed and liquored-up cowpokes, came barrelling up the stairs.

They took in the situation with interest – the smoke was now unfolding itself in cloudy waves – and proceeded to do exactly the wrong thing. Wanting a closer look at the problem, Dad and Eddie seized my bed at either end and flipped it over. Instantly, a sheet of flame went shooting up the curtains. The ragged webbing on the underside was all ablaze, the whole bed a little rectangular sea of burning. The two men staggered slightly at the assaulting flames and started beating them pathetically with my clothes, my grey corduroy school shorts, my striped football jersey, my sensible long socks.

Mother told Madelyn to ring the fire brigade and tell them the address. She herself stood wringing her hands, a frontierswoman in the middle of an attack by Indians, whose flaming arrows had landed in the haybarn.

I was, shaming though it is to admit, entranced. It was the damnedest thing I'd ever seen. On Boxing Day, in calm, suburban South London, during the jolly rituals of eating and carousing, this extraordinary man-made disaster was occurring right before my eyes, and it was all my fault. I was an arsonist, a dangerous and wayward desperado who couldn't be trusted with guns, a self-immolating trasher of the family homestead. I felt both a terrible villain, and an exultant anti-hero. It was heady stuff. I moved across the room, behind where the grown-ups were flailing away at the blaze with bits of my school uniform, the Cash's name-tapes ('J.H.M. Walsh' in red copperplate) blackening and cindering. I flattened myself against the wall. 'I'll get you for this,' some celluloid Mini-me promised in my head. 'You torched my house, destroyed my property and tried to kill my family. Wherever you go, I'll track you down and kill yuh . . .'

'John,' said my mother, crossly. 'Come away from there. Come out of the room.'

I looked at her across nine feet of untouched shagpile carpet. 'I can't, Maw,' I said thickly. 'Ah'm trapped.'

'No you're not, you stupid boy,' she said. 'Come out here this minute.'

And, tail between legs, I went.

The rest of the afternoon is a blur. We children stood in the garden crying and watching as my bedroom windows cracked and burst in the heat, and smoke poured out into the cold December afternoon light. The fire brigade arrived – *two* fire engines – like the cavalry arriving too late to save the wagon train and its blazing canvas homes, their metal struts standing naked in the smoky air. As the men in their gleaming uniforms rushed up the stairs with the first of the fire hoses, I was struck by the hatchet each man carried in his belt, like an Apache tomahawk . . .

It was the end of my Western dreams for a while. The

house stank of fire damage for weeks and weeks. The final days of December were miserable, as I slept in the spare room beside the now-redundant equine chest of drawers. I didn't want to ride them with the herd to Missouri any more. The fire had ruined all my presents, especially the expensive Meccano set, whose little car tyres had perished in the blaze and left a disgusting pong of burnt rubber all over the house. And in a gesture that was both noble and resigned, I handed my fabulous new gun over to the town's marshal.

'Could you get rid of this?' I said to my mother. 'I never want to see it again.' And I didn't. The Lonesome Kid had had enough of bravado. There was no point, I decided, like a suddenly rather grown-up cowboy, in pushing your luck.

4

GIRL IN THE GAZEBO

The Sound of Music (1965)

'If they didn't show it on the screen, most people would
never know about oral sex'

– Mary Whitehouse

'Let me give you some advice,' said my friend Chris. 'The
key to pulling girls is *The Sound of Music*.'

'Whaaat?' I said. We were walking across Clapham
Common one Saturday afternoon in autumn 1967.

'Oh yeah, trust me,' he said. I had to trust him. I was
thirteen. He was fifteen and terrifically cool. The age difference was crucial (no fifteen-year-old at school would speak
to a kid two years younger), but it was as nothing compared
to the gap between us when it came to the fair sex.

Chris was a friend of some family pals in Battersea, and
we met a couple of times a year. He would always talk to
me as if we were equals. He smoked roll-ups with brown
liquorice Rizla papers. He wore a tiny gold stud in his ear.
He read books. He thought about things. He was always
recommending stuff. After an evening in his company I

would seek out anything he'd talked about, in a fever of hero-worship. I stayed up nights, puzzling over epic Old English poems or Russian SF classics in a fog of incomprehension. He was the first person I ever met who knew the names of film directors and went on about them as if they were painters or novelists, people who stamped a personal signature on a film. But now and again Chris descended to ground-level emotions and his recommendations were of a more practical kind.

'Have you actually kissed, I mean, *really* kissed a girl, yet?' he would demand.

'Well, no,' I would concede. 'Not exactly.'

'Don't give me that "not exactly" stuff, John,' he said. 'Either you've done it properly or you haven't done it at all. Because the point of kissing somebody properly is that you both know what you're doing, you're both thinking of what you might be doing instead of kissing. You want to give her one, and she knows it too, and you're trying to make her feel all right about that, and the kiss is a kind of shorthand for saying, "Do you fancy it then?" and she's saying, "Yeah, kind of", and you're both getting beyond conversation and arranging for the moment when it might be OK for you to stick your hand inside her shirt, because obviously you can't say, "Is it OK if I stick my hand inside your shirt?", you just can't come right out and say it because it's just too embarrassing, and –'

'Chris,' I said. 'This is all in your head, isn't it? They don't let you do that stuff until you're older.'

'Yeah?' said the seen-it-all Lothario. 'I've done it. Piece of cake . . .'

And that's when I heard about the *Sound of Music* Big Kiss Strategy.

'You know the scene where Liesl, the eldest girl of the Von Trapp family, goes off with her boyfriend beside that summerhouse-gazebo thing?' Chris explained. 'You know, where she sings that thing, "Sixteen Going on Seventeen", yeah?'

'I can't believe you like that crap,' I said, with the confidence of a thirteen-year-old sceptic. 'I mean, *The Sound of Music*, it's all nuns and Nazis and those creepy children, and whiskers on kittens and the Lonely Goat-herd, isn't it?'

'That's where you're wrong,' said Chris. 'You have to think about the psychological implications.'

'Oh, right,' I said.

'Absolutely. When the eldest girl sings about being sixteen-going-on-seventeen et cetera, you do realise, don't you, what she's singing about? All that stuff the boyfriend sings about her life being an empty page which men will want to write on?'

'Uh-huh,' I said, baffled.

'It's *screwing*, John. Her empty page is basically the knicker department. The song is all about sex, for God's sake. And when she goes on about how "eager young lads and roués and cads will offer me food and wine", she's thinking about screwing. What else could she be referring to?'

I was lost. I thought the movie was all about a governess learning to be brave and getting off with the terribly stiff Christopher Plummer despite him having a posh girlfriend.

'So there she is in this summerhouse,' continued my sophisticated pal, 'away from the house which is full of rules and good behaviour and so on, and she's thinking about screwing and what it'll be like, and who to do it with, and who might be worth losing her virginity to, and who else she might do it with afterwards, you know, who'll be next, who might be worth a try, and, most importantly, who she can trust. And her boyfriend, what's his name, Rolf, he's worried about her thinking of all the *other* men in the world, so he sings to her that he's the one she can rely on. Stick with me and screw me and nobody else, he's saying, and I'll show you a good time, because I *really care* about you, not just because you're dead pretty and all. He saying that he's a Real Boyfriend. You get it?'

Chris subsided. I had never heard such a searching analysis of a movie scene before. It was brilliant. It radiated hard-won wisdom. My fifteen-year-old chum clearly knew, not just the dark heart of a seemingly innocent movie, he knew a thing or two about girls, who were still a mystery to me.

'But what did you mean,' I asked, 'about the key to getting off with girls being something to do with the film?'

'Ah, well, there's the beauty of it,' said Chris. 'It's all to do with the setting. You know my parents' big house on Clapham Common, and how the garden goes on for miles? Just outside the French windows there's this patio thing with a big yew tree on the left, and it's where people sit outside on chairs in the summer. You with me so far?'

'Sure.'

'Well, my parents have parties twice a year, summer and Christmas, and they invite people's children if they aren't too noisy or too childish. So there's always half a dozen girls there, all nervous and shy in their party dresses, sipping Tizer and wondering who to talk to. I usually get some friends from school over to the party, and we talk to the girls about records and clothes, you know, the usual stuff.'

I didn't.

'Anyway, last summer the parents rigged up some Christmas tree lights in the yew tree to make this sort of fairy-glade effect. And that evening, there was this girl at the party, Camilla, she was lovely and had these big trusting eyes, like Rita Tushingham only not so funny-looking. She was wearing a pink dress that came up to her neck, but it had a hole in it around here' – he gestured towards his spindly upper sternum – 'like a porthole, like it was asking you to look inside it, so she obviously wasn't all that inno-cent. I worked out she was about fifteen.

'So there she was at the party with her fat sister and a

couple of friends who giggled a lot, but she knew I had my eye on her and we talked for ages about exams and books she'd been reading. There were lots of grown-ups getting drunk and standing around in the living-room near the bar or by the record player. About 10 o'clock, I found Camilla in the kitchen, eating a packet of crisps by herself, and I said, "Oh, this is where you are. Isn't it a terrible crush and what awful music," you know, the things you say . . .'

I didn't.

'. . . and I said, "You fancy a walk outside?" I didn't think she fancied me or anything, because she was always looking round the room when we were talking, but she knew I liked her, so maybe she came with me because she was bored. Outside, I steered her under the fairy lights and we stood there and things were suddenly all different. All I said was, "So you're fifteen, now – how do you see things working out in your life?" It was all I could think of. I didn't realise I was talking like Liesl's boyfriend. And the next thing, you know, she was going on about how nobody took her seriously and how she wanted to be a fashion designer, and she had this dream about living in a big house in the country with dogs and servants, and having a big airy studio, and someone to understand that she might be in a mood sometimes, but that was because she was so creative – it all poured out of her. She kept asking if I knew what she meant, and I said, "Yes yes, absolutely, me too, nobody understands how I want to be a doctor, but I can't because I got really lousy results in my science O-levels," even though I made up the doctor stuff on the spot. But the next thing, you know, she's looking deep in my eyes and she's putting her hand on my face and saying, "Oh, Chris." I thought of Liesl, and said to her, "You need someone to take care of you, someone who understands you properly," and she nodded like she was going to cry, and my heart was going like the clappers but I kissed her right on the mouth, and there we were, having this snog under the fairy lights, and she pulled away and I was going to say something about the moon, but before I could, she said this fantastic thing, I mean this really *glorious* thing. I didn't realise two simple words could be so, well, fantastic . . .'

He paused, tantalisingly.

'Go on,' I said. 'She didn't tell you to eff off, did she?'

'*Naow*,' said Chris, in an exasperated voice. 'No, of course not, you mug. She said, "Not here." It was just brilliant.'

'I'm lost,' I said. 'Did she want to go back inside the house?'

'John,' said Chris. 'She was saying, I. Am. All. For. The. Kissing. But. Let's. Do. It. Properly. You know, somewhere where it's dark and secret and no one could see us.'

'So what did you do?'

'I took her off down the garden, of course, and we had this fantastic snog in the bushes at the end. The thing is, once they've agreed to snog you, you don't have to say anything else, or talk at all. You just kiss them and squeeze them and say, "You're lovely," and so forth. Surely you know that?'

I waved my hands in wordless admiration.

'Though I didn't really get anywhere,' said Chris, the connoisseur of female abandon. 'Just Upstairs Outside. I tried to get my hand through the hole in her dress, but she said I'd tear the material. And after half an hour her bloody mother started yelling, "Where's Camilla gone?" and her fat sister grassed on us and they were sending search parties out to look for us, so we had to come back to the house and pretend we'd been checking that the goldfish were still alive. But you see my point? The general principle?'

'No,' I said, my head full of equal parts envy and dreamy rapture. 'What point is that?'

'The scene under the fairy lights. It was straight out of *The Sound of Music*. She wouldn't have gone for it like that unless she'd remembered the scene with Liesl and her boyfriend. It was a subconscious thing. Get a girl out underneath something that looks like the gazebo in the film, and they'll subconsciously imagine themselves back in Austria, wondering about sex and what's going to happen to them, and they'll look up and it'll be you they want to do it with.'

'Gosh,' I said. I was *so* impressed.

'Have you tried it again?' I asked. 'Or was Camilla, like, your girlfriend after that?'

'Nah,' said Chris. 'I met her once or twice but she wasn't interested. Kept banging on about bloody fabrics and dress designing. It worked with a couple of others, though. One was called Mandy. Then there was Samantha . . .'

I left him to it. He was streets ahead of me in these matters. But I resolved to try out the Big Kiss Strategy as soon as possible. I didn't manage it for a whole year.

Although it had seemed terribly old-fashioned when I was dragged to see it by my mother two years earlier, I tried to remember everything I could about *The Sound of Music*. It was populated by characters who were either too old or too young to be interesting. I couldn't work up much empathy for Christopher Plummer, playing the crochety, smirking martinet Von Trapp, or his matronly, meringue-haired girlfriend (Eleanor Parker) or their chortling, bow-tie-wearing, allegedly raffish pal Uncle Max, who ran the local singing festival. They all seemed like figures from some leaden Fifties B-movie, the kind of thing that surfaced on TV on Sunday afternoons, all yellow lighting and soupy soundtrack and mystifying exchanges of tearful emotion. As for the nuns – well, I'd had it up to here with nuns at my primary school, the co-ed Ursuline Convent in Wimbledon. The nuns' 'problem with Maria' didn't seem very problematic – so *what* if she turned up late for Vespers?

It was all so bloody *wholesome*. I guessed that you were supposed to find Julie Andrews's scatter-brained behaviour in the convent endearing. It just left me wondering what a full-grown woman was doing acting like the madcap of the Fourth Form. And the Von Trapp children seemed a pretty emetic bunch: the young ones were sweetly hopeless, like the kids in the Mabel Lucie Attwell pictures that turned up on the bathroom walls of my friends' houses, while the older ones radiated a creepy infantilism I found positively disturbing.

When the older boys clambered into Ms Andrews's bed during a thunderstorm, to be comforted by their governess's little song about brown paper packages tied up with string, I had started to wonder, Why is everyone in this movie acting the wrong age? The father was too old to have a girlfriend. The girlfriend was too old to *be* a girlfriend. The governess behaved like she was in a Malory Towers story by Enid Blyton. The teenagers were pretending to be about nine. Everybody seemed to be pretending. Captain Von Trapp, singing his 'Edelweiss' song, accompanied himself on a guitar without (I sternly noted) actually playing any recognisable chords. The children performed a puppet show (the rather jolly 'Lonely Goatherd' number) with wild manipulations of the strings that never actually corresponded to what was happening to the puppets down below. It was the first movie in which I delighted in identifying everything that was wrong with every minute of it.

But the gazebo scene – I had to concede that Chris had a point. There was a strange abandon in the way Liesl, the eldest girl, danced across the wooden benches and seemed to climb the walls, while her boyfriend hurled himself to and fro and the rain hammered down on the windows, that seemed to have strayed in from some quite different film. And there was a crucial detail. Right at the end, when the two of them meet, face to face, in the middle of the summer-house, Rolf the Nazi *does* kiss her on the lips for exactly one second, before briskly disappearing – and she raises a hand to her mouth, and widens her eyes in amazement, as if something spectacular has happened. I hadn't remembered it because, at twelve, I hadn't realised its importance. Liesl had just had her First Kiss.

As screen kisses go, it was no great shakes. But it evidently meant a lot to her. And there before me was an essential secret of teenage interpersonal relations: that for girls, your first Big Kiss was a colossal Big Deal. And that girls – all of them, every girl in Christendom – was keen as mustard for it to happen. It wasn't just that they might *allow* you to brutalise them with your hungry mouth. They might actually desire it.

I thought about it a lot, as the Beach Boys' cover version of 'Then I Kissed Her' (then in the charts) danced in my head. Did girls feel the same way as you did? Were they as keen as I was (now I was fourteen) to crash their mouths against yours and see what happened? This was spectacular information. The very prospect made you feel like singing (which I did, regularly in the street, 'Well, I walked up to her and I asked her if she wanted to dance . . .').

I knew very few girls of my own age. They tended, mostly, to be my sister Madelyn's friends – Jackie and Liz and Sally and Anne (my favourite, with her fabulously bee-stung lips and air of Frenchified wickedness) and Sarah and Gerry and the other Madelyn – all of whom were a year older than me, and therefore completely out of girlfriend-reach. But I found I could talk to them, when they visited my sister in Battersea, provided I didn't stick around too long and become annoying. With them, and the daughters of my parents' friends, I found I had a small talent for farci-cally elaborated stories about disastrous holidays or terrible train journeys or embarrassing things that had befallen my pet tortoises. I could even make them laugh.

But who was I kidding? I could just about get on with

girls because I had no prospect of getting off with them. To them I was just someone's younger brother who had to be endured or humoured for as short a time as possible. But inside I was a man, a sufferer from sudden hormonal aches and sweatily guilty dreams – and pretty well all of them came from films.

My passionate connection with movie goddesses started early. Although no women in Battersea looked or sounded anything like the lipsticked, marcelled, arch-eyebrowed dames that swanned through the old Hollywood spectaculars I saw on TV, I managed to incorporate them into my night-time excursions. At ten, I was allowed to stay up and watch *A Connecticut Yankee in King Arthur's Court*, the 1949 version of Mark Twain's story about a chap (Bing Crosby) who dreams he's back in Camelot, where he teaches the thunderstruck medievals some modern tricks. The climax was brilliant – sentenced to be burnt at the stake for witchcraft, Crosby works out that there's a solar eclipse due that evening and threatens (from the stake) to blot out the sun unless he is released. But when I went to bed, the face of his red-headed, Guinevere-ish girlfriend came along too and invaded my dreams so comprehensively that I spent all the next day at school in a dizzy rapture of romance. I checked the film's cast details in the previous day's newspaper, and discovered her name was Rhonda Fleming. Rhonda . . . Was it too late to fly out to Hollywood and ask her to marry me? (Yes it was. She would have been forty-five by then, only a few years younger than my mum.)

I spotted Lana Turner a few times, and admired her air of sultry, put-upon wickedness. She always seemed to wear a white jumper pulled tight against her chest. The scene in *The Postman Always Rings Twice*, when she and her boyfriend (who are planning to kill her husband) find themselves up-ended in a ditch after a car accident, led to my first-ever erotic fantasy. In it, my friends Thimont and Armfield and

I rescued Ms Turner – whose face kept morphing into that of our golden-haired form teacher Miss Goldsborough – and we carried her across a field, where we proceeded to remove her clothes. Finding nothing under her dress but a blank, formless absence (I mean, c'mon – I was only nine), we threw her down a nearby well. I crept guiltily past Miss Goldsborough next day, and couldn't meet her eye, relieved to find that she had emerged from my dream apparently in one piece.

And I had a real *thing* about Dorothy Lamour's lipstick.

The Bob Hope/Bing Crosby *Road* movies represented the pre-Sixties orthodoxy of sexual encounters. The films – *The Road to Singapore/Zanzibar/Morocco/Utopia/Rio/Bali/ Hong Kong* – were regularly shown on TV around Christmas and Easter and guaranteed a happy ninety minutes of male rivalry, exotic settings, incomprehensible allusions to jazz and Republicans (or was it Democrats?), gunplay, chases, slightly-boring songs, captive princesses, foolish villains to be outsmarted, talking camels, a happy air of inconsequence and the feeling that some God-like fabulist in the background was making it all up as he went along.

In every *Road* film, there was a scene where everything slowed down, the soundtrack became a sighing dream of Hawaiian strings, the backdrop was a glowing sunset with Arab dhows or Polynesian skiffs in a harbour, and one or other of our heroes would tell Dorothy Lamour (whose very surname, to anyone studying basic French, suggested a lifetime of romantic encounters) how special she was to him, as he moved ever closer to her.

That was how it was with girls, it seemed. If you told them sufficiently flattering things about themselves, and threw in some information about your home town or some dream you'd always lived for, the girl would just sit there meekly, in her multicoloured princess frock, and – if you kept talking long enough – you could move your face towards hers, and finally, like a magnet finally meeting a metal plate, your mouth would clamp over hers.

Dorothy Lamour had a long, equine face and invariably wore a fat pout of red lipstick. I wondered constantly about the crimson smear. Imagine, I thought, kissing that – what would it be like? It must taste of . . . jam? Strawberry jam, or possibly damson, spread on the female mouth like some breakfast preserve on toast, so you could eat it, and it would make the lady whom you so admired taste a lot better than would her undraped gob (yuk). The idea that tongues might ever enter the kissing fray was never suggested. The notion that Hope or Crosby might ever actually lie down and perform sex upon Ms Lamour's unassailably coiffed, upholstered and tightly-laced person never entered my head.

The *Road* movies were about romance, not sex. The kiss was only a momentary interruption of their headlong, gentleman-adventurer gallivanting. It wasn't a sign that you'd won a lady's heart and must now stay with her forever and raise a family; only a sign that you were, temporarily, her champion, like a knight being allowed to carry a lady's colours impaled on the end of his lance. Getting to kiss the girl was, it seemed, simply part of the larks of being on an extended holiday with your friend, fighting nasty foreigners and stupid policemen, living to sing, go to bars, cheek the authorities, free some local beauty from imprisonment and move on. It was exciting stuff, no matter how old-fashioned it looked. There was nothing like it in the pages of *Valiant* comic. It made you wonder how soon you too could take off, one day, with your best pal and find, among the Pyramids or the South Sea Islands, someone to rescue and claim a trophy kiss from.

It's embarrassing now to recall how I tried out a trophy kiss on my first trip to America when I was thirteen. We went across the Atlantic, *en famille*, to stay with my mother's County Sligo sisters and their extended family in Boston, where the Irish exiles had settled into parallel streets in the moneyed suburb of Brighton, Massachusetts and made a good living selling wire-mesh screen doors and the like.

Madelyn and I went out on a boat in Cape Cod for the day with our cousins and their children – a fantastic treat for the London-bound teenager – had a picnic, basked in the glittery sunshine, ate ice-cream from the ship-board portable fridge, talked about films and records and got along unexpectedly well.

Madelyn had seen photographs of our cousins in their handsome, sporting-jock, college youth and was disappointed to find that they were now middle-aged and comfortable suburbanites with children of their own. I was pleased to discover, among the children, a girl called Francie with whom I bonded from the start. She was my age and wore tight purple trousers cut off in mid-calf and a sweet pink T-shirt, and freckles dotted her cheeks like Doris Day's. We swam around in the warm Cape Cod shallows, and she held my hand as we tottered across the rock-pools, past the crab-catcher pots, and we sat together on the seat of an old-fashioned, blue-and-red-painted fishing boat that had been pulled up on the beach, and chattered on. Even when the other kids came to join us, she stuck close to me, as I talked with airy familiarity about the Beatles, the wonders of Carnaby Street and other bits of modern London that all Americans seemed to know about, but I'd never personally encountered.

At the family homestead, my ancient uncle Tom recklessly offered me my first-ever alcoholic drink, a small can of Budweiser. It tasted horrible, but I knew I had to knock it back without complaint and join in the world of grown-up amusements. After a day on Cape Cod, transported into a new element of excitement, I felt a foot taller.

That evening, a long trestle-table was laid out in the cousins' back yard, and we sat and ate soft-shell crabs and barbecued pork and chicken. Somebody wedged garden candles on long metal spikes into the gravel when it grew dark, and lit them so we could see what we were eating. Francie sat beside me. Uncle Tom handed me another Budweiser, and I told her that of *course* I'd seen the Rolling Stones walking down the street in Chelsea, and yes, as it happened, I *was* just about to buy some fashionable bell-bottom trousers, and grow my hair over my collar, and I'd been learning the guitar and would probably start my own pop group very soon.

Francie seemed entranced, though her urgent questions about the fab-ness of London eventually tailed off into silence. I belched discreetly, after my two cans of alcoholic fizz, and looked around me. There was a moon, directly overhead, and a soft backyard breeze. From the gramophone in the dining room, sentimental Irish melodies wafted through the tranquil night air. The charcoal from the barbecue was turning to feebly-glowing ashes. It had been the most brilliant day, out on the ocean, and now there was a sweet-faced girl beside me, avid for news of exciting London. Bing and Bob, those reckless adventurers, would have taken advantage of such a situation. I turned to her.

'Kiss me,' I said blearily.

'Pardon me?' she said politely.

'Kiss me,' I said. 'It's such a lovely night. I think you're terribly pretty.'

'Oh, OK,' she said. And she kissed me with the enthusiasm of a small child, right there on my cheek. 'I think you're nice too,' she said. 'Do you want another chocolate brownie?'

'No thanks,' I said. 'But I meant, kiss me properly. You know, on the lips.'

'What?' she said. 'You being funny?'

'No, really,' I said, putting my face right beside hers, and closing my eyes. She was, admittedly, a bit young to be

Dorothy Lamour, and her tiny mouth had no trace of the all-important lipstick, but after all the adventures we'd shared that day, and the warm, musical breeze, and the moon over the back yard, she must surely have known what I was expect—

I opened my eyes. She'd gone. Just as I was moving in for the kill, the bloody girl had disappeared.

Maybe she'd gone to the loo. Perhaps she was feeling sick after the soft-shell crabs. They were pretty disgusting. In fact I was feeling a bit pukey myself . . . I looked around. Everyone else was talking to each other and ignoring me. She'll be back in a minute, I told myself, and you won't feel so sick provided you keep your eyes open.

A cross grown-up appeared beside me. 'John,' he said, 'Francie's a bit upset. Did you really just try to kiss her?'

'I, er – only in a friendly way,' I said. 'We were just talking about the boat and the, er, crabs' – God, I felt rough – 'and where is she anyway?'

His big handsome face was grim. 'John, look,' he said, putting it disturbingly close to mine. 'I don't think it's very nice of you to come into our home and upset little girls like this. Maybe it's what you wild fellers do back in Swinging London and all, but it's a little gross. Do you know what I'm talking about?'

'I did *not* kiss her,' I said, with outraged dignity. 'I wasn't really going to. We were just talking . . .'

'Francie is only *eleven*,' said her father with admirable self-control. 'She's just a kid. I don't think it's very nice for you to come here and try to make her do things she's not comfortable with. OK?'

'Blimey,' I said. 'Sorry.'

I was going to say something else, perhaps offer to apologise, but it suddenly occurred to me that I was about to be amazingly sick. Which I was two minutes later, mostly into cousin Marion's kitchen sink when I finally reached it.

Nobody sympathised, or indeed spoke to me at all for the rest of the evening. From being a raffish adventurer, in my own private screening of *The Road to Boston*, where I whizzed about on boats all day, drank beers like Errol Flynn and got to snog the heroine in the moonlight, I'd become an unpopular, pushy child-molester. It put my romantic ambitions back several months.

Back in London, I went to the cinema every Saturday and lived a vivid fantasy life in the new atmosphere of daring and (for a Catholic boy) sinful screen encounters. The old *Road to Bali* world of comedy romance was well and truly over. The Sixties cinema had buried it for good. This was a different era, the time of *Lolita* and *Darling* and *Un Homme et Une Femme* and *Bitter Harvest* and *Girl on a Motorcycle* and *Chelsea Girls* and *Blow-Up* and *Belle de Jour* and *Breakfast at Tiffany's* and *Love with the Proper Stranger* and *Sex and the Single Girl* and *The Thomas Crown Affair* and *Our Man Flint* and *Dr No* and *From Russia With Love* and *Thunderball* and *Goldfinger* and *Barbarella* and *Alfie* and *The Italian Job* and *Billy Liar* and *Women in Love*.

Movies weren't about romance any longer. They were mostly about girls who'd let you do anything to them because you were a Hero.

If the new movies told you anything, it told you that girls were not a race of beings from which you picked a special friend to fall in love with. The new movie posters featured men who didn't have to do any old-fashioned wooing to find a lady friend. Men who assumed that every female in the world was available to them, because they were already so utterly, confidently heroic. Wherever you looked, the movie male was a grinning, gun-fingering, sassy sexpot who seemed to have exclusive rights to a troupe of swooning *odalisques*.

It had started, of course, with James Bond. The poster that accompanied *Dr No* showed a smiling Sean Connery in a tuxedo and cuff-links (the last word in posh suavity in 1962) leaning forward, left elbow resting on knee, right hand holding a phallic smoking pistol with a fat silencer, the smoke curling up the suntanned thigh of Honey Rider (Ursula Andress), the gun's black hammer silhouetted against the white triangle of her knickers. It was the most shame-less advertisement for male sexual triumphalism. Connery's raised eyebrow* seemed to ask the idle watcher, 'You think I'm satisfied with just one? Why, no. I have lots more to blast away at with my enormous gun.' The bulk of the poster was taken up with girls. There were four of them: one blonde, one redhead, one brunette and one black-haired oriental. They were dressed in various stages of dishevel-ment – the blonde in a bikini, the redhead in a bath-towel (back view), the brunette in an abbreviated pyjama jacket falling off one shoulder, the oriental in a *cheong-sam* slit to the thigh. To the least horny viewer, the image suggested a simple proposition: this is a film in which James Bond gets to go to bed with every woman in the world. The supposedly frightening villain, Dr No (Joseph Wiseman), appeared at the edge of the picture, tiny, marginalised among all these strutting, leggy, legs-apart dames. He lurked half-seen in a corner, like a nervous dentist in the doorway to his antiseptic, I'm-not-shagging-anybody consulting room.

The iconic image of the master-spy male was set for a generation – someone who didn't just encounter a girl companion to help to safety, but who *deserved* half-a-dozen whorish handmaidens to play with. Double-bills of James Bond movies were all the rage – three or four hours of adventure, cars, master criminals, planes, helicopters being

* Anticipating, by seventeen years, the famously limited acting reper-toire of his successor in the James Bond role, Roger Moore in *Moonraker* (1979).

blown up, chases, exotic locations – and the film posters featured the same image of the suave Connery smirkingly fondling his long pistol or harpoon-gun, while a seraglio of gossamer-draped sirens reclined and cavorted by his side. In 1967, I stood in front of the Odeon, Brixton and gazed at a double-bill poster for *From Russia With Love* (1963) and *Thunderball* (1965) and counted eight of them. Eight girl-friends! I could barely imagine getting even one.

In 1965, *Our Man Flint* had appeared and sent us all into pubertal overdrive. Derek Flint (James Coburn) was not only a spy, he was a karate champion, a brain surgeon, a nuclear physicist and swordsman, and he lived with four pouting 'playmates' all of whom he kissed in his swimming pool before breakfast every morning, before going out to save the world. A year later, Dean Martin (then forty-nine) played Matt Helm in *The Silencers*, surrounded by a coven of similarly wanton girlfriends.

When *Alfie* opened in 1966, it fed straight into my pubertal dreams: one bloke (Michael Caine) wandering his cocky, unfettered way through the lives of seven women, offering themselves like a smorgasbord of desire objects: the slapper (Millicent Martin), the brainy nurse (Eleanor Bron), the domestic slave (Julia Foster), the good-time voluptuary (Shelley Winters), the older woman (Vivien Merchant), the posh bird (Jane Asher) and the nurse (Shirley Anne Field).

I sneaked, under-age, into the Imperial cinema on St John's Hill to see it, guiltily and alone, and was startled, not by the sexual activity (there wasn't much of that), nor the film's atmosphere of jaunty degeneracy, but by Michael Caine. Nobody on any screen had ever addressed you, sitting in the audience, like that before – like a confiding older pal, a smugly irritating friend like Chris, bringing you tales of rampant conquest and airy wisdom that left you hanging somewhere between awe and furious jealousy. 'Sometimes, it gets a look on its little face,' he confided about Julia

Foster, as she busily holystoned the floor of her new boyfriend's reeking pad. 'It looks all mumsy . . .'

Nobody in my life had ever said such things about girls, women, lovers, before. It was appalling, but excitingly so. It sounded like the truth about human relationships. Between the figure on the screen and the palpitating pubescent in the ninth row, there was no mimetic filter. It wasn't like watching an actor playing a part. It was so *real*. It meant that you listened to everything he said, as if you were attending a lecture on How to Treat Girls. It meant that, to acquire a girlfriend, you didn't need courtship, romance, attentiveness, weeks of getting-to-know-you stuff followed by a polite request for permission to kiss them, and whatever lay thereafter. It required only cheek, worldliness, confidence, availability and a curious vocal trick, in which you said things with a wounded, half-bullying emphasis and ordered women around. It was wonderfully liberating, but upsetting at the same time, because you knew you could never be like Michael Caine yourself – so selfish and cruel and, for want of a better word, so masterful.

A year later came Clive Donner's *Here We Go Round the Mulberry Bush* (1967), taken from Hunter Davies's sweet, moralising novel whose final Author's Message was that seeking random 'bits of sex' was no substitute for a serious commitment to monogamy. The film, when I finally saw it, tried eventually to urge the same sensible, temperate path through the modern jungle of permissive claspings and sunderings, but its prevailing mood was quite different. I caught the trailer, when I was spending a boring afternoon in the Imperial, watching Shirley MacLaine and Michael Caine in a so-so heist movie called *Gambit*.

The trailer to *Here We Go Round . . .* was cunningly edited to ignore the fact that the hero (Barry Evans, that sad case with the dark-brown eyes and one-note range who starred in TV's *Doctor in the House* and ended his life as a milkman) was in fact an innocent provincial virgin desperate for a début shag. Instead the trailer featured a blizzard of racy vignettes – intercut scenes of foxy Sixties girls, orgiastic parties, fumblings with brassières, *al fresco* encounters in the park, the trendy music of Traffic on the soundtrack – and climaxed in one brief moment that stayed in my head all through my teen years.

It was a scene set inside a bus. Barry Evans, dressed in fashionable white jacket and trousers, was surrounded by half a dozen gorgeous females in their early twenties, strap-hanging around him as he stood – the centre of attention – in their midst and told them that they would all, sooner or later, have sex with him. 'First you,' he said with unanswerable confidence to gorgeous Adrienne Posta, 'then you [Judy Geeson], then you [Sheila White], then you [Vanessa Howard], then you . . .'

In the actual film, which I saw in its entirety two years later, this is just a fantasy sequence, a classic wet-dream scenario of bloke-as-Sultan talking dirty to his harem. But watching the trailer was like watching a documentary of what was supposedly happening all over London. Girls, *girls* . . . They weren't, after all, the strange little parcels of school uniform, floppy felt hat and satchel that I saw demurely walking up The Downs in Wimbledon to the Ursuline Convent, one street away from my own school on Edge Hill. Once you'd grown up, the film promised, they would become lissom, enervated, sexy wallflowers in tiny, knicker-skimming skirts, waiting for you to show up in your white suit and easy manner, whereupon they would greet your offhand overtures of seduction with an OK-all-right-then shrug . . .

It was the heyday of bare-faced sexism, and all the would-be seducers in town must have lapped it up. To this day, I've carried that idiotic, teenage harem-fantasy in my head, and it's done me no good at all. Should you chance, in

2003, to meet a compulsive middle-aged flirt at a party, who, despite his white hairs and 38-inch waistband, is convinced that he's in with a chance of having sex with any attractive woman in the room, try asking him if he lived near a cinema in England in the mid-to-late Sixties.

The trouble was, none of this was any practical use to me in 1967. These movies might haunt your daydreams but they left you no closer to finding a girlfriend than if you'd been watching re-runs of Laurel and Hardy. They dealt in sex rather than love, and the first requirement of the teenager (despite all signs to the contrary) is to fall helplessly in love with *somebody*, to find a single object for his fixations on the whole female gender. I had no focus, even in the screen world. I didn't know what kind of girl I might fall for, though I knew she must be out there somewhere. But that was where the movies came to my aid.

I was too young to see *Billy Liar* when it was released in 1963. But I caught up with it four years later, at the Streatham Odeon, and left the cinema with my heart pounding with love for Julie Christie.

You must know the plot, about Billy Fisher, the under-taker's clerk in a dismal Northern town who dreams of a country called Ambrosia – where he is dictator, adored popular Presidente, army general, bandleader, liberator, tank commander and grenade-throwing, granny-obliterating commando – and who tells fibs to everybody, from girl-friends to employers, to make life more bearable. The whole film is about getting away, leaving everything behind, running off and finding a new home away from the awful-ness of the home you're stuck with, and Ms Christie is correspondingly portrayed as a creature constantly in transit.

The first time she appears, her fabness is signalled by the faces of Tom Courtenay (Billy) and his friend Rodney Bewes as they glimpse her in the cab of a lorry in which she's bummed a ride. 'Isn't that that bird,' breathes Rodney

Bewes, 'that bird who wanted you to go to France with her?'

His excitement is understandable. The rest of the town's womenfolk want from Billy only an engagement ring and a promise of urban domesticity. Billy's two girlfriends are nightmares of extremity. One is the wholesome, keep-your-hands-to-yourself, orange-scoffing Barbara, to whom Billy lays siege, unsuccessfully, in a graveyard. The other is the vulgar, blonde hoyden-bitch Rita, who has (we assume) let him have sex with her as a form of entrapment. Beside these harpies, Liz is the epitome of liberation.

She'd like to be married, but can't stand to be stuck anywhere for long. She has a sexual history, and might sleep with Billy but only on her terms, and she keeps leaving town, suddenly disappearing in search of new adventures. She is the kind of girl who invites men to accompany her to France simply because that's what she fancies doing (an unheard-of phenomenon in 1963).

'Where's she been?' asks Rodney. 'I dunno,' says Billy, in admiration. 'She goes where she feels like. She's crazy . . .'

With hindsight, you could marvel at the prescience of Keith Waterhouse (who, with Willis Hall, wrote the screenplay from his 1959 novel) in anticipating a decade of people trying, or longing, to be thought 'crazy'. The free-wheeling quality of his almost-girlfriend is spelt out time and again. 'She works as a waitress, a typist, last year she was at Butlins – she works until she gets fed up and goes somewhere else,' breathes Billy. 'She's been all over.' A whole Sixties dream of unfettered behaviour, a whole genre of road movies, lay unborn in those words. And as a visual corollary, we get a scene that had never appeared in any movie before.

Julie Christie walks through the streets of her home town, tracked by a long-zoom camera. She is dressed in a white shirt, some kind of jacket and short skirt (not a mini-skirt – this was 1963) and she swings a bag, smokes a cigarette and runs her fingers along metal railings, while her face registers a succession of smiles, frowns, grimaces (she gurns at herself in the reflection of a bank window – crazy or what?) and snatches of song. What is being filmed is not just her beauty, but her preoccupation with her own thoughts – the visual equivalent of the stream of consciousness. Lorries and cars obscure our vision of her as she waits to cross a busy road. As pre-war houses are knocked down by a wrecking-ball, she sails on regardless. The camera watches her pass by a shop window, but watches from *inside* the shop, like an appreciative onlooker. She affects a little dance step on the pavement, a tiny movement like a passing thought, and just as briefly abandons it, bringing to mind that line from Yeats about the young Cleopatra: 'She practises a tinker shuffle/Picked up on the street.'

What was memorable about this scene, a thing of wonder despite its ghastly jazz soundtrack with hyperventilating cymbals, was the director's shameless adoration of his leading lady.* For we weren't watching the action through Billy's eyes (he saw her only glancingly, remember, in a truck a mile down the road), but through Schlesinger's. In this classic piece of benign stalking, he gave you an emblem of independence, a girl unfettered, unchainable but hungry for connection with someone who is prepared to join her quest for excitement. Why it should be Billy – well, I thought, God only knows. Why such a sexy pilgrim should waste her time with the mendacious loser Billy Fisher was a mystery. But the movie's climactic moment, and the reason

* Call me a dreamer, but I swear John Schlesinger had a few Yeatsian moments of his own about Ms Christie. The whole transit-of-Venus character he gave her in this scene reminds me of a stanza in 'When You Are Old': 'How many loved your moments of glad grace/And loved your beauty with love false or true/But one man loved the pilgrim soul in you/And all the sorrows of your changing face.'

I fell in love with Julie Christie in the Sixties, is the ballroom scene. Billy has witnessed a fight between his two awful girlfriends, has had a row with his friend Rodney Bewes (who tells him to 'grow up') and has retreated, hurt, on to the balcony, where Liz puts a supportive hand on his arm. Tom Courtenay's face is a mask of rage at everything he hates in this town. Behind him, on the dance floor, the patrons of the Locarno Ballroom are joining in a conga line that snakes its foolish way across a harsh spotlight. The dancers, pathetically high-kicking and all-join-in-ing, look like mad stick figures, like ants or drone bees out on the razzle, backlit by the spotlight's glare, a chiaroscuro nightmare vision of the local Northern community he has no wish to join.

Billy's face is obscured by his hands and his floppy, sweaty hair; but it expresses an agony that's an Ilkley Moor version of James Dean in *Rebel Without a Cause*. And suddenly the camera cuts to Julie Christie's face. She looks away to the left (at the conga), then looks centre (to the table) and her eyes flick upwards, directly at Billy, and they shine with an unearthly light. She never looked more beautiful, more sympathetic or more desirable.

The camera fixes on her and won't let go. Schlesinger is so entranced, he returns to the same shot a moment later, then once more. Here is Billy, beyond words, realising that his footling inventions and his Ambrosia *schtick* won't work any more. Here are the idiotic dancers in their stark spotlight, symbolising the world he must leave behind. And here, looking at both, is the face of beauty that could offer him a way out, if only he had the balls to accept it. And here was me, utterly enraptured. The movement of Julie Christie's head, the look on her face, its sympathy and radiance and strength, fell on me like a blessing. I didn't share much with Billy, beyond a tendency to daydream and a desire to leave home soon, but I decided, then and there, that I'd spend my life looking for a woman who turns her perfect face from the ghastliness of the everyday to the trouble in your eyes, and resolve to make it better.

I remember what a change the vision of Ms Christie made to my life because of a simple domestic row: the *Photoplay* Incident. In the summer of 1967, when the first heady scent of Flower Power was wafting across the Atlantic from Haight Ashbury and the convent girls I met at my sister's friends' parties suddenly began drawing little marigolds in ballpoint pen on their virgin cheeks – the summer that was christened 'the Summer of Love' by the newspapers because of a modest, Home Counties 'love-in' at Lord Montague of Beaulieu's stately home – my Irish Catholic parents had been shocked by an epidemic outbreak of immorality in the suburbs. Rumours of unfettered behaviour at teenage parties had driven my mother into spasms of suspicion that the world of decency had gone to Hell.

She and my father grimly surveyed the evidence. Convent girls now routinely folded the waistbands of their skirts over and over until the hems lightly brushed their upper thighs. My father's teenage patients arrived like coach parties at every surgery asking for prescriptions for the contraceptive pill, which he politely refused on religious grounds, while tut-tutting (none too sternly) about their wilful, sinful presumption. The early-evening news carried stories about a new fashion called the 'monokini' or one-piece swimsuit: it featured a pair of aquatic knickers and a wholly redundant piece of string that went round the wearer's neck, leaving her breasts wholly exposed. Mary Quant, the fashion designer, casually mentioned the then-unspeakable topic of pubic hair, and told the world that she'd had her own jungly pudenda topiaried into the shape of a heart to please her husband. My parents looked on, appalled, at this new cultural focus on bosom and vagina, and didn't like it one bit. Myself, since I'd just reached puberty (or, to be more accurately, had it crash down on my awakening consciousness like a stricken helicopter), I greeted every fresh evidence of sexual licence – of what the papers at the time called 'the new permissiveness', though nobody was clear who was doing the permitting – as if it were a personal gift from some benign providence.

Then one evening, home from school, I was unloading the physics homework from my satchel when my mother seized the June issue of *Photoplay* from its leathery depths and proceeded to flick through it, aghast, in the kitchen. This benignly jolly, down-market movie magazine, full of previews, film-star interviews, studio gossip and the like, happened to carry a feature on *You Only Live Twice*, the 1967 James Bond, and splashed Sean Connery's new line-up of bikini-clad Japanese cuties across a double-page spread. There was, I swear, not a scintilla of smut in any of the pictures – no nakedness, not even the suspicion of a nipple, no Quant-style groinal hairdressing – but my mother hit the roof. She had, apparently, discovered her son's secret cache of pornography. Not only that I possessed something so vilely inimical to the Sixth Commandment (which forbade, along with Adultery, all wilful pleasure in titilla-tion or in, as it quaintly termed erections, 'the irregular motions of the flesh'), but that I'd been showing it off at school. In tones of mounting hysteria, she called my father in to witness the spectacle of their only son suddenly revealed as an impresario of porn, a libidinous wretch, a (presum-ably) closet masturbator who was probably running a secret cadre of pustular onanists in the bike-sheds and locker-rooms at (hah!) playtime.

There was hell to pay. She even rang my friends' parents (while I stood mortified in the kitchen beside her) to ask if they knew that their sweet Papist children were caught up in an enslaving maelstrom of sexual iconography. For a heady few days in 1967, the inoffensive *Photoplay* magazine enjoyed a reputation, round Battersea way, as something just short of *Knave* or *Fiesta*, the authentic porn magazines available to desperate men from the top shelf of corner shops.

With awful vindictiveness, she tore *Photoplay* in half right there in front of me, then folded the savaged sheets of glossy A3 paper and tore them again, right down the middle. Mr Connery's lissom associates were split in half, their bursting bikini tops unceremoniously parted from their innocent, peach-coloured briefs, in a sudden blaze of maternal violence.

'But Mum,' I protested, 'it's a *movie* magazine. There's nothing wrong with it. It's about films and directors and, er, cinematography.'

'You are not to bring this kind of *filth* into the house ever again,' she shouted at me. 'I can't believe, after everything you've been told by your teachers and priests and your parents, that you can like this sort of . . . *awful stuff*.'

'He told me he bought it just to read the reviews,' said my sister scornfully. 'But that was before he started taking it to school to laugh about the girls in bikinis with his little pals.' I looked at her with amazement. Such treachery, even though it might have been about 40 per cent close to the truth.

'I did *not* buy it because of the bloody Bond girls,' I yelled. 'I bought it because I like the bloody *films*.'

That pretty well did it. I'd never used the word *bloody* in front of my mother before. It wasn't much of a swear-word, but it apparently carried some freight of religiosity, some conflation of By-Our-Lady, in its plosive depths.

'Go to your room,' said my mother with quiet menace, 'and stay there, and think of the shame you've brought on yourself. I'm very disappointed in you, and so is your father. We did not bring you up to be looking at pictures of naked women in filthy magazines. You are not fit for the company of decent people, so you aren't.'

And so I slunk off up the stairs to my bedroom at the top of the house, where the only picture on the wall was of a glum-looking Jesus Christ standing in a foggy doorway. I did my homework sitting on my bed, balancing a Physics textbook on one knee. I tried to think of the shame that had brought me to this low ebb. And I concluded, with a certain satisfaction, that, while I liked looking at the bosomy swimwear and the sweet faces of the undifferentiated girls who surrounded Sean Connery, I was past all that stuff. From now on, I knew I was really keen on looking at only one girl – Julie Christie – and that I would henceforth move heaven and earth to find someone just like her, and make her mine. It was, I told my newly grown-up self, a matter of *taste*.

It was a tremendous liberation to discover that I now had a Dream Girl in my head, someone to look out for in the real world. I looked for Ms Christie everywhere. At parish-hall dances, at school debating-society evenings, when the Ursuline Convent girls were bussed in after school hours to propose the motion, 'The Female of the Species is Deadlier than the Male', I gazed at the girls on display, noting their sensible grey cardigans, their serious navy-blue felt hats, the sheen-free nondescriptness of their ironed-straight, not-quite-chestnut hair, the lack of erotic promise in their grey flannel skirts and thick, wool-hosiered thighs.

I took to visiting Oxford Street by bus, to mooch around the department stores, marvelling at all the things I couldn't afford to buy, and to spend a couple of pounds on a record in the HMV music shop. But after a desultory half-hour in Selfridges, I found myself just walking in the street, caught up in the million-headed bustle of the heartland of London consumerism, just walking and looking, inspecting the vast gallery of faces that briefly passed by. The girls in town, unlike the schoolgirls at home, at least looked as if they knew that movies existed, and dressed like supporting actresses.

That girl over there, wearing a short, sky-blue dress with a metal belt made up of linked circles, from which the last four or five circles dangled down like the crucifix end of a sexy rosary – she was being Judy Geeson in *To Sir With Love*. The shrill, plump one over there with the piled-up blonde hair and the white lipstick, she'd evidently just seen *Up The Junction* and had turned overnight into Adrienne Posta. Lots of girls, especially the smaller ones, now adopted a short, bobbed hairstyle, flicked up at the sides, that had originated with Doris Day and was now worn by Jane Asher in *Alfie*. But none of them had the mile-wide mouth of my beloved Julie, the light, dancing step, the straw-blonde tumble of hair, the liquid eyes that crinkled so intelligently, so sympathetically when she smiled . . .

I pounded the endless, clanging, bus-wheezing, shoulder-barging, tumultuous thoroughfare of Oxford Street week after week, without knowing quite why I was drawn there. There was a department store down the road from my house, if I'd wanted one to mooch around in. Come to think of it, if I'd wanted urgently to buy a new record, I could have gone to Readings, the record shop beside Clapham Junction. Instead I went to Oxford Street to lose myself in the throng. Sometimes, I'd sit down on a cold metal bench and narrow my eyes until all the people thundering along the pavement became an out-of-focus blur. Sometimes, I watched a woman on the other side of the road, tracking her progress for a hundred yards, as buses and lorries and the occasional tall pedestrian briefly obscured my view of her. Then one day I realised I was, unconsciously, placing myself in the scene from *Billy Liar* when Julie Christie swings her way down a Northern street and the camera secretly watches her, adoringly, from a distance. There I was, making myself into a camera – turning my head, my eyes and brain together, in one long tracking shot. All that was missing was my leading lady.

As I pondered how I could ever make a Julie Christie-type

ever fall in love with me, two insuperable problems reared their heads. One was who I was; the other was my lack of conviction about who I was trying to be. It was clear enough who I was – a spindly, gangling, middle-class Battersea boy with a vestigial Irish accent, the legacy of two west-coast-Irish parents, and a face that, while pleasant enough to pass muster among the doting coven of Catholic matrons who populated my mother's kitchen, could not conceal its growing resemblance to that of a friendly horse. But which of the leading-man role models of the modern cinema should I be emulating?

One day, when I was fourteen, the cheekiest of the matrons suggested, more out of kindness than strict accuracy, that I was the dead spit of James Coburn. It was an absurd but life-changing moment. I gazed in the bathroom mirror and willed it to be true. James gazed back – the cool and lanky cowboy with the fancy knife action in *The Magnificent Seven*, the suave brain-surgeon-turned-special-agent in *Our Man Flint* – and shook his head, sadly, back at me. Undismayed, I began to affect his easy swagger. I checked out that cocky, all-American strut with which he comes on screen in *The Great Escape*, and tried it on for size on the daily walk from school to Wimbledon Station. My friend Hodkinson, who walked beside me to the station, confiding his heady dreams of growing up to be an in-demand archivist in a university library, would find himself talking to thin air as I fell behind on the suburban pavement, trying to reproduce Coburn's rolling gait. 'For God's sake, Walsh,' he'd say, 'try to keep up, can't you? Are you . . . *lame* or something?'

In my blue rayon shirt, ineptly twinned with an orange sports jacket, I once posed for photographs in our garden, a threatening hard case, holding a small pen-knife that had once been a flick-knife, complete with dagger-hilt and pearly button, but had had its flick mechanism removed. I looked vaguely nasty but wholly weedy, like a psychopathic school swot, whose blade, if directed at the least accomplished playground fighter, would soon end up plunged through my own heart.

We all had James Bond to aspire to, but it was never really going to be much use. We understood that, no matter what caprice of Fate befell us, we could never flirt with older women whom we'd address by their surname ('I have eyes only for you, Moneypenny'), nor race around Caribbean islands, dodging bullets while clasping the hand of an uncomplaining Ursula Andress. The trouble was that Bond was a hero, not a role model: a crucial distinction. He was not someone from whom you picked up tips about how to get off with girls. He did not exist to show you how to do sex properly – but to assure you that you could do it with beautiful girls *only* if you were already a reckless hero, who spent his chosen career escaping penis-scorching lasers and ponds full of piranhas.

Role models needed to be different – more awkward, more nervous, more domestic and weedy – more, in short, like you. And that's why I gravitated towards cowards.

Woody Allen once admitted that he owed a large debt, film-persona-wise, to Bob Hope. Me too. I've talked about the *Road to . . .* movies as the *locus classicus* of pre-Sixties romance. But Hope's influence kept up a curious tenancy in my emotional make-up, even in the new decade of Steve McQueen and Paul Newman. Hope remained an attractive male lead for any weedy, middle-class kid to emulate because he took on the world of film heroics and beat it at its own game, by being a hopelessly unheroic, pathetically ill-equipped, urban nerd who survived through natural cheek and nothing else.

I yelled with laughter at *The Paleface* on television, in which Hope plays 'Painless' Potter, a dentist faced with casually efficient professional killers in the Wild West.

Confronted by ugly gunslingers, he gibbers and prevaricates. In a saloon bar full of evil-smelling, saddle-weary desperadoes, he orders 'Lemonade . . .' and when they lean towards him, halitotic and suspicious, he adjusts the order to '. . . in a *dirty glass*'. He meets Calamity Jane (Jane Russell, sending up her role in *The Outlaw*), and marries her without realising he's being used as a blind, a cover for her Federal mission against the bad guys.

In winning the right to bed down with the most baroquely bosomed dreamboat of the lawless prairie, he is sweetly oblivious to the fact that he's surrounded by danger, mendacity, lethal plots and faithless women. He is not an innocent who learns to be brave; he's an innocent who defeats the bad guys and wins the girl by being foolishly lucky in a world which doesn't understand his innocence. The only remotely brave thing he does is to sing a jaunty song called 'Buttons and Bows' while playing a squeeze-box on a covered wagon. But his screen presence, his reliance on fatuous charm among the murderous cowpokes and screaming Injuns, was a potent influence.

You don't need to relate Bob Hope's influence solely to Woody Allen (although the scene in *Play It Again Sam*, when Woody meets a gang of Hell's Angels while dating Susan Anspach, couldn't have happened without *The Paleface*) because you could see it everywhere. In the Sixties, his modern descendants were the charming rogues Terry-Thomas and Leslie Phillips. They were never, by any stretch of the imagination, heroic figures. They were predators, like Hope; keen on girls, like Hope; louche and silly and *faux*-charming and affectedly worldly, but clearly too silly to be taken seriously by any girl with half a brain – like Hope, in other words, only in spades. Admittedly, Terry-Thomas could be a sinister presence, a cad and a rotter and a gap-toothed swine, but he resembled Hope in his endless, predatory fascination with the ladies, his breathless – and essentially teenage – amazement ('I *sayyyy* . . .') at everyone in possession of a pretty face and a pair of tits that passed his way.

Leslie Phillips was more my kinda guy. He chortled and brayed and neighed and swooned about girls, through a dozen forgettable comedies – *Carry On Nurse*, *Doctor in Love*, *Doctor in Clover*. He was the chap in the MG sports car, his hair slicked with Brilliantine, his Ronald Colman moustache quivering with desire to get off with somebody – anybody – who might fall for a pick-up line or a glass of Madeira. He was a chronic would-be seducer at whom everybody laughed, except me. I thought he was a delightful character, a breath of naughty air amid the terribly British cast of stiffs and termagants and authority figures (Dirk Bogarde, Hattie Jacques, James Robertson Justice) who populated those early comedies.*

It may seem perverse to admire someone so universally perceived as a lecherous twit, but there you have the central mystery of this book. We do not choose, on any rational level, the things that influence us. They tend to be chosen for us by some inner impulse, one that winnows out whatever will not work in the real world. The movies are the reason why boys who grew up after the war didn't grow up to become their fathers. Unlike our dads, we did not want to be Cary Grant or Gary Cooper; unlike our grandfathers we had no wish to turn into George Raft or James Cagney. Despite the presence of authentic new stars like Michael Caine and Peter O'Toole, my need for a hero with whom to empathise was satisfied more by the cowards and craven Lotharios and the wordy, hero's-best-friend roles.

There was something undeniably camp about Hope and

---

* Strikingly, Leslie Phillips and Julie Christie starred together in my dream girl's first two movies, *Crooks Anonymous* and *The Fast Lady*, both directed by Ken Annakin in his *annus mirabilis*, 1962.

Phillips and their cowardly ilk. Surrounded by macho types with no trace of humour, their affectation of satyriasis seemed to express an enthusiasm for the world that was, in the old sense, gay. Women were creatures to be ogled and wooed and eventually won – but you got the impression that neither Hope nor Phillips would be dynamite in the sack, once they'd got past the kissing stage. Me too: while I wanted, at thirteen and fourteen, to embrace every single one of my sister's rackety friends at the Convent, anything beyond such preliminaries seemed stunningly problematic, like a trip up the Zambesi spent ducking poison arrows that might come randomly flying at you in the mad, unimaginable jungle.

The Alfies and Flints and Bonds presumably all did the dangerous, life-threatening stuff (and you must remember the peril in which a Jesuit-educated Catholic boy put himself with what were called 'occasions of sin'; you were, in Kate Saunders's happy phrase, 'always one fuck away from perdition'), but we were content with the lesser turmoil of 'getting off with' any girls who might fancy some limited oral engagement.

The movies supplied everything for the nervous teenager – hot James Bond/Alfie sex (for your hot, unsettling dreams), mild Billy-and-Julie-Christie romance (for your swoony daydreams) and craven, furtive sex in the real actual world, the one bequeathed to you by Painless Potter (Hope) and Dr Gaston Grimsdyke (Phillips), who looked for girlfriends all the time but ran away from any encounter that might confront them with the real thing. And in their energetic ogling, flirting, swooning, clasping and running-away, there was a camp theatricality that appealed to me. It wasn't heroic, but it was amusing and it made girls laugh and men scoff a little nervously, as if this soppy git with the sleek moustache (Phillips) and the startled expression and nervous patter (Hope) might be more tuned in to female sympathies than they were. Armed with these wildly conflicting impulses, of bravery and cowardice, lust and apprehension, I went off to do battle.

I was fifteen when I put the *Sound of Music* First Kiss Strategy into action. I was a late starter, and it was hardly surprising. My brief resemblance to James Coburn had evaporated. I hadn't mutated into the handsome leading man that had once been promised. Instead, a small street accident (bicycle, car, bollard, swerve, tarmac) had left me with a split lip that never seemed to heal. For nine months I walked around with a lower lip brutally bifurcated and bloodied. My mother brewed up herbal infusions of boiling water over which I would bend my suffering face, my head arrayed in a kitchen tea-towel featuring picturesque Irish shop doorways, so that I looked like a mad tinker woman reading fortunes in a seething liquid crystal ball. Savlon and Lipsyl and a dozen other special-issue, weapons-grade holistic unguents from far-off Latvia and Connemara were confidently smeared across my devastated gob, but to no great effect.

My father, a doctor, looked with distaste at the oral wreckage and said, 'If you'd try and keep your mouth closed for five minutes together, it'd be a help. Saliva is the best remedy, if only you'd stop talking long enough.' But when I took his advice and spent whole days in sulky silence, my swollen lip hung heavily, pendulously in the air. I sat, lipsticked with exotic balm, open-mouthed like a village idiot, willing myself to become handsome.

Then one day it all cleared up. I looked in the mirror and saw that my features had changed for good. 'Your brother's very *unusual*-looking,' my sister's sexy friend Anne Johnson said to her one day, 'with those Mick Jagger lips.' I was dizzy with excitement, to think I resembled the impossibly cool singer, though I knew Anne was just being a tease, like the way she'd smoke French cigarettes in our house to make everyone think she was on marijuana. But suddenly, reflected in the shop windows of Battersea Rise, I decided I looked OK – a horse-faced schoolboy, yeah, but one with this fat labial cushion to recommend him. Perhaps.

My parents were planning a New Year's Eve party. It was tremendously exciting. I was fifteen and two months, and dying to get off with someone. Anyone would have done, to be frank, but I had my eye on Eve, the pretty daughter of my parents' friends Sally and Joe. Eve had large, trusting blue eyes. She was about my age. Her chest, behind her sensible gingham blouse, seemed dismayingly flat, but logic dictated that she must have breasts in there some-where, lurking like pale prisoners inside the gloom of her Aertex vest, dying to be let out and savaged by an action hero with a huge lower lip.

The house was swept, vacuumed, festooned with bits of post-Christmas greenery. I eyed the swag of mistletoe that dangled from the chandelier in the hallway. It promised embarrassing, drunken lunges from desperate adults, stolen kisses at midnight by grown-ups who were about to depart into the night in their expensive winter coats. It wouldn't be enough for what I had in mind.

At the back of our house, there was only a cold, bricky yard, ignorantly littered with brooms, empty bottles and dustbins like the back end of a slovenly restaurant. Sure, we had a back garden, but to get to it you had to negotiate your way through the noisome yard, squeeze past the bins, go up a step and work your way round to the tiny patch of green that was overlooked – dismayingly – by the upper deck of the No. 19 buses that groaned and strained their way up Battersea Rise. It was phenomenally unpromising. I raged, inwardly, at Chris and his parents' grand rolling acres and their bloody patio, strung with fairy lights. He was born lucky. How could I possibly re-create his arena of seduction? It was hopeless.

Then I looked at the front of the house, where there was, in the space between the dining-room window and the hedge, a little concrete arena. A welcoming light over the front door cast Gothic shadows over this seductive bower. Could it be possible? It could. It damn well could.

I found an extension lead, a huge cardboard yo-yo of white flex that could be run from the mains socket in the dining-room right out to the front hall. From there, you could plug in a string of spare fairy lights, whose wire emerged unscathed from being squeezed under the front door. I told the parents I was rigging up a lovely welcoming tent of lights around the front door – as innocent as the display of multicoloured balloons that traditionally announced the venue of a children's party. Outside in the front garden, I stood on a rickety garden chair and nailed the lights to the house wall, whacking five-inch nails through the crumbly grouting around the bricks. Then I trained the remaining string of fuschia-shaped illuminations across to the silver birch that loomed over the garden gate, and dangled the last ten miniature electric flames across to the honeysuckle trellis that marked the end of the front garden.

It took hours. The first-ever beads of honest sweat twinkled on my forehead as I laboured to create this tacky bower – and at the end, as I surveyed my handiwork, it seemed as far from a chamber of seduction as, say, the departure hall at Gatwick Airport. But then I stole inside the house, switched the lights on at the mains in the dining-room and – miraculously – it all sprang into life outside the front door. The dullest front garden in South London was abruptly transformed into a glade, no less, a vivid little cave of red, green and yellow lights strung, with all its wires showing, across the modest front pathway outside No. 8 Battersea Rise.

I assured my suspicious parents it would help any straggling, drunk, uncertain Hogmanay guests to find their way, should they turn up late. And that it looked incredibly stylish and modern. And that it would convey the message that our house, more than any other in the Rise, was fully alive to the seasonal convivium.

The party got under way. The Turners from Leathwaite Road were the first to arrive, bearing champagne. Mr Kalsi, the tall Sikh who ran the chemist's shop across the road, showed up without his wife but with a bottle of non-alcoholic blackcurrant cordial, which my father gravely inspected for several minutes, willing it to turn into a litre of Hennessy cognac. Sally and Joe and their beautiful daughter Eve arrived at 10 p.m. She was wearing a spidery display of mascara and a white angora jumper, through which her modest bosom protruded in a 32B-cup fashion, and she said 'Hey, John' with annoying off-handedness.

'Fancy a drink?' I asked, a worldly connoisseur of barman lore.

'Yeah, OK,' she said. 'Got any rum and Coke?'

Thank goodness, we did. I found a long glass, extruded three ice cubes from their rubber coffin in the freezer, poured in a triple slug of Lamb's Navy Rum, topped it up with Cola and handed it to her with a meaningful look. Skinny and lithe and utterly oblivious to my suave bartender ways, she drifted off to talk to my sister and her cool friends, all of them a year older than me.

The dining-room began to fill up with people, most of them Irish friends of my parents, chattering and laughing and determined to knock back as much canned Guinness and as many slugs of Jameson as could be crammed in before midnight. In search of my lovely prey, I went to the kitchen, which was now under a fog of nicotine fumes, as the hard-core arrivals drifted past the elderly slices of turkey and ham, looking for more drinks.

I was nervous. Despite all the seductive illuminations I'd strung up over the front door, the prospect of actually kissing somebody for the first time was bothering me. The practical details – deciding on the right moment to pounce, gazing into her eyes, wondering if you'd been given, as it were, permission – were an impossibly difficult series of protocols. I wanted to do it, I had to do it – and I was scared to death. So much could go wrong. I poured a Dutch-courage glass of Schweppes Bass shandy ('guaranteed 1.5% alcohol', the bottle promised) and went looking for safe female company on which to practise some conversational preliminaries.

Some of my sister's friends were standing in a circle, a little awkward and shy in their cool Sixties frocks, trying to find a conversational opening that would stimulate them all into speech. It was a mystery, what girls wanted to talk about. So I decided to provide them with one.

'I've been to see this wonderful movie,' I said to Bernadette, the plumpest and least obviously attractive girl there, reasoning that she might be grateful for the attention even of a fifteen-year-old. 'It's called *2001: A Space Odyssey*. It's really amazing.' Why, yes, she had seen Kubrick's chilly masterpiece, but she hadn't understood what the hell was going on in it. So I explained. I'd read the book by Arthur C. Clarke. I knew the story, such as it was, about the long-haul exploratory trip to Saturn on which the ship-board computer goes mad and tries to kill the astronauts, and about the intelligent life that lay in wait for them on the far side of the universe. It was a hellishly difficult film to describe, but an easy one to chat knowingly about, because this was the Sixties and you could fill in any problematic moments by saying this bit was totally, like, *heavy*, and that bit was *really cool*, and the other bit was just *amayyyy*-zing. So I persevered, as Bernie, and then Sally and Anne and Liz, gradually became (a lovely sight) just-about-interested in my stumbling exegesis.

They were smart convent girls with lively minds, who could take a few minutes off their hunt for a partner at a

New Year's Eve party to chat about a new movie, provided it didn't take too long. So, for perhaps four or five minutes, I had the undivided attention of four – count 'em, four! – sixteen-year-old babes, as I explained about the monolith, and the Star Ride with all the weird psychedelic colours and patterns, and why the astronaut found himself in an eighteenth-century hotel room at the furthest reaches of the universe, and why he turned into a star-baby at the end.

It was a pretentious little speech that mingled insight and complete fabrication, but I had their attention. Can you imagine how I felt? Can you guess which movie star I'd suddenly turned into? Yes, it was James Coburn in *Our Man Flint*, surrounded by his posse of live-in handmaidens, as they (briefly) hung on my words and wondered if it was worth the bother of arguing with me.

As I looked at their faces – Sally with the short blonde curls, Anne with her fabulous, sexy pout and a Gauloise Disque Bleu hanging off her bee-stung lower lip, Bernie the plump one with the huge brown Italian eyes, and Liz the tallest with her Polish-countess demeanour – and banged on about computers and the Rings of Saturn, I was falling utterly in love with the idea of girls *en masse*. I was suddenly Barry Evans in *Here We Go Round the Mulberry Bush*, turning from one female face to the next on the immemorial bus, and telling them I wanted to have sex with them all. Under cover of my pretentious little film critique, I was applying for the job of shag-monster, of pasha and sultan and James Bond rolled into one.

All it would have taken, in theory, was to stop talking about Kubrick for a moment and say out loud: 'I would like to have sex with you, Sally/Anne/Bernie/Liz, and kiss you on the mouth for hours and remove your acrylic pink cardigans and yellow swirly cotton frocks, and run my hands all over your soft and bulging curves until we . . .' But that probably wouldn't have worked. They'd have been shocked.

More likely, they'd have laughed. Or, much worse, just told my sister that her little brother had picked up some ideas well above his station. So instead I kept talking about the film, and the soundtrack, and the moment when Hal 9000, the mad computer, eavesdrops on the astronauts' discussion of how they're going to have to dismantle him, and I kept my crazed fantasies of lust to myself.

But I've never forgotten that moment in the kitchen, with that audience of four girls who were, for five minutes, the seraglio of my dreams. After a few minutes, they made excuses and drifted away in search of more promising male partners, but I didn't mind. I felt empowered, long before the word was ever used. A foolish confidence, steeled by half-pint draughts of minimum-strength Bass shandy, made me put my plan into action. It was time for the Big Kiss.

When I tracked down the gorgeous Eve, she was standing with my father, who was talking to her father, Joe. Dad was becoming genially sloshed on gin-and-orange, and his hand was encircling Eve's waist with a crushing arm, as he said, 'She's a great girl, Joe – you must be awful proud of her,' thereby excusing his snaky fondness for the young female form. I talked to Joe (a librarian) for a moment about some work of philosophy he'd recommended I read, tried to persuade him of my fascination with epistemology (his subject), and finally said, with the utmost innocence, 'Eve – there's something happening in the kitchen that Madelyn and I want to show you. Come with me.'

I seized her arm and steered her through the herd of revellers in the hallway. I experienced a crawling sensation in the bowel region, as I guided the object of my dreams to her fate. I knew I would run out of conversation, of inspiration, at the crucial moment. But I relied on Chris's words: 'Once you've actually snogged them, you don't have to say anything else for the rest of the evening. You just have to find somewhere else to do it.'

We found the kitchen. As I'd hoped, Madelyn was nowhere to be seen. She'd ushered her troop of friends upstairs to watch television and sneer at the White Heather Club ushering in Hogmanay with naff kilts and wholesome songs about Loch Lomond. 'Oh, Mad isn't here,' I said. 'Never mind. We've hidden a bottle of my parents' pudding wine, and we thought you'd like a drop. It's called Muscatel. It's really nice. It's sweet and it tastes of raisins. Do you fancy some?'

Eve did fancy some. She accepted a glass of the orange-hued sweet nectar, sniffed it professionally and took a swig. 'Nice,' she said, 'though I prefer Cointreau.' Evidently, she was a connoisseur of sticky things. My heart began to pound. Now I had her to myself, and was plying her with orange aphrodisiacs (shades of Billy Liar's irritating girlfriend in the graveyard), could I now persuade her to . . .

'It's awfully smoky in here, John,' she said, wrinkling her perfect nose. 'Could we go somewhere else?'

I was stunned. Could it really be this easy? 'Come for some air outside,' I said. Enfolded suddenly in an anti-fag conspiracy, we threaded back through the chattering revellers, glasses of marmalade wine in our hands, and suddenly I was pulling the front door shut behind us. Outside, the fairy lights over the lintel glowed with Christmassy sweetness against the dark sky. It was 11.30 p.m., New Year's Eve 1968, and I was a soul in bliss, a spindly vision in blue slacks and cotton shirt, with a genuine, living, breathing girl in a white angora jumper beside me. I guided Eve sideways, away from the door, into the heart of the bower.

'Oh, this is nice,' she said. 'I like what your dad's done with the lights.' Hah! She was wrong but, already, she was falling under the spell of the summerhouse in *The Sound of Music*.

'All those people in the hallway,' I said airily. 'You wonder how grown-ups get like that, don't you? Getting drunk, and smoking and talking bollocks about nothing. I sort of know you don't want to turn into anybody like that, do you?'

'Mmmm?' she said. 'This wine is lovely.'

'I mean,' I persisted, 'I get the impression you, er, want more to life than to be like people around here. You're different. You probably want to be, er, more wild and free, and, you know, just disappear one day and go to France . . .'

'What *are* you talking about?'

'I mean,' I said, trying to banish Julie Christie from my thoughts, 'that you've got your whole life ahead of you, and you're young, and you'll have lots of, ah, keen boyfriends who'll want to go out with you. But you're probably too smart to want to live like everyone else.' I was getting desperate. That ridiculous song was going round and round my head.

'Well, yes,' she said suddenly. 'I *do* want to be different. I don't want to wind up in a library like my dad, or be a housewife. I'd quite like to go to South America, and travel around and see things, and maybe get a job in a polo stable.'

'You'll meet a lot of men there,' I said. 'Eager young, er, stable lads and roués and, er, terrible seducers will offer you drinks all evening,' I said. 'I expect.'

She looked at me more closely. 'You seem terribly interested in my welfare, John,' she said.

The traffic outside on Battersea Rise was reaching a crescendo – what were all these bloody cars *doing* out so late, crashing up the South Circular Road on New Year's Eve? I could barely hear what she was saying, though we had reached a moment of promising mutual understanding.

'We've known each other for ages,' I said, clinking our glasses together in what seemed a gesture of astounding sophistication. 'I just wouldn't want you to be . . . hurt by some horrible boyfriend who didn't really care about you . . .'

She was eyeing me strangely. I put my hand on her angora-sleeved arm.

'. . . as I do.'

'Oh, John,' she said. 'Why should you worry about me?'

'You are fifteen,' I said flatly, 'nearly, er, sixteen. I would love to take care of you myself, if you'd let me.'

'Hang on a minute,' she said, starting to laugh, 'this is a film we're in, isn't it? You know, *The Sound of Music*? And in fact I *am* sixteen going on seventeen, thanks very much, whereas *you* are fifteen, going on sixteen, and you're younger than me, and you haven't even done your A-levels yet.'

'Eve . . .' I said, thickly.

'And I have a perfectly nice boyfriend called Art, who's eighteen, going on nineteen, and who's somewhere in the jungles of Peru studying agronomy, and he'll be back in February, and I can't wait to see him.'

'Oh,' I said. The world crumbled around me. The whole New Year spirit, the cinematic dream of willing girls and horizontalised Sixties dolly-birds, the easily-charming Alfie figures and master-spy Lotharios, the whole foolish canopy of sexy dreams collapsed on the spot. The evening chill finally penetrated my shirt and made me shiver. The romantic gazebo over my head now seemed a pathetic little string of fairy lights, as tacky as my pathetic advances to this angora-clad girl – no, this grown-up woman with a real boyfriend in tow, adventuring somewhere in the Machu Picchu jungle. How could I have been so self-deceived? I felt about ten inches high.

'Oh, John, don't look so sad, you silly twat,' she said. 'You don't want to be my boyfriend. You just want to get off with someone. If I wasn't here, you'd have steered someone else out on the front doorstep and tried it on with them. All that stuff about me – you don't really mean it. You're such a dreamer.'

'I . . .'

She looked into my eyes. 'You're a sweet kid. And you have this humungous lower lip. You'll find someone inside to get off with. Lots of girls are going to want to snog you, just to find out what it's like with an enormous gob like that.'

Inside the house, a ragged cheer went up from the hallway. I could dimly hear the bongings of Big Ben, chiming in the new year from the TV in the upstairs living-room.

'It's too late,' I said pathetically.

'Oh no it's not,' she said, and put her hand behind my head, her fingers in my hair, and drew me to her lovely face, and our lips met for the first and only time they ever would, and we kissed with a deep, adolescent hunger that was more passionate than it might have been because she was being so kind and tartily generous to a virgin of the Big Kiss and because it meant nothing to her but it meant that I could just live in this extraordinary moment of saliva and tongues and Muscatel grape-juice and become lost in its secret, cavernous chambers, and care about nothing beyond its dreamy, absorbing, extravagant rapture, and the way her busy tongue flicked and fenced and seemed to grow in a fat and lazy abandonment, which meant that she liked the experience for itself alone without expecting it to be the start of anything special. That was the best lesson ever – that girls sometimes wanted to be kissed from an impulse of pure pleasure rather than from a culmination of everything that had happened in the last ninety minutes of a film, a climactic clinch that insisted on a perfect future. It wasn't lust that made her do it, only a desire to check out a chap's mouth at close quarters. Even if it was someone she wasn't going to marry. Even if it was someone she wasn't going to have sex with. Even if it was me.

I opened my eyes when it was over. 'Don't,' I told myself, 'don't for God's sake say "thank you".' Instead, since it had gone so well, I placed my hand brazenly, experimentally, on her angora chest, right there on her breast. It was so soft . . .

'Don't push your luck, sunshine,' she said and pushed me away.

We went inside to the noisy strains of 'Auld Lang Syne'. My father approached us, ignored me completely, and swept Eve away under the mistletoe. But I didn't care. The Big Kiss Strategy had worked, though not quite the way I'd envisaged it. I was a boy who'd become a man, who'd tasted Muscatel rapture on somebody else's mouth, and the sharper, bitter-sweet joy of thwarted love, all in the space of half an hour beside the honking discords of the Battersea night.

Nothing could touch me now. Nothing could improve on this moment, not even if the entire Ursuline Convent quartet of my sister's friends were to reappear, minus their clothes, begging me for further information about the special effects in *2001: A Space Odyssey*. I nursed a passion for Eve after that night. It went on for weeks. But then I saw a lot more movies, and gradually forgot about my almost-love, and about *The Sound of Music*, and about Liesl and her problematic boyfriend, plighting their childish troth in the lamplit gazebo.

5

WHITE HAT AND GOLDEN SHIRT

Bonnie and Clyde (1967)

It was a May evening, and I was walking down The Avenue that bisected the twin patches of Clapham Common, on my way to a date with Kathrina Fitzpatrick. Kathrina wasn't my girlfriend, but she was unquestionably my Dream Girl in the early summer of 1968. She was the eldest daughter of my parents' best friend in the neighbourhood, a Bohemianly thrilling Irish dame called Jo, who lived with her six children in a huge house on the fashionable west side of the Common. The sitting-room was full of ancient furniture – the armchairs and sofas seemed to sprawl in languorous disarray because so many people had flung themselves down upon them in extremes of devastated romantic emotion – and the kitchen, where Jo and her family held court, featured a decadent mural of a swarthy, Hendrix-faced gypsy that had been painted one day by Georgina, the second daughter, a tall, rope-haired *Beata Beatrix* with huge green eyes and six-inch crimson fingernails.

The Fitzpatricks were in the vanguard of everything new that was happening in cool metropolitan circles in the late Sixties. Their house was the place where I first heard wailing guitar solos by Eric Clapton, first danced to Thedorakis's bouzouki music on their ancient gramophone, had my first arguments about the Permissive Society, learned about the availability of marijuana to enterprising teenagers, and first learned to take the mick out of people whose ambitions stopped at chartered accountancy. The whole family was fantastically cool. In the year when the Rolling Stones brought out *Beggars' Banquet* – whose sleeve artwork yoked together posh, stately-home decor and sprawly, narcotic, rock-star misbehaviour for the first time – I looked at the Fitzpatricks' elegantly trashed living quarters and wondered how they had managed to anticipate Jagger and Richards and their friends in the iconography of decadence.

That evening, as I walked down The Avenue to their house, I was proud to have been co-opted into the mysteries of trendy London. The call had come at 6 p.m. Kathrina, the eldest daughter (then seventeen; I was fourteen and a half) needed a partner to take her to a discotheque in Roehampton. Her young man had been struck down with gastro-enteritis. She couldn't go to the dance by herself. Where was she to find a partner at two hours' notice?

Jo, in her kindly way, had thought that I might do. I was tall, I could walk and talk and just-about dance in a not-too-embarrassing way, and could be relied on to stay on the sidelines of the evening, should some more suitable beau catch Kathrina's eye. Jo and my mother agreed it might be nice for me to go dancing with a family friend, with whom I had no earthly possibility of having sex. I'd been sent to the bathroom to scrub up, anoint myself with after-shave, and find some clothes that would pass muster at a fashionable bop on the outskirts of Richmond. There was a complication in these arrangements, however, one that only I knew about. I was head-over-heels in love with Kathrina, the way you are at fourteen and a half, when you look away from the dream girls on the movie screen and suddenly notice the attractions of beautiful neighbours right there in front of you.

I admired her long, slender, model-girl body. I never tired of gazing at her Russian-heroine cheekbones. I stole glances at her amazingly pretty face when I dropped round on Sunday afternoons to catch the end of her family's *al fresco* lunches. She looked nothing like Julie Christie, but her face, when she laughed, was full of helpless, crinkle-eyed warmth. She had no idea about the passion burning inside my Marks & Spencer's shirt.

This evening, I was to be her date. I was to pick her up, compliment her on her hair, clothes, et cetera, be driven to the dance, buy her non-alcoholic drinks, squire her around, and make myself scarce if – all right then, *when* – appropriate.

I'd given some thought to my clothing, of course. A white shirt, obviously (this was a proper dance), and a tie that was neither too boringly patterned nor too alarmingly psychedelic to cause offence. My only pair of non-school trousers were navy blue (from the Army and Navy Stores in Victoria, where my mother bought all my clothes), but had smart turn-ups at the bottom, so I wore those. I'd brushed my sensible school brogues until they shone, even the front bits with the holes all over the place.

In the bathroom, I'd borrowed my sister's 'Hide 'n' Heal' cream, and covered a couple of incipient spots with the flesh-hued moisturiser. I'd shaved my chin and slapped on a handful of cigar-scented Aramis aftershave. Walking down The Avenue, I felt like a million dollars. I wondered about Kathrina – would she grow tired of the conversation of other boys? Might she, in fact, return to my side by the end of the evening, and say, 'These guys are all very well, John – but can't we just slip away together somewhere? The night is still young . . .'

I reached her house. I banged on the door. The importunate

lover (I told myself) has come a-calling, and you'd better be ready, doll, wearing something gorgeous . . .

The door opened. Kathrina's youngest sister, Fiona, a foxy twelve-year-old, stood on the threshold. 'John,' she said. 'Come in. Lovely to see you.' She looked me up and down. 'Kate's nearly ready,' she said encouragingly, 'and you can change in the front room.'

'Oh, good,' I said. 'I was afraid I might be late. But what d'you mean, change?'

Fiona gave me a funny look.

'Change into your party stuff,' she said. 'I mean, obviously you're not going out looking like that . . .'

God, the tactlessness of the young.

'I'm *wearing* my party stuff,' I said. 'Why would I need to change?'

Fiona let out a stifled shriek and fled into the kitchen.

I followed her. 'Hi, Jo,' I said to their fabulous mother, as she sat, as always, smoking untipped Players and reading *The Times*. 'Kathrina all set?'

'Darling, how lovely to see you,' said Jo, giving me a kiss. 'So *heroic* of you to step in at the last minute like this. Have a drink.'

She was always doing that, asking you to have a drink, as though you were likely, at fourteen, to say, 'Gin and tonic please.' Then I realised she was looking at me with something less than approval. 'You look lovely, darling, but are you actually planning to go to the dance in that?'

'You mean the tie?' I said with a smile. 'You think it's a bit much?' I considered the swirly purple Paisley design that hung down my chest. 'My mother said it might be a bit too wild . . .'

'No, it's not the tie, John darling, it's the –' and then she broke off and said, 'Excuse me a minute.'

There followed a ghastly silence, as Jo went up the stairs, and I stood in her kitchen wondering where I might have gone wrong. Were my shoes insufficiently polished? My white shirt disastrously creased in its brief journey across Clapham Common? As I stood in the Fitzpatricks' *demi-mondaine* den, Fiona reappeared, bringing her brother, Anton, with her. They regarded me like a brace of tourists inspecting a waxwork in Madame Tussauds, then burst into giggles and left the room.

What? (I asked myself). What was *wrong* with everyone?

From upstairs I could hear a row in progress. One voice was Jo's – I could tell her fag-drenched, smoky contralto – and the other was Kathrina's, saying, 'No . . . no . . . I'm not going. I'd rather shoot myself. If he's so *dumb*, to wear something as crass as *that*, I'm not going anywhere with him.'

Mutter, mutter, went Jo's low pleading voice. I caught the words '. . . don't want to hurt his feelings'.

'I don't *care*.' Kathrina's voice was muffled by several inches of plasterboard ceiling. 'I'd rather stay at *home*.'

It wasn't a happy five minutes, standing alone in the kitchen, waiting for my dream date to conquer her revulsion and appear before me. When she did (looking gorgeous, in a white-and-blue mini-dress), her mother stood uncomfortably by her side. They nudged each other, insisting the other should break the news.

Kathrina looked me up and down. 'John . . .' she said, then turned to her mother. 'No,' she said shortly, 'ab-so-lutely not.'

'Is something wrong?' I asked.

'No, darling,' said Jo. 'But we're a little taken aback by what you're wearing.'

'I did my best,' I said. 'I didn't think I should go to a dance in jeans.'

'It's not about jeans,' said Jo, at last. 'It's about the school blazer.'

I looked down my front. I *always* wore my school blazer,

every day, including weekends. Except in winter, when I went around in diamond-patterned jumpers my mother had bought for me in Arding & Hobbs. But none of them had seemed quite right for a posh dance, in a roomful of twirling lights, where you might get too hot.

'Oh dear,' I said, aghast. 'What shall I do?'

'Fiona is upstairs at this very minute,' said Jo, 'looking through Patrick's stuff' – Patrick was the eldest boy, a handsome, streetwise kid a year older than me – 'I'm sure we can find something for you to wear that's not quite so . . . *school-y*.'

'Oh God, it's hopeless,' said Kathrina, leaving the kitchen in a flurry of womanly distaste. But it wasn't. They finally located a T-shirt with a picture of Bob Dylan on the front. Instead of my sensible navy-blue slacks, I was slithered into a pair of Patrick's black flares. My fatuous school blazer was stripped from my shoulders and replaced with a leather waistcoat. Amazingly, they didn't try to replace the school brogues with some fashionable moccasins.

After half an hour's induction into trendy dressing-up, I was deemed just about OK. Kathrina was talked out from behind the locked door of her bedroom, and persuaded to accompany me to the dance as planned, though she was noticeably distant all evening. I kept no memory of that night of strobe-lit, noisy darkness beyond a desire, as urgent as a call to war, to get connected *pronto* with the complicated, trendy new world that lay out there, where you either joined in, or died in the attempt.

In order to join in, three things were essential. I had to grow my hair, I had to acquire a T-shirt and I had to find a rebellion to join. Revolution had been in the air for months. In England it was purely a social, or rather style phenomenon, evolving quite naturally from the post-Macmillan world of amplified music, shocking fashions, swirly designs, recreational drugs, trendy restaurants, the contraceptive pill, young millionaires in customised Bentleys, the heady sub-culture of London shops called Kleptomania and Granny Takes a Trip and Biba, the silver façade of the Chelsea Drugstore. The design leaders of this colourful revolution were a tiny throng of elegant pop stars, moody actors, wayward young Royals and skinny models with their entourage of high-earning courtiers – photographers, stylists, fashion designers, advertising men, gallery owners and a few journalists – who moved in a small area of fashionable London.

The rebelliously inclined could lay claim to a more serious dimension of political upheaval, but most of that was supplied from America. The 1967 hippie summer of Haight Ashbury, California had transformed some of my friends into hairy Christ-figures or Afro-headed oddballs, and made everyone use the words 'man' and 'heavy' all the time. On television we watched student riots in Paris, that mirrored the demonstrations in Washington and New York against the Vietnam War. These events didn't mean much to my apolitical, suburban soul. They were big physical upheavals about things I didn't understand.

You could, however, buy into the revolutionary miasma of 1968: it meant a poster of Che Guevara gazing into the far horizon of liberation, it meant Jimi Hendrix's squealing, chaotic guitar, and a band called Thunderclap Newman, whose song 'Something in the Air' briefly commanded the top of the charts, advising the listener to block up the streets and houses, call out the arms and ammo, and generally prepare for imminent social meltdown. At ground level – at home and at school – it meant letting your hair grow long, and wearing jeans with badges sewn onto them, and spearing the lapels of your school blazer with little tin badges saying 'Legalise Pot' and 'Drop Out', and having entirely bogus conversations with your chums in the fifth form about how you'd tried smoking cannabis and how it had made you feel like you were, you know, flying (we may have got it mixed up with LSD, which none of us had tried either).

The trouble was, I hadn't yet become a real player on this trendy stage. The son of two naturally conservative, God-fearing Irish Catholics, living miles from my school-friends, I had no instantly available spur to rebellion, no posse of friends on the doorstep with whom to organise a generational revolution. I looked at the fifth- and sixth-formers who grew their hair way down past their collars, and wondered how on earth they got away with it. I could never (I just knew) withstand the pressure from my mother to stay a nice, decent, soberly dressed, church-attending, homework-loving kid. She was far tougher than I. She disapproved of ever pop star she clapped eyes on. She tut-tutted about displays of 'immodesty' in female dress. She was not the kind of mother who would look on indulgently as I rolled joints in the living-room or put up posters of rock chicks on motorbikes in the study. I was having my own private rebellion issues because of the awkward fact that I no longer believed in God, and had no idea how to communicate this information to my parents without stirring up a tidal storm of trouble. The revolution was, for the moment, going to have to proceed without me.

But that was before the Saturday night I saw *Bonnie and Clyde*.

I caught it at the Wimbledon Odeon with my friend Harry. We weren't technically old enough to see an 'X' film (he was fifteen, I was fourteen), but we butched it out, lighting cigarettes and doing a lot of noisy, grown-up laughing to impress the girl behind the box-office grille.

'I read in the *Evening Standard*,' said Harry darkly, as we took our seats, 'that it's dead violent. People were fainting in the stalls at the premiere in the West End.'

'Gosh,' I said. 'What happened to them?'

'Got taken out on stretchers,' said Harry. 'They had to call an ambulance. In fact it happened again and again, until they had to have ambulance men standing by at every performance, just in case.'

'Blimey,' I said. 'Just couldn't take all the blood, eh? *Tchuh*, some people . . .'

We were sitting miles back in Row R of the stalls. I craned forward, wondering if I could spot any uniformed St John's Ambulance paramedics, standing in front of the screen scanning the audience for signs of nervous disposi- tions. Could they, I wondered, see me, so far back in the crowd? Or would Harry have to haul my slumped and comatose form all the way down the stairs himself?

'Not nervous, are you?' he asked, with a hint of mockery.

'Nah,' I said. 'Thought I spotted someone I knew.'

The film began, with a succession of old monochrome snapshots of Depression-era types – worried-looking share- croppers, skinny, harassed mothers with dirty-faced kids, gormless young men in Sunday-best suits gazing proudly into the camera. Between them came the credits: the names of Warren Beatty and Faye Dunaway appeared in white against a black backdrop, the white gradually turning to pink, then to a threatening blood-red.

Ms Dunaway's lovely face appeared, framed by pillow- tousled, blonde hair. Her shoulders were naked. She was in her bedroom, radiating agitation, gazing at herself in a mirror, throwing herself on the bed and looking through its dull metal bars like a gorgeous prisoner. I gulped as she stood up and moved to the window, displaying her perfect, naked back, her arms concealing the modest swell of her breasts. Outside in the street, a man in a white hat was hovering around the family car, glancing guiltily from side to side. 'Hey, *boy*,' she shouted. 'What you doin' with my momma's car?'

The man looked up and saw – and was as astonished as

I to see – the most amazing sight: a naked blonde girl crushed against a grimy window, her bosom conveniently concealed by the wooden sash, her lower bits obscured by the opaque glass, yelling at him with half-serious indignation.

'Wait there,' shouted Faye, and ran about her bedroom throwing on some clothes. I assumed she was going to remonstrate with the would-be thief. I was sure he was going to run away. But when she stood before him, closing up her dress, upbraiding him for trying to steal a little old lady's car, something in her voice suggested she admired his cheek. As they walked along the road, she walked backwards facing him, her legs giving her body a little bounce of anticipation, her whole attitude an approximation of dancing.

The man was wearing a mint-condition white hat, which conferred on him an instant glamour, and tilted his chin as if he owned something terribly valuable. He asked what kind of work she did. 'A movie star? A lady mechanic? A maid?'

She frowned. 'What do you think I am?'

Flatly he replied, 'A waitress,' and she is crestfallen to think it's so obviously the truth.

Soon we learn that he is just out of prison for armed robbery. She tries to laugh it off ('Mah, mah, the things that turn up in the street these days'), but is clearly intrigued.

'So what you-all do for a good time around here?' he asks, reclaiming the initiative. 'Listen to the grass grow?'

But now she is walking like a demure schoolmarm, handbag clutched before her, keeping company with someone who might be a genuine desperado. 'What's it like?' she asks.

'Prison?'

'No,' she says, caressing the next words, 'armed robbery.'

'It ain't like anything at all,' he says.

Soon they were drinking sodas side by side. He had a

match in his mouth, which he kept there even while drinking. It was a curiously ornate match, as matches go, with a white tip surmounting the bulbous black head, and he jiggled it up and down with his tongue. I'd never liked the look of Warren Beatty before – there was something conceited about him – but I was impressed by the match trick. That and the white hat, and his air of unshakeable cockiness. Everything about him was integrated and well-proportioned in a way I never was. He seemed like a man whose life fitted together like a well-cut suit.

'Shoot – I knew you never robbed anything, you fake,' she says, a little too sassily.

So he shows her his gun. The camera follows her eyes into a close-up of the man's waist, and the long-barrelled gun that he holds so casually, so listlessly, pointing it flaccidly downwards. 'Yeah,' she says, 'but I bet you wouldn't have the gumption to *use* that thing.'

The match between his teeth flickers up and down in irritation. Then – 'Ahright,' he says. 'Wait here, and keep your eyes open.' For the first time, there's a long-shot of the small town. Warren Beatty crosses its empty, deserted main street into the first act of outlaw bravado we witness. Seconds later, he's back, brandishing a wad of stolen dollars and shouting, 'C'mon!' He fires a single gunshot and they run to a parked car, where Beatty opens up the hood and somehow starts the engine with the minimum of fuss.

'Hey,' she says, 'what's your name, anyhow?'

'Clyde Barrow,' he says, hurling himself into the driver's seat, to which she replies, 'Bonnie Parker – pleased to meet you,' and they roar off to the jaunty strains of 'Foggy Mountain Breakdown' played on fiddle and banjo by Flatt and Scruggs – a pair of ancient bluegrass-hoedown musicians – as the car jerks away in a cloud of dust, and the empty street becomes briefly alive with townsfolk who have never seen nothing like *that* before.

It was a wonderful opening scene, with a texture all its own: a heady mix of amorality and humour. I liked the way Beatty and Dunaway had done a little mating dance around each other down the street, she so apparently contemptuous of his conceited talk, but fascinated by his lawlessness; he scoffing at her small-town waitress job but desperate to impress this Lone Star Venus. The key moment was the robbery of the general store. It took place out of our sight, without drama or bravado, and was clearly about as heroic as taking a lollipop from an infant; but as Clyde brandishes the wad of dollars and they roar away, revealing an election poster for a grinning Roosevelt on the wall behind the car, this pair of frustrated loners had already become heroes of a kind, in bringing some action, some life (and a fistful of money) to the dead town. The blue-grass music was pure Keystone Cops, the stuff of farce, signalling the police would never catch them – and suggesting that the film we were watching might, after all, be a comedy. It was a huge relief to discover that this wasn't going to be a blood-boltered gangster movie after all, but a *Crooks Anonymous* jape. But then the film lurched into seriousness, the fun stopped, and something else took over – something potentially life-changing for all us suburban revolutionaries in the stalls.

Their car comes to a halt in a grassy clearing (Bonnie and Clyde are always driving off the road into fields, in a repeated motif of wayward pastoralism) and, although she is sexually turned on by the robbery, he fights off her advances. He ain't, he says, much use as a lover-boy ('I could never see any percentage in it') – but stops her from flouncing home by telling her how, together, they could 'cut a path right across this state, and Kansas and Missouri and Oklahoma, and everybody'd know about it'. On the grassy plain, she smokes aggressively, furious at being turned down, but gradually her head tilts like a listening canary, her eyes crinkle with seriousness, and she sidles back towards his stream of seductive patter.

We cut to the crucial scene in a fly-blown diner, where Clyde tells Bonnie about her life by simple, horribly accurate guesswork. It was brilliantly written (by David Newman and Robert Benton) and went straight to the soul of anyone who ever feared their life was heading down too straight a path.

'You were born somewhere around East Texas, right? Came from a big ol' family? You went to school, o' course, but you didn't take to it because you were smarter 'n everyone else so you just upped an' quit one day. Now, when you were sixteen – *seventeen* – there was a guy, worked in a, a . . .'

'Cement store,' puts in Bonnie unhappily.

'Cement store, and you liked him because he thought you were just as *naaaace* as you could be, and you almost married that guy, but then you didn't think you would, and you got the job in the café, and you wake up each day and you just hate it. You *just hate* it. You get on down there, and you put on your white uniform . . .'

'Pink,' says Bonnie.

'. . . and the truck drivers come in and eat your greasy hamburgers, and they kid you around and you kid 'em back, but they're stoopid, dumb country boys with their big ol' tattoos, and they ask you out on dates and sometimes you go, but they mostly just wanna get into your pants whether you want 'em to or not. So you go on home, and sit in your room and you think: When, and how, am I ever gonna get away from this?'

He stops this merciless recital of the smallness of her life, and looks into her crumpled, beautiful face. 'And now you know.'

The film's bloody succession of robberies and shoot-outs, with the genuinely shocking slow-motion carnage at the end, ran in a loop in my head afterwards, but the café scene stayed with me far longer. It seemed to contain a shocking truth. People's lives had simple trajectories. People could get stuck in a life the world arranged for them, without being able to do a thing about it. It reminded me of a song that turned up on Saturday morning radio, a much-requested little number on Ed 'Stewpot' Stewart's family request show, 'Little Boxes' sung by Burl Ives:

Little boxes on the hillside,
Little boxes made of ticky tacky,
Little boxes on the hillside,
Little boxes all the same.
There's a green one and a pink one
And a blue one and a yellow one,
And they're all made out of ticky tacky
And they all look just the same.
And the people in the houses
All went to the university,
Where they were put in boxes
And they came out all the same.

And *Billy Liar*, I recalled, opens with a brilliant tracking shot along the 'little boxes' of identical Northern terraces, while on the soundtrack we hear – yes – a radio request show, like Stewpot's, bringing the same mindless little songs into a couple of million faceless homes . . .

The word 'conformity' had been dinging around my brain for a while: conformity, not revolution. Revolution – the kind of thing going on in America – was too grandiose a concept to be entertained at a personal level. Conformity was different. It meant being like everyone else. And the message of the times was: don't be like everyone else. Be yourself. Find your own reality. The trouble was, everyone around me chose to non-conform in exactly the same way. Something was in the air, all right, in the streets and houses of 1968, and it meant everyone growing their hair the same way, wearing white T-shirts and denim jeans, and saying the word 'heavy' to mean absolutely anything – good, bad, musically progressive, socially embarrassing, emotionally draining, mentally challenging . . .

The movies were slow on the uptake when it came to the late-Sixties revolution. By the time Hollywood woke up to the power of the student dollar, and the fortune to be made from dramas about campus protest, it was almost too late. In 1969, when *Easy Rider* came out, with its ambiguous investigation of the hippie dream, hippies were already old hat. When MGM tried to capitalise on student unrest with *The Strawberry Statement* in 1970, student unrest was about as hot a subject as ballroom dancing. Rock 'n' roll, with its behavioural excesses, from rock-star hotel-trashing to naked writhings at open-air concerts, was the *locus classicus* of Sixties rebellion, a far greater influence on the groovy young than anything on celluloid.

What the cinema did brilliantly, though, was to portray non-conformity. Closeted in the dark, I could respond on a personal level to movies which showed my parents' genera-tion as boring, clueless, shallow, craven, herd-following, smug suburbanites, obsessed with material things, from whose dull lives any youth with a spark of life would run screaming away. That's why *The Graduate*, which came out in the same year as *Bonnie and Clyde*, had such an effect on me and my friends.

Benjamin Braddock (Dustin Hoffman) began the film as a desperately uncool, high-school straight, a high-achieving dork in a sports jacket (I felt an embarrassed twinge of iden-tification), whose academic triumph was celebrated by his awful parents with a party to which nobody young – nobody his own age – had been invited. At twenty-one, he was surrounded by grown-up complacency, forced to listen as a pissed family friend passed on some adult wisdom: 'I have one word of advice to give you, Ben: *plastics* – there's a great future in plastics.' It was depressing advice from the representative of a plastic generation. The only sign of life was the low-level thrum of seductive promise from Mrs Robinson, who cut through his adolescent sulkiness by demanding he drive her home and tossing her car keys into the aquarium into which he'd been glumly staring – a watery prison that recurs in the image of the family swimming-pool where he later stands, in his pathetic birthday-present scuba-diving suit, and resolves to telephone the dangerous Mrs R to chase the promise of her dark-eyed, contemptuous sexiness.

For Ben, she offered the same promise of adventure and escape from dull conformity as Clyde Barrow held out to the small-town waitress Bonnie Parker. Both films were an education in raging against the machine. But if *Bonnie and Clyde* finally seemed more seductive to me than a dozen Mrs Robinsons, it was because the movie made the invitation to join the gang seem so irresistible.

C.W. Moss, played by Michael J. Pollard, is the gargoylish Texan motor mechanic that Bonnie and Clyde enlist along the way as getaway driver and automotive genius. He was the least prepossessing gang-member in the history of armed robbery, but he had a lot of charm. He was every doltish schoolboy who longed to have a glamorous gang of robbers turn up one day and spirit him off to a life of lawless roistering. The scene when he meets Bonnie and Clyde and blows, cheeks-distendingly, down a plastic fuel pipe, while Bonnie lies languorously across the front seat of their four-cylinder Ford coupé, sucking a cigarette, is a classic in the annals of wannabe heroism.★

★ I was probaby too young, at fourteen and a half, to appreciate what was going on, but the whole movie is suffused with oral sex. Clyde's toothy match-flicking, the way he and Bonnie hungrily fellate bottles of fizzy pop while flirting together, the desperation with which she sucks a cigarette after Clyde refuses to have sex with her

He motions to Bonnie to try the engine. She turns the ignition, and it fires into life. Clyde, who's supposed to know everything, is enraged that anybody but he could have fixed the engine. 'Now you just tell me,' he shouts, 'what was wrong with this car?'

'Dirt,' says Pollard in his abbreviated Southern way, the word more a parping noise than an explanation. 'Dirt in the fuel-pipe. Ah just blowed it away.' You had to admire the chutzpah of this baby-faced oddball, as he airily asked Bonnie, 'Anythin' more Ah kin do for you today?' like a waiter at the New York Ritz-Carlton.

Bonnie knows instinctively how to impress him. She has learned from Clyde the value of shameless bragging. She asks him to identify the car they're sitting in. 'This here's a four-cylinder Ford Coupé,' he says. No it isn't, she replies. 'It sure is,' he says firmly. 'No,' says Bonnie. 'This here is a *stolen* four-cylinder Ford Coupé.' The effect is fantastic. C.W. goes into a gobsmacked display of head-shaking, fist-punching respect. 'I'm Miss Bonnie Parker,' says the sleek odalisque, 'and this here is Mister Clyde Barrow. We' – infinitesimal pause – 'rob banks.'

C.W. redoubles his awe-struck dumb-show, impressed beyond words, except the words 'Ah just knew it . . .'

In the reaction of one simple country-boy, stuck in a

---

in the opening scenes, the way she devours a burger after hearing about how her life is about to change, her casual appropriation of his half-smoked cigar, which she clamps between her own lips to be photographed, with gun and beret, on the front of his stolen car . . . But since these Freudian images are supposed to be embedded in the subconscious, who can say if they didn't work some magic on my emergent libido? There was always something intrinsically rude about Ms Dunaway, even when she was trying to look severe and sceptical – that just-out-of-bed hair, those astonished eyes, that eloquent mouth . . .

one-horse town in Texas, I suddenly understood the glamour of fame in Depression-era America, even if it was the fame of criminality. C.W. offers his credentials – that he spent a whole year in a reformatory. Clyde mocks his vanity, and asks him if he's got what it takes to pull off an armed robbery – you'd think he was the personnel officer at a big corporation, dealing with the modest CV of an aspirant middle manager. And C.W., spurred into action – just as Clyde was egged on to his first post-prison robbery by Bonnie's scornful challenge – bravely raids the till (the owner wasn't around to be petrified by his reckless behaviour) and tosses a wad of dollars all over Bonnie's lap. As Clyde yanks down the rumble-seat in their stolen Ford Coupé, to let C.W. take his seat as the newest gang member, and they cruise away into the golden afternoon, C.W. sits with his arms folded, transformed into an unlikely hero.

I could feel Harry beside me, sitting forward in his tip-up rumble-seat, right there with C.W., triumphantly recruited into this glamorous gang. I felt the same, wholly assumed into the on-screen action, redeemed from the boredom of my ordinary life, keen to experience whatever wild excesses were to follow, heedless of the consequences. C.W.'s recruitment, the fact that this ugly, dough-faced nobody could join the Olympian team of Beatty and Dunaway, played straight into my schoolboy's fantasies of joining the cool fraternity of fifth-form rebels. All of us fourteen- and fifteen-year-olds had been applying for the same job as C.W. Moss from the moment he appeared.

All three of the film's main characters were figures pitched somewhere between Innocence and Experience, nobodies longing to be somebodies, people bored to death with their lives, whose anxiety to find a wider, public identity hurled them into a life of danger, and pursuit, and the retribution of society.

Harry and I emerged from the cinema wildly impressed

and deeply shocked by the violent end of two people we'd come to know well. The fact that they were robbers and killers, thieves and murderers, meant nothing to us. We'd been on their side throughout. The picnic scene, where Bonnie was reunited with her daffy old mum, where family members hung out together as if attending some *al fresco* Thanksgiving, where children tumbled in slow motion down a hill in the honeyed light, and Clyde reassured the lined and querulous Mrs Parker that he'd take care of her precious daughter, was as enfoldingly romantic as a Mateus Rosé commercial. The law, which eventually tracked them down and totalled them both in a hail of bullets, was the enemy. Their deaths were the result, not of a court action that had arraigned their bloody felonies as a social outrage, but of a deal struck by the whiskery Texas Ranger, Frank Hamer, with the bug-eyed, treacherous father of C.W. Moss – a man who made the cardinal style error of criticising his son's tattoo, which Bonnie had chosen for him.

Harry and I, that night, became transgressive souls. We didn't realise it at the time, but we'd joined the ranks of the Sixties revolutionaries. We might not have been among those students on the cobbled streets of Montmartre or the campus of Kent State University, but we were determined, from now on, to be different.

But how? How could you establish your difference in a world where every oik in the street was convinced he was Che Guevara, where everybody listened to the same records, watched the same TV shows and wore the same things to signal their rebelliousness? I kept my eye out for opportunities for rebellion, but there weren't many.

Sometimes I'd visit the local library in a PVC mackintosh, whose unyielding material was perfect for purloining books and walking out with them clamped under my armpit, but I wasn't stealing them – I'd already borrowed up to my limit of four, and needed four others because I was such a swot. Sometimes, when leaving Clapham Junction station, I'd stand at the bottom of the double stairs that led to the exit and, with shocking rebelliousness, walk up the flight of stairs where it said OTHER SIDE UP, defiant, magnificent. If only there had been someone around to yell at me, it would have been perfect. Or to notice me at all.

But the big clue the movie gave about being different was all about clothes. All through the movie, Warren Beatty kept changing his outfits, acquiring significant new threads as his life moved from brash cockiness into suave criminality and then down the slide into hell. In the opening scenes, just released from prison, he wears a white shirt and a tie, grey pants and a double-breasted burgundy sports jacket, topped by a stylish white fedora. It hardly seemed like standard wear for the recently released convict. When he and Bonnie set out on their life of crime, he swaps the burgundy jacket for a cool, navy-blue pin-striped suit jacket, rather cheekily counterpointed by a peaked cap.★

Waistcoats and hats were Clyde Barrow's speciality. God knows when and where he bought them. We never saw Bonnie and Clyde shopping at all, except at the very end, when she shows him a tiny china shepherdess she's bought. But however he did it, Clyde was never short of sassy headgear and fancy vests. I absorbed the lesson without any trouble. Fine feathers make for bravado. Heroism is about getting your way with a swagger, and tipping your hat to the ladies while doing it. Fancy clothes were your best expression of personal defiance against a world of grey financiers and waitresses who have to wear pink uniforms every day.

After the Kathrina fiasco, I had resolved to make an effort

★ Coincidentally, the same kind of peaked cap Bob Dylan used to wear in the early Sixties, a look temporarily borrowed by John Lennon.

to dress like a modern kid. I visited the Great Gear Trading Company in Chelsea, gazed at the rows of plain T-shirts, the round-neck ones that looked like school sports kit, the ones with three buttons that looked as if they should be worn by dockhands, the ones with druggy cartoon jokes on the front, the ones covered in Californian hippie flowers. Which should I get? I had no idea. I'd never worn a T-shirt in my life.

Finally I bought a pale-blue one, the button-necked kind. I brought it home and sneaked it up to my bedroom. In the mirror, I gazed at a puny figure in a stupid little blue vest that only confirmed how skinny and inconsequential I was. A week later, I tried on my first pair of blue denim jeans. They looked all right, but felt absurdly stiff and unyielding; whenever I ventured out of doors, everybody else seemed somehow more comfortable in their jeans than I did in mine – as if they'd been wearing them for years. I looked at the hundreds of post-hippie, floral-patterned shirts now on sale, but even I could see that having half a dozen scarlet peonies blooming all over your front was not a happy design choice.

The summer's end-of-term Parish Hall Dance was coming up in two weeks' time. It was a Saturday-night bop at the draughty hall beside my school in Edge Hill, and girls from the Ursuline Convent in the next road were expected to attend. My friends and I didn't express any enthusiasm for the event, because we were unconfident, single-sex-school boys, and knew we would spend the whole three hours of its duration slugging Coca-Cola, shouting inane small-talk at each other, and prowling the room in circuitous walk-abouts, trying and failing to ask Rosie Nicholson if she'd like to dance. But though we didn't talk about it, there was never any likelihood that we wouldn't actually *go*. We were as edgily passionate, as ambiguously excited, as romantically fatalistic as kamikaze pilots waiting for the signal to take off.

A troubled mantra started up in my head:

I am going to the dance.

I am going to the dance but I'm not going to actually dance with anyone.

I am going to the dance and I'm going to dance with someone but not get off with them.

I am going to the dance, and will ask several girls to dance, but will be rejected by all of them, except the one right at the end with the hideous spectacles, and we will dance to 'Nights in White Satin', but she won't let me kiss her even if I wanted to.

I am going to the dance wearing my jeans and my blue T-shirt, and I will look a spindly prat.

I am going to the dance wearing my beige slacks and a flowery shirt, and I will look like an upholstered sofa, and anybody I ask to dance will shriek with laughter like Fiona did, or just curl their lip and say, 'No *thank* you, I'd sooner die.'

I am going off the dance.

I am *not* going to the dance.

I laid out on my bed all the clothes I possessed. As wardrobes go, it was pathetic. White shirt, grey shirt, other white shirt, blue shirt, green check shirt with button-down collar (never worn), blue-striped shirt with football logo stitched on to breast pocket (never worn – I wasn't keen on football), new blue T-shirt with three-button display emphasising pigeon chest; also my Sunday church-going navy blue trousers with turn-ups, grey school trousers, cricket flannels, new (incredibly stiff) jeans. School blazer. Two jumpers, one thick (orange), one thin polo-neck (black). One pair black school brogues. That was it, apart from an elastic belt with a snake-design clasp that not even I would seriously wear in the street, for fear of being taken for a Boy Scout.

I thought of Warren Beatty in his array of waistcoats, hats, sporty jackets, stylish tweed suits. How, and when, could I start getting stuff like that?

I went to Arding & Hobbs that afternoon and mooched around, wondering why none of the new flowery shirts that lined the rails could make me look convincingly modern. I fingered their expensive cotton sleeves where they hung on the display rails. They were meant for somebody else. Whatever they did for other almost-fifteen-year-olds, they just wouldn't work for me. I flicked the hangers along the rail.

Flick. Not this cascade of blue, red and yellow Paisley patterns, falling like a blizzard of hundreds and thousands on a sherry trifle. *Flick*, not this emetic, pinky-orange thing with the ruffled front. *Flick*, not this bilious purple-leaved bougainvillaea design, thanks very much. *Flick*, not this flowering clematis design, meandering all over a black-night background. *Fl—*

And then I stopped. The most amazing shirt was hanging under my fingers, hanging discreetly, a touch sulkily, in smouldering contrast to its brash neighbours. Its very shoulders appeared to be hunched, like a brooding bird of prey.

I pulled out the hanger and stared at the gorgeous shirt. It seemed to flow under my fingers in a slow, liquid cascade, quite unlike its trendy cotton associates with their flower patterns tackily spread all over their tits.

It was gold. Not like a gold bar is gold, but as a long shimmer of golden moonlight would reflect off the surface of the blackest lake in a jungle. It had depths. It had mystery. It curled and coiled itself slowly in the air as I turned the hanger around and gazed at the slinky, gold-black back of this wondrous second skin. It had an oily shimmer that I'd never seen on any shirt before. I didn't know what kind of material made it shimmer. All I knew was that it would transform anyone who wore it into somebody instantly attractive, spectacularly modern, fantastically cool.

All next week, I wondered how to buy it. It cost two pounds, nineteen shillings and sixpence (£2.97 in modern money), a huge sum for a kid whose weekly pocket money was five shillings (25p). A week later, I dragged my mother to Arding & Hobbs and showed it off, the first time I'd ever displayed an interest in any garment whatsoever.

'That thing?' said my mother, horrified. 'Are you out of your mind? It's *harble*. Don't *ever* let me see you wearing the likes of that.'

'But it's gorgeous, Ma,' I whined. 'Why can't I have it? I don't have a single trendy shirt to my name.'

'I'll buy you a nice cotton shirt right now,' she said. 'You can have any one you like, provided it's a nice sensible colour. But not that awful, stupid, slimy thing. One of them over there would be just fine.'

She pointed to a rack of nondescript *chemises* in pale yellow, pale green, pale purple, pale beige, pale vomit, pale spew (I was by now getting *really* cross) . . .

'But they're so boring,' I said with feeling. 'They're just like everyone else's.'

'And what's wrong with that?' she asked. 'I don't see Paul or Harry or any of those nice boys walkin' around in horrible slimy gold shirts, lookin' like nothing on earth. Like that awful feller on the television.'

'Who?'

'That awful feller, you know, on *Top of the Pops*.'

Who could she mean? Jimi Hendrix?

'That Engelbert Humperdinck.'

I was quiet for a while. She seemed, annoyingly, to have a point. The frog-faced crooner with the unfeasibly Bavarian *nom de guerre* did indeed favour terrible, shiny satin blousons in which to sing 'Save the Last Dance For Me' on Saturday-night variety shows on television, and one did not want, under any circumstances, to look like him. With either rat-like cunning or dumb luck, my mother had landed a blow smack on my Achilles heel. How could I look different, without looking like a circus act? I imagined walking into Wimbledon Parish Hall at 8 p.m. in my dance-extravaganza gold shirt to shouts of raucous laughter.

But I still loved it because it was obviously a one-off design. All the week that led up to the dance night, I kept a beady eye on what every male under thirty-five on television was wearing. There were lots of dark-brown jackets in fashionable corduroy, and lots of flowery shirts, sometimes accessorised by a tie made of exactly the same material, for the ultimate I'm-a-pillock look; the men who presented *Blue Peter* at teatime wore pastel shirts and V-necked jumpers. At no point thank God, did Engelbert Humperdinck make an appearance – even on *Top of the Pops* on Thursday night, where the Beach Boys' 'Do It Again' was at Number One.

Coming home from school on Friday, the day before the dance, I looked at the teenagers in the streets around the station. A few were in denims, but absolutely no one was recklessly wearing a gold shirt with a shimmery surface. But then, this was Clapham in the late Sixties, when it still mostly resembled Clapham in the late Fifties. It was only in Chelsea and Carnaby Street that you'd find groovy young men in psychedelic patterns and shoe-concealing, two-feet-wide bell-bottoms. The streets around the Junction were grey and litter-strewn, the shop windows nondescript, the women at the No. 19 bus stop head-scarved and defeated-looking. Passing Arding & Hobbs, the venerable department store, I noticed how badly the plaster under the windows was chipped, how weather-beaten the paintwork looked, how neglected it all seemed, like the rest of my home suburb. I could stand beside the traffic lights, where Lavender Hill became St John's Hill, and look round at the whole panorama of late-Sixties Battersea, and register how dowdy it all looked – so many telegraph wires and TV aerials, so much dampness and traffic fumes, so many cracked paving stones, such a wholesale lack of glamour.

And yet, there, inside Arding & Hobbs, on the second floor lay something that could change my world completely. One single piece of material, cut to feature a pair of sleeves, a collar and lots of sewn-on buttons. It would take everything I'd become – the hopelessly straight schoolboy swot with his charcoal-grey slacks and school blazer, everything that Kathrina and her family had laughed at – and slough it off like a snake's tired skin. I would emerge as a glittery rebel, with a shirt both girls and men would die to own, and I would be such a hero, my fame spreading through the metropolis and beyond, into Kansas and Missouri and Oklahoma . . .

No, *of course* Clyde Barrow never wore a gold shirt like the one I craved at any time in his career; there weren't any around then. But the way he wore his white hat, and his cool black waistcoat *without a jacket*, and his succession of caps, meant that he'd surely have admired it, had he been standing on the second floor of Arding & Hobbs beside me.

'Clothes that draw attention to yourself, boy,' he'd have told me. 'That's what you need. You wanna earn people's respect, you gotta look like you deserve it. You gotta look different from them. You gotta look like a hero, and you gotta start *now*.'

I had to do it. I had to buy the shirt but I had to do it quick. There was so little time. There was so little *money*. I checked my cash supply. Fifteen shillings. I still needed two pounds four and six. It was hopeless. I couldn't ask my mother for extra cash, because she'd demand to know what it was supposed to buy. So I went to my father at the end of his Saturday-morning surgery.

'Pocket money, please,' I said. 'And can you let me have a bit more this week?'

He was writing some complicated instruction, in his tiny doctor's squiggle, on a hospital form. 'What for?' he said.

'I, er, want to buy some clothes. Sort of special ones. For the dance tonight.'

'I thought your mother always bought your clothes,' he said, 'at the Army and Navy Stores. Ask *her* if you want some clothes money, why don't you?'

'Dad, *please*,' I said. 'This is different.'

He looked in his pockets. There's your five bob,' he said, 'and here's another two-and-six out of the kindness of me heart. And' – he gave me a sidelong glance – 'good luck gettin' the special clothes with your mother.'

Had she told him about the gold shirt? Oh blast. So he wouldn't help me, for fear of reprisals.

I looked for Madelyn. She was in the living-room with Father John, my father's eldest brother. Our venerable Irish uncle was now a parish priest in a small town in Yorkshire. He came down to London from time to time to flee the gull-shrieking solitude of the Whitby outlands, to check out my mother's cooking and to say Mass very *very* quietly round at our local Catholic church. A strange, unclassifiable eccentric, he talked in an indecipherable mumble, nursed random passions (for obscure mathematical formulae and mutton chops and Sophia Loren), wore cheap, all-over-polythene raincoats in wet weather, the kind that enveloped you in transparent plastic as if you were wearing a tent, and affected a jet-black hairpiece which fooled nobody and slid all over his balding, snow-white pate like an ice-hockey puck across a frosty rink.

'Mad,' I said. 'Can I have a word?'

'I haven't *got* one pound, seven and six to throw around,' she said. 'You should have saved up. But Father John just gave me a quid when I walked round to the church with him, so you could try being extra nice to your uncle . . .'

She was right. Back in the living-room, the devout man was already deep in his breviary (a kind of leather-clad compendium of 'Thoughts for the Day').

'I see *Solomon and Sheba*'s on TV tonight, Uncle John,' I said sneakily. 'That's a favourite of yours, I remember you telling me.'

'It is *not*,' said the priest, without opening his mouth. 'You're thinking of *Samson and Delilah*. It was directed by the great Cecil B. De Mille years ago, and is a very *interesting* portrayal of the Philistine race. The lady playing Delilah was Hedy Lamarr and, of course, many liberties were taken with the Old Testament story because she was portrayed as quite an attractive woman rather than a murderous Jezebel. 'Twas very enjoyable. Now *Solomon and Sheba* was quite different, full of awful irrelevant stuff, awful romantic slush that got in the way of the story. And what were they doing at all, having the Queen of Sheba played by Gina Lollobrigida, when Sophia Loren would have done it so much better? Did you see her, John, in *El Cid*? Marvellous. Very Spanish. And she was in *The Fall of the Roman Empire*, but they made her wear this awful nun's get-up, so she had bits of cardboard pressing into three sides of her face at once. And I was surprised not to see her playing the Queen in *Sodom and Gomorrah*. She'd have been a sight better than that French woman.★ Now, *that* was an interesting film, about a Bible story that many people have very half-baked ideas about. A number of details that were wholly erroneous. As far as I know, none of the Sodomites ever . . .'

And on he went. I'd forgotten that one of my uncle's random passions was for Biblical and Roman epics, especially films that combined both strands, like *Ben-Hur*. I bowed to his expertise, although I didn't care for these films. They all featured the same two scenes: an interior shot of some plush Roman boudoir crammed with red velvet

---

★ I checked: it was Anouk Aimée.

furnishings, where men in plumed, chin-constraining helmets plotted with elderly emperors in nightshirts or snogged women with kohl-drenched eyes and plum lipstick; and an exterior shot of massed Roman crowds shouting like football fans and waving their arms in the air, while a battle-wearied hero acknowledged them with a wave, and leant over to his sidekick to whisper, 'Any news of Drusilla?'

I wanted to tell him all about the new world of movies, where the gangsters were the good guys, and you sympathised with them from first to last, but I desisted. It wouldn't have gone down well with a priest, even a film-buff one.

'Do you want to come for a walk, Uncle?' I asked. 'I'm going off to the shops. There's some, er, books I was going to look at.'

'Books?' he said. 'I thought you lads spent all your money on records? I was going to buy you a record token for your birthday in, when is it, October.'

'No, no, Uncle,' I said, in a plausible impression of Goody Two-Shoes. 'I'm doing this reading programme. From now on, I'm reading only classics. Modern ones, then old ones, then modern again. I started with *Gulliver's Travels*, then *The Great Gatsby*, then *Bleak House*, and now I'm on *To Kill a Mockingbird*. I got bored reading stupid spy stories, you see. And . . .' I took a deep breath. Would this work? 'And so I'm going down to the bookshop now to buy *War and Peace*.'

His kind eyes lit up. 'Tolstoy? Are you not a little young to be reading the great Russians?'

'I heard it was the best novel ever written,' I said neutrally. 'So of course I'd want to read it straight away. I think I can afford it,' (I added pathetically) 'although I hear it's *really* long.'

'John,' he muttered, as a thought struck him, 'I wonder if –'

'And of course, I was wondering if I should buy *Anna*

Karenina as well, because some people say it's even better than *War and Peace*.'

'John,' he said. 'I've just had a very good idea. Why don't I introduce you to the wonders of the Russian classics? It would be my pleasure and, indeed, my duty as your uncle to endow your young library with such pieces of literature.'

I practically stuck out my hand and said, 'Come on, then.'

'How much would it cost, *War and Peace*?'

'At least a quid,' I said hurriedly, before he decided for himself.

'A pound? For a paperback book? I'd be very surprised if it was anything over ten shillings.'

'I was thinking of the, er, Norbiton edition,' I said, casually pinching the name of a Surrey suburb which was familiar from platform announcements at Clapham Junction. 'It's the best translation, so I'm told.'

'Oh, very well,' he said. 'You need a copy that'll last, unlike these flimsy softbacks.'

'Can I get *Anna Karenina* as well?' I asked greedily. 'So I can think of you in the future, every time anyone mentions Tolstoy?'

'All right so, John,' he said. ''Twill be a pleasure. I will definitely send you a two-pound book token for your next birthday.'

Bloody hell. It took ages to get the cash off him. I had to persuade my kind uncle that, when you feel the urge to read a brace of thousand-page Russian epics, you *really* feel it. You need that stuff with the snow, the battles and the patronymics *right now*. But half an hour later, mission completed, I set off with two pounds nineteen shillings and sixpence crackling and jingling in my pocket. Going through the swing doors of Arding & Hobbs, I was seized by a terrible conviction that somebody would have bought the shirt – that, indeed, gold shimmery chemises might recently have become a uniform all over South London. But all was well. The shirt hung where I had first seen it two weeks before, still glowing, still sleek and sultry, still looking a little hunched and secretive and wicked. In a changing-room, I tried it on and stared into the mirror, where my face, my torso – hell, my whole being – was transfigured. I could see it was a rich, deep, black-and-gold colour and it seemed to ooze and slither around me as I stood there. And I knew suddenly that I loved it because everybody else in the world would absolutely hate it.

I bore it home in secret. I hid it behind the garden hedge so that nobody could confront me in the hallway and inspect my purchases. Upstairs I considered the option of wearing a completely different shirt, and bringing my fabulous new one along in a carrier bag – but wouldn't that look a bit girly? And where would I change? Then I realised what to do. At 7.15, I came downstairs wearing the gold shirt, cunningly concealed beneath my skinny black roll-neck sweater. The parents were in the kitchen, where I stuck my head round the door for a millisecond and said, 'I'm-off-bye-now-back-at-11-see-you,' before departing. My father hardly glanced up from his gin-and-orange and the *Irish Post*. My mother said, 'Have you money for the train? And don't be late or I'll start to worr—' But I was gone.

Madelyn was coming down the stairs as I headed for the door. 'You aren't seriously going to wear that jumper to go dancing, are you?' she said with a sneer. How come people had been saying that to me all my life? 'You'll boil like a lobster. It's June, you dumb kid.' I opened the door. 'I'll take it off when things warm up,' I promised. Oh yes, I thought, indeed I will, and then the world would see . . .

By the time I got to Wimbledon, I was indeed uncomfortably hot. At 8 p.m., it was still light. A gorgeous marmalade glow bathed the brickwork of the houses in Worple Road as the bus rocked along with all its windows winched halfway down. The other passengers sat with their sleeves rolled up, or wore the new T-shirts with the three front buttons undone. Trendiness was coming to the politest suburbs of Sixties London, assisted by the liberating warmth of summer nights. At the Edge Hill stop, the windows of nearby houses were open. From one of them, the strains of the Beach Boys' 'Good Vibrations' sailed out on the tranquil breeze: 'Ah-I . . . I love the colourful clothes she wears, and the way the sunlight plays upon her hair . . .' I felt marvellous, despite the rivulets of perspiration that were coursing down my front, and the insane scratchiness of the wool that tortured my neck. I sweated up the hill, feeling underneath the jumper, every so often, to touch the slithery second skin of the gold shirt, to reassure myself how miraculously *fab* it felt.

The Parish Hall was packed with teenagers but nobody was dancing. Aretha Franklin's 'Respect' was on the sound system, but it was still light outside, and anyway the army of spotty boys hadn't yet done enough drinking cream soda and sizing up the talent to feel bold enough to ask anybody to dance. Girls from the convent stood around in knots of five or six, talking urgently together in their flowery cotton frocks or their psychedelic-patterned tops. The air was thick with the fruity pong of Aqua Manda. I soon found my throng of classmates – Harry and Paul and Chris and Bill and Stephen and Tony and the brothers Jeremy and Geoffrey – and we greeted each other cautiously. Boys in their fifteenth year, caught together out of uniform, have an achingly self-conscious look about them, which can only be alleviated by their commenting on each other's dress sense like bitchy divas. They were all wearing pastel shirts and light-coloured summer slacks that evening, and looked like a group advertisement from the Young Moderns section of Elys department store, across the road from Wimbledon Station.

'You look a bit . . . *hot* in that thing, John,' said Paul with glee.

'At least you're not wearing your school blazer, like last year,' observed Harry.

'Girls like a bit of sweat, I believe,' said Stephen, regarding my glowing forehead. 'I'm sure you'll be a big hit.' He seemed strangely confident, for a fat vision in lilac Ben Sherman.

'Give me a minute to get my breath,' I said, 'and I'll show you something dead cool.'

The soul music got louder, to still the flow of soignée conversation in the hall, and we tried a few experimental dance steps together, waving our arms around in modest abandon.

'Have you seen what Margaret Coburn's wearing?' Harry yelled in my ear. 'She's practically *naked*.'

'Why don't you go and do something about it?' I yelled back. Any minute now, my new self was due to appear, and I didn't want to present myself to this gang as if requiring their approval.

'Reach Out, I'll Be There' by the Four Tops had got several girls dancing around their handbags. Paul, the leader of the playground pack, went to talk to his future girlfriend Liz and her Aqua Manda-scented pals. Our little crew was breaking up, into the first of the night's many wanderings around the dance floor, the boys trying to summon up the courage to ask, and the resilience not to mind being told that the lady in question would rather stick pins in her eyes. It was time.

I went outside to the cloakroom, yanked off my sensible black polo-neck and looked at my reflection in the Gents mirror. The shirt looked a bit crumpled and steamed, but its extraordinary shimmer was unaffected by the five-mile journey by train, bus and foot in 87-degree heat. Beside me, a couple of younger boys stopped dead in their tracks and stared. I ruffled my hair and straightened my collar. The boys disappeared, giggling.

Resplendent in black gold, I came back out into a blast of strobe lights. It was suddenly hard to get my bearings, but I knew a few of my pals were beside the bar. As I got there, with a cheery 'That's better . . .', Tony, a large Anglo-Polish kid, turned, saw me glowing towards him like an ambulant mirror-ball, and let out a yell. 'Bloody hell!' he shouted, over the music. 'Look at Walsh!'

They turned. And they looked. They flinched, quite physically. They actually backed away from me, as though in danger of contamination.

'What?' I asked innocently, as if my new shirt were the most natural dance-hall garb in the world.

And then something awful happened. As the others laughed at me – not just laughed, but clutched each other by the arm, and pointed, and laughed some more – one boy, Jeremy, a future school captain, looked into my face with a terrible seriousness. 'How can you *possibly* wear such a – ridiculous – *thing*?' he asked in a kind of fury. 'What are you playing at? What's going on?'

'Jesus, Jeremy,' I said. 'It's just a shirt. You don't have to like it.'

He shook his head. Whatever was bothering him, he really meant it.

'Go back,' he said thickly, 'and put your jumper back on.'

'What?' I said, bewildered. 'What are you, my mum?'

'Go and cover that up,' said Jeremy, with a steely something-or-other in his voice, 'or nobody will have anything to do with you.'

It was terrible. I looked at my friends, my classmates, my generation. They had got over their convulsions, now, and looked back at me with the utmost contempt.

'The trouble with you, Walsh,' said Jeremy, reverting to the playground rule of surnames-only, 'is, you're the kind of person that we all take the piss out of.'

I was stunned. It was the most shocking thing to hear.

Did they all think that? All my friends? Had I become a figure of fun without realising it – and all because of clothes? Stuck for a reply, I turned round and walked, ears ringing with embarrassment, back towards the swing doors with the twin port-holes and back to the cloakroom, where I would find my sweaty but acceptable jumper, and pull it over my glowing gold chest and cover up my shame for always like a terrible secret.

I hung my head. This had all been a terrible mistake. I'd spent two pounds nineteen and six just to feel wretched and discover my friends all thought I was a complete pillock. My feet were heavy. My shoulders ached. A last drop of sweat ran, mockingly, down my right cheek and dropped off my chin . . .

Just as I was about to push the swing doors, I passed Mick Chamberlain. He was in the sixth form, a tall skinny prefect whom I knew a little because he was friendly with my pretty sister. He was friendly with all the convent girls, in fact, because he was funny and was in a band called The Dark Riders. He'd been the first boy in school to buy the Beatles' *Sergeant Pepper* album the previous summer, before the rest of the world caught on. We'd had a conversation or two.

'Hey, Walshy,' he said, as I slunk past. 'Blimey, look at you.'

Please don't say it, I thought. I can't stand any more of this.

'Fan*tastic* shirt.'

I stopped. 'What?' I said.

'Fan–fucking–tastic shirt,' he said with real enthusiasm. 'Where the hell did you get that?'

I looked at him guardedly. Was he taking the piss, like everybody else?

'I've never seen anything like it,' he enthused. 'I've got to get one. Really. Where was it? The King's Road?'

'Er, no,' I said, feeling a tiny surge of ego. 'Around

Clapham, actually. It's just something I thought I'd wear to the dance . . .'

'Well, yeah, damn right,' said Mick. 'It's not something you'd wear for a visit by the school governors, is it? But where in Clapham? Tell me the address and I'll go and get one.'

'Mick . . .' I searched his face for signs of sarcasm. 'You really think it's OK?'

'I've got a band practice on Wednesday,' he said. 'I really want to turn up wearing something amazing. The others are so boring. They dress like a crowd of undertakers. Where –'

'Mick,' said a blonde girl in a Julie Christie bob. 'Did you get me a Coke? Are you ever coming back?' She looked at me. 'Who's your friend?'

'This is Walshy,' he said (I don't think he ever knew my first name), 'the man with the *best* shirt. Walshy, this is Charlotte. Charlotte, why don't you dance with Walshy while I get you a drink?'

'Oh, OK,' she said. 'Come on, then.' I followed her, disbelievingly, into the central crush of bodies. Suddenly pulled back from the brink, I was dancing with a girl at least two years older than me, who had blonde hair and a dress with a cleavage inside it.

The sound system was pounding out 'Jumpin' Jack Flash'. I put a lot into the dance. I plonked a hand on my hip like Mick Jagger, and extended my right arm like an Austrian countess flapping her hand at an admirer. Charlotte ground her hips like a belly dancer and hardly looked at me once, but that was OK. Every time I raised my arms, I saw a snaking line of flashing gold that was my sleeve. My own sleeve! Under the hot lights, it had become a special effect.

When Mick returned with Charlotte's Coke, I was exultant. 'You're a brilliant dancer,' I told her. 'You should be on *Top of the Pops*.'

'You really think so?' she said. 'Mick says I can't dance for toffee.' A girl friend appeared by Charlotte's side, another blonde in a bosomy blue halter-neck, to shout something in her ear.

'Clare, this is Walshy,' Charlotte shouted back. 'Check out the shirt.'

And the brazen Clare did so, running a finger across my chest and scraping it, once, twice, with her fingernails. 'Very nice,' she yelled. 'Very tactile.'

'Would you like to dance?' I said, with reckless confidence. She would. She even stuck around for a second go, to an idiotic but catchy song called 'Judy in Disguise'.

I'd love to say that I won the dancing competition that night, was named Best Dressed Man in a Parish Hall 1968, and won the love of the Prom Queen, but it wouldn't be true. What is true is that I danced with a couple of older girls until I was genuinely ragged with exertion, met a couple of girls my age who wanted to talk about clothes without a trace of satire, and at 10.30, when the music slowed down, experienced the thrill of having a girl called Fiona dance to 'Nights in White Satin' with me, her arms around my neck, as her hands touched the slithery material of my shirt, and fingered it with steady, rhythmic pleasure. I even copped a small, liquid, corner-of-mouth kiss as the lights went out at the end.

I didn't see Jeremy again. Paul and Harry and Stephen and I walked out into the cloakroom together, soaked in sweat, talking about everything except the clothes we were wearing. Nobody mentioned the sartorial atrocity I had committed, as if we'd agreed to leave it as an unmentionable subject, since I'd successfully managed to dance with girls in the ridiculous thing.

But a major battle, it seemed, had been won that night. I'd entered the other world beyond the world of home, been abused for trying to be different, and survived, and emerged in a new land where some people liked other people to be a bit flash and cocky and vainglorious. It was a long way from seeing Clyde Barrow walking down the main street of Small-town, Texas, with his sassy white hat and his gangster insouciance, trying anything to impress Faye Dunaway, but the journey had been worth it. From then onwards, I invested regularly in clothes which guaranteed I stuck out of the crowd like a flamingo in a rookery, and wore them with a shrug of indifference to the Jeremys out there, the cautious squad who were born to take the piss out of show-offs like me.

I got home at 11.15. My mother had gone to bed, but my father was still up, watching the end of the late-night movie. I was too hot, and too pleased with myself, to bother putting on the concealing jumper. Dad surveyed my glittery shirt, now wrecked with sweaty endeavour. 'My God,' he said. 'You look like a victim of the *Torrey Canyon*' – namely, the giant tanker that had split open in the seas around the Scilly Isles, leaving an oil slick several miles long that had distressed seabirds and local bathers.

I stood in front of him, exhausted from dancing, elated with girls and music, and the thrill of having been an outlaw who'd almost died on the dance floor but had somehow been reborn. He smiled at me, secretly complicitous about the arrangements you have to make to impress women when you're fourteen and a half. I smiled back. There had been a lot of dirt in the fuel-pipe of my life, in my connection with trendy young Grown-up Land. But to my surprise, I'd blowed it away, in the end.

6

DANCING WITH
DECADENCE

Cabaret (1972)

It was the summer of 1972, the year I was going up to
Oxford University. I was now eighteen, tall and gangly,
socially sophisticated (in that I could hold conversations
with almost anybody without pretending to be Bob Hope
or Leslie Phillips), intellectually chaotic, well-read in a
neurotic, must-have-read-everything-by-now sort of way.
All around me, people were in motion, just like in Scott
McKenzie's 'San Francisco' song. My chums from school
had ventured off all over the world, heading out into the
blue yonder of the Grand Canyon, the beaches of Thailand
and Turkey, the hippie trail to Samarkand. Some had taken
summer jobs as jolly *gentils organisateurs* with Club Med.
Others, the post-hippie rebels, had travelled all over the
place. They were like latter-day fans of Jack Kerouac's *On
the Road*, who didn't quite know where to go in their gap
year, but knew that all they really wanted was to come
back from there with a photograph of themselves sitting,
unshaven and wild-eyed, on the bonnet of a pick-up truck
in Africa or Ceylon or Yemen with a copy of *Lonesome
Traveller* dangling from their sunburnt fingers as they

regarded the lens with the look of One Who Has Seen Many Things.

I hadn't wanted to do that. No way. I'd already been away to exciting foreign places, to America and the USSR, and I didn't have the same wanderlust that seemed to pitch my co-scholars into a fever of excitement about going somewere other than Europe. The hell with all this *travelling*, I thought. I will be cool, stay in London, and get to know the place, earn some money, cruise around Soho as a guy with cash to spend, rather than as an oikish schoolboy with his pockets full of bus tickets and conkers.

I'd turned into a proper grown-up in the last year. I'd grown to six-feet-one. I'd become a fashion casualty of the Great Gear Trading Company, Chelsea's trendiest shop: I now wore loon pants in vivid yellow, 28 inches at their widest point, skimming my two-tone, fake-snakeskin boots, and a purple *Oz* T-shirt to show my solidarity with the groovy Underground magazine editors who'd been on trial the year before for falling foul of the Obscene Publications Act. My head was full of *Exile on Main Street*, the Rolling Stones's finest hour. I was rangy, stylish, sussed and street-familiar, if not exactly street-wise. There was only one thing missing from my life as a metropolitan hero. I was still a virgin.

I had, however, acquired a girlfriend. I was going out with Lucy. She was gorgeous. Short but wiry, *jolie laide* but with long, luxuriant hair, slender but with enormous breasts like her mother, she was a clever, guardedly acquiescent partner in the business of finding out how sex might feel with somebody else doing things to you.

I would walk across Clapham Common to her house in the mid-afternoon during the summer holidays, when both her parents were at work, and she would greet me fondly, with her hair pinned up, in the hallway of their huge, echoing house. In the kitchen she would offer me 'a coffee', as though I cared a flying fuck for caffeine-based stimulants at this moment of charged, hormonal dizziness.

I'd try some puny conversational opening ('So how's your physics revision coming along?') and she would talk about her school with bored detachment, and I would nod, and wonder if the damn kettle was ever going to boil so that she could pour the seething water over the brown crystals and do this *thing* she did, which was to stir the resulting mixture this way and that, clockwise and counter-clockwise, as if to make it – what? more authentically coffee-ish? That lovely hand of hers, holding the silver spoon so angularly, so correctly, like a baton, parting and re-folding the steaming waters like a conductor on a podium, calling together the woodwinds and the brasses of this overture to our love, tantalised me to madness. It was coffee foreplay, pure and simple, toying with the moments of chat that had to elapse before I could slide my arms around her tiny waist – where-upon she would put her hands on my forearms and say, 'Wait!' and unclasp her unruly long curls from a pink bull-dog clip, and shake her head to let them tumble all over her T-shirted shoulders, a shake of the head like a drugged no-no-no while the rest of her was expressing a heady yes-yes-yes, a tumbling unloosening of hair that suggested that, OK then, it was time for our relationship, young and awkwardly polite as it was, to progress into a silent nego-tiation of desire.

And so we'd twine together, and kiss each other hungrily, lying on the sofa in her family living-room, where I'd spent a score of evenings with her parents and mine, chatting, arguing, listening to their jazz records, eating smoked salmon canapés and cheesy pretzels, and I would be regularly trashed at chess by her loud, ebullient, civil-engineer father.

It felt deliciously wicked, on those afternoons with Lucy, to violate the serenity of both their silent house and their innocent daughter, in a kind of revenge against polite suburbanism, as if I were Benjamin Braddock in *The Graduate*. The coffee, that frightfully urgent preliminary, grew cold and untasted on the table beside us, an emblem (it seemed) of how little we really cared for the conventions of tea-time, as we lay there for an hour or two in the sunny afternoon and talked and kissed.

Unfortunately, that was as far as it went. Ours was a basic relationship of teenage sweatiness with no climaxes. Lucy was also a virgin, but a sensible-minded one, as keen to preserve the status quo as I was to corrupt it as soon as I possibly could. If I clamped my hand for too long on her mountainous bosom, she would remove it, gently but firmly, non-negotiably. We could kiss like lust-maddened savages, but any attempts to investigate her tremendous body were sternly repelled. It was a classic problem of both class and religion. You couldn't undo the bra-strap of an almost-girfriend without being treated like an aspirant rapist. There were rules of engagement with young Catholic girls. The mouth, the chin, the cheeks, the ears were OK. Anything else was heading too disturbingly in the direction of Filthy Sex, and that was the territory of mortal sin.

I went along with it. (I couldn't do anything else.) Terrible straining sensations might distend my jeans, as I lay with eight stone of flushed, seventeen-year-old Lucy flesh writhing beneath me, but the chances of persuading her to do anything about it were unimaginably remote. Girls didn't acknowledge the existence of the male member in those days, nor encourage you to get familiar with anything below their waists. Your bolder friends might tell you about the female regions they'd successfully invaded – 'upstairs inside' and 'downstairs outside' were the most extreme terms used by the coy lechers of my acquaintance. But I could no more have clamped my hand on Lucy's tight-denimed seventeen-year-old crotch than I could have goosed her mother.

Sex, as far as I – as we – were concerned, was hygienic,

labial, salivatory, all tongues and urgent promises, and a mutual understanding that we were sworn to each other in a polite rapture of kissing as another form of (and a blessed relief from) talking.

Of all the hundred things we never did, lying there in her parents' front room, we never played music. Why not? Music could have spurred us into action – especially musical films, if only I'd known then what I knew a few weeks later.

I'd always hated musicals. They were full of phoney emotions and crappy sunsets and chocolate-boxy landscapes and people singing at each other. You'd watch the faces of the people being sung at, and appreciate how much they had to act looking really delighted about having some guy trilling and emoting into their ears for five minutes. It was all so *fake*.

South Pacific was the worst. I'd heard the soundtrack a thousand times on the family gramophone at Sunday lunchtimes. It was pretty enjoyable, the way any hepped-up orchestral extravaganza can be enjoyable when accompanied by roast beef with roast potatoes and peas and strawberry jelly and ice-cream through a thousand undifferentiated Sundays. It was OK, listening to the guy with a deep voice singing 'There is Nothing Like a Dame' on a rising note of hysteria: 'There ain't a *thing* that's *wrong* with *any* man *here*/That *can't* be *cured* by *puttin'* him *near*/a something-something, female, feminine *dame*.' You could endure the idiot whimsy of 'Happy Talk', the lush Polynesian chorale of 'Bali Hai', and the gruff romanticism of 'Some Enchanted Evening', even though it made the idea of true love sound like imprisonment ('Once you have found her, never let her go'). It was just about bearable on the gramophone. Then one day my mother made the mistake of taking me to see the film. I sat dumbfounded with boredom, while the American sailors pranced about, the Technicolor sky turned everything boiling orange and sickly red, and the grizzled charmer Rossano Brazzi cradled the dismally unattractive Mitzi Gaynor in his elderly embrace. Everything about it was old, old, old. Nothing about it held a shred of interest for a cool young desperado in the Sixties.

Other musicals were almost as bad. *Showboat* was a stage-bound, sterile bore, mostly filmed in a proscenium arch, framed and fringed with fake trees, into which people in primary-coloured frocks and frock-coats came and went like mobilised waxworks. *Seven Brides for Seven Brothers* featured lots of energetic jumping around by brawny halfwits in rural threads, with the same solidly dislikable lead man, Howard Keel. *West Side Story,* for all its street-gang *realismo*, failed to engage my sympathies (was I a Jet or a Shark? Did I care?). *The Sound of Music*, despite its appeal for the aspiring kisser, left you drowning in sentimentality. *Oklahoma!* had one terrific song, when the girls in the dormitory float about in their nighties singing 'Many a New Day Will Dawn Before I Do'. It fixed itself in my head for years as the image of the way querulous girls complained about their nasty ex-boyfriends and the awfulness of men in general, but the film itself sent you to sleep in the dream sequence. *My Fair Lady*, another big hit at Sunday lunchtimes, was full of good songs, especially 'Wouldn't It Be Loverly' with its humming Cockney intro; but seeing it was an endless, three-hour ordeal with Audrey Hepburn going '*Owwwwww*' all the time in an adenoidal wail.

I had, in short, no time for musical films. They were mostly over-produced, tiresomely spectacular, emotionally gaga spectacles for a generation who needed some respite from the years of war, a kind of polymedial balm for hurt minds. Musicals? Pah. Who needed them?

And it was in that frame of mind that I went to see *Cabaret*. The reviews in the *Daily Telegraph* and *Evening Standard* were ecstatic. The film contained songs and dance routines, true, but they all took place inside a club. Nobody would be found declaring his love in song while walking down a street or while meeting his girlfriend outside a gazebo. And I knew the Berlin novels of Christopher Isherwood, on which the story was based. So I rang Lucy and asked if, instead of an afternoon on the sofa, she fancied a real date – a hot new movie, with a tasty meal at the Stockpot (Soho's cheapest restaurant) afterwards. Why yes, she said, she would *love* that.

We went to see *Cabaret* in the Haymarket on a July evening in 1972. We agreed to meet at Clapham South tube station at 7 p.m. My parents were elated by this evidence that I could, without any prompting, fix up a date with a nice Catholic girl, and a friend of the family to boot, to see 'a show in town' (my mother seemed under the impression we going to see a stage update of *Showboat*). My father pressed a five-pound note into my pocket and said, 'Buy her a programme, and an ice-cream at the interval, and for God's sake let *her* do some of the talking.'

Programme? Interval? Neither of them had been near a cinema, singly or together, in years. But they liked Lucy. My mother approved of her cool, hands-on-hips stroppiness. My father enjoyed their conversations about her prowess at Biology and was not, I fear, unmoved by her phenomenal bosom. Both parents saw me out to the front door, flittering with advice and encouragement, and stood leaning over the gate, waving and beaming like a small fan club, as I strode away in my rainbow-striped summer jacket towards my first proper date.

I walked across the Common, where the late sunlight was glowing on the trees, and got to the station early. Lucy turned up promptly at 7 p.m. full of smiles, wearing a white cotton summer frock with a lilac jumper tied around her waist in case the evening got cold. She kissed me on the lips, so fleetingly I might have missed it, were I not alive to any tiny hints that Lucy was turning from a snog partner into a Proper Girlfriend. We talked about holidays (she was just back from Barcelona) and held hands as we crossed the street from the bus stop. We did not stop to kiss in a doorway. This was a proper date. We were a Serious Young Couple going out together to check out the first X-rated musical in film history . . .

I sat in the stalls with my left hand fingering Lucy's knee during the credits, and watched as Joel Grey's face appeared, tilted against the wobbly, metallic sheen of the Kit Kat Club's far wall. A buzz of conversation in the Club had gradually increased during the initially silent and downbeat credits, to be silenced by a drum roll and the first ghastly smile of the Berlin club's sexually ambivalent MC.

His first appearance was a fantastic sight – a malevolent sprite in a bow-tie, a white mask of make-up, a rouged, cupid-bow mouth, his tiny skull-head plastered with black brilliantine, his leer of complicity, his light, cutesy-pie delivery. Mr Grey was, from the start, an impresario of shocking things, a damaged cheerleader.*

'*Meine damen und herren, mesdames et messieurs*, ladeez *unt* gennlemen – leave your troubles outside . . .' I stared at this apparition, entranced. He was a music-hall turn with a nasty streak. You couldn't take your eyes off him as he introduced the show. On the line, 'Even zer orchestra is beautiful', my life began to change. The gang of ladies

* Joel Grey was a classic example of the one-hit wonder; he was forty and unknown when he won a Best Supporting Oscar for *Cabaret*, and virtually disappeared thereafter, apart from minor roles in two 1976 films, Robert Altman's *Buffalo Bill and the Indians* and Herbert Ross's Sherlock Holmes farrago, *The Seven Per Cent Solution*.

revealed against a bright, hurt-your-eyes spotlight were stunning in their grotesque radiance, as they swung into a dirty, honking, Weimar-Dixieland riff. The MC, and the camera, prowled among them as though inspecting hookers in a brothel (the MC poking his knobbly, music-hall stick meaningfully down the open mouth of the saxophone) and my eyes settled with fascination on the toad-like figure of the banjo-player.

She sat, or rather squatted, on top of the piano with her legs apart, her skirts drawn over her knees, looking like an old peasant woman shelling nuts in the sunshine, revealing her long, slatternly black socks. They were *socks*, for God's sake, rather than cabaret fishnets, but that made them all the more gross; you could imagine that she hadn't changed them in weeks. She played the banjo with a fat, listless, uncaring, rhythmical vagueness, a slow, masturbatory strum like a hooker servicing a client. You could hardly see her face, but she was smiling, entirely at home doing the same routine night after night. She was gross, no doubt about it, but there was something triumphant about her at-home squatness. It was like watching a bloated queen sitting on a lavatory.

I stole a glance at Lucy. In her sweet white cotton frock, with tiny blue cornflowers at shoulder and hip, she was the polar opposite of the lady on the piano. It was amazing to think that two people so different could inhabit the same gender. Her face was tilted up to the screen with utter concentration. She crossed her legs. I reached out and tickled her knee again, as I'd been doing before. She glanced at me with the weakest smile of encouragement, and went back to the screen.

The film had cut to Berlin station, where Brian Roberts (the Christopher Isherwood role, played by Michael York) was arriving, in his felt hat and tweeds, to make a living teaching English conversation to well-off Berliners. As he rose from his seat on the train for his first sighting of the city, the camera came along the platform and squinnied up underneath his wondering, pasty English face, so that we too were leaning upwards from beneath him, checking out his ordinariness, his gawping innocence.

Back in the club, the MC introduced the dancing girls as they bent over the lip of the stage, looking like whores in a market. They were – reading from right to left – Heidi, Kirsten, Mousie, Helge, Betty *und* Inge, and unlike the girls in any chorus line in any movie I'd seen, they appeared, at first sight, slightly horrific – unsmiling, dead-eyed, bored to death with the MC's routine, his ironic flattery of their beauty. He confided to the audience that they are 'Every one – a *wergin*'. The elderly bourgeois audience rocked with laughter. The MC, pretending shock at their lack of gallantry, said, 'You don't believe me? Don't take my word for it – ask Helge.' But I didn't want to ask Helge. I wanted to see Mousie again, and the camera obligingly returned to her. She was the girl in the middle, a cold, black-eye-shadowed vamp in a sailor-suit top and black pants. Her eyes were deader than the others, and she stood with her back arched and her rump stuck out as if it were her natural posture, as if waiting to be fucked from behind had become second nature to her.

An uncomfortable heat began to build up, in my head and elsewhere. This was not pornography we were watching, I and my sweet, bosomy, keep-your-hands-where-I-can-see-them girlfriend; this hardly even counted as erotica; this was a mainstream musical film. But something about the fat ladies in the orchestra and the slave-market vamps in the chorus line had hit my libido amidships. How could I possibly fancy this girl on the stage, in her enveloping black pants and her arrogantly bendy, used-and-abused body? But I did. *God*, I did. The camera seemed determined to play on my discomfiture, lingering on the swaying bottoms of the dancers as they wiggled and twitched and fled from Joel Grey with his tickling stick.★

As the first number, 'Wilkommen, Bienvenue', approached its climax, the dancing girls linked arms around each others' shoulders and plunged forward for the final chorus, and the camera did the same trick it had pulled with Michael York at the station, and went in *under* the action, twisting its head to look up wonderingly at the girls as they sashayed above it to the front of the stage in a stamping, triumphant goose-step. I'd never seen anything like it before. I wasn't watching a slick bit of showbiz polish, but a line-up of six beefy tarts in plunging *realismo*, crashing amateurishly across the foot-lights because it was their job for the evening, raising dust and temperatures. Although all you could see of the Kit-Kat Club was the stage, the harsh lighting and some faces in the audience, it seemed to have got the amateur-hour raggedness of Weimar decadence absolutely spot-on, until its very tackiness became, like zer orchestra, a thing of perverse beauty. As for the girls – well, what I was looking at there, as the chorus line stamped and surged above my head, was sex, impure and simple, in all its gross and messy wonder – the first time I had an inkling of what it was really all about.

★ Behind the scenes at the actual cabaret, the (never named) MC stays a silently sinister figure. He is never out of character. He is never off-message. On-stage and off, he is a gurning satyr but a worryingly attractive one: when he extends his wiggling tongue, like a cunnilingual memento, to Sally (just as she's protesting her fidelity to Brian), you could imagine a night in the past when she went to bed with him by mistake, and spent hours thereafter trying to forget her folly. There's a poignant air of resignation about Ms Bowles when the MC comes up behind her, as she stands wretchedly in the wings, and clamps his claw-like hands on her breasts . . . He is the genuine article, the epitome of the corruption which Sally childishly impersonates.

What did I know? I was a Catholic *wergin* at eighteen. Until then, I'd taken sex to be a thing you did round the front, all lips and breasts, all kissing and sucking and trying to get your hands in between the buttons and under the straps. After *Cabaret*, things changed. Sex became something darker and ruder, it was about rumps and bottoms, and legs enfolded in stockings, and flesh bisected by black straps. It was my first intimation that there was nothing polite about sex at all, nothing sweet or romantic, nothing for which you can decently ask permission. My first inkling of the true nature of Eros unmasked – how undignified and smelly it could be, how insatiable and cruel and impersonal it might be, how Shakespeareanly lust-in-action, the tangled, reeking sheets of the student hovel, the hurly-burly of the hotel bedroom – came from the first fifteen minutes of a movie. It was a spectacular education, there in the plush, velveteen stalls of the Odeon Haymarket.

Liza Minnelli was a revelation too. She wasn't a great beauty (that long Grimms' Fairy Tales nose, that funny mouth, those fathomlessly huge, slightly mad eyes), but she was sexy as hell. She was always swaying, always humming, always twirling her hands and beckoning you in, as if her whole life – every minute of her whole existence – was an invitation to a dance, whose choreography was designed to suck you in to being her partner, and to trap you there with her, trap you actually *inside* her, for ever. She was slightly comical, of course, because she was always scheming and plotting and dreaming of her big break, but her energy was profoundly exciting.

My favourite view of Ms Minnelli was not a front view of her suspender-belt routine, but a back view of her body backstage, just before she goes on for the 'Mein Herr' number. Sally is listening to the MC's patter, murmuring the lines of his little joke ('I said to her, "I vont you for my vife," and she said, "But what would your vife possibly vont with me?"'), and, with adrenalin coursing through her, raises her arms in the air and waggles her hands, like a parody of Al Jolson doing 'Mammy'. Just one simple gesture communicated such waves of life-energy, such vivid enthusiasm, such hectic, yea-saying delight in being alive, I fell in love with her on the spot.

You also had to admire her determination. When she tries to kiss Brian (Michael York) as he lies in bed, reading a book, he rejects her advances and she flounces away out the door of his tiny room. We think she is acting the Woman Scorned – but she leaves the door open, crosses the hallway and goes into her own flat, leaving its door open as well. We and Brian watch, with mild fascination, as she wrestles with her hefty walnut gramophone and, staggering under its weight, carries it across the hallway, back inside Brian's boudoir. She winds it up, puts on a record, applies the ancient needle to the ancient shellac, and does another of her little twirly-hands dance routines – a slightly ridiculous Salome, performing for a chilly Englishman, as he lies there in his knitted jumper reading a German porn novel which he is due to translate.

Finding he doesn't leap up and smother her with kisses, she sits down and discusses her body. 'Is this bit too fat?' she inquires, guiding his hand to her stomach, then her hip, then her right breast. Brian responds with the chillingly English reply, 'Isn't it a little early in the morning for this sort of thing?'

I wondered, Did I, despite her flapperish ways, find her resistible? No, I didn't. Any girl who went to that much trouble to impress a somnolent male, who took such a masculine line of attack (a truck driver might have balked at being asked to heave that old gramophone around), and then asked for his view of her soft and spreading flesh, deserved, I thought, a medal. Would Lucy one day take my hand and place it on one of her mountainous breasts and say, 'Go ahead, you've put in the hours, be my guest, we both know how much we fancy each other?' It seemed unlikely. She was not the kind of girl who would take the initiative. She seemed more the kind of girl who would stifle the initiative in others. But maybe I was wrong . . .

On screen, Sally had taught Brian to scream under railway bridges. She'd introduced him to the suave but impecunious Fritz Wenger. And she'd sat in on his first lesson in English conversation with the divine Fräulein Landauer, played by the glacially ravishing Marisa Berenson. It was a marvellous scene, played for laughs, that matched the well-bred innocence of the Fräulein with the worldly directness of the American *chantoose*. Sally Bowles wears too much make-up (red lipstick, blue eyeshadow, beauty spot) and plays the bad fairy who could, at any moment, wreck the gentility of the language lesson. Fräulein Landauer's elegantly inept small-talk ('I have had a cold, but it is better now . . . Der plegm is in der toobs.') is hijacked by Sally, who steers the conversation round to sexually transmitted diseases. Why yes, says Fräulein Landauer, apparently you can catch such things from teacups, and towels.

'And of course,' says Sally, 'from screwing.'

'*Zcrewing*?' asks Ms Landauer. 'What is zis?'

'Oh it's . . .' Sally tries to remember the German word. Brian prays that she will not.

'I know,' she says at last. '*Boompzen.*'

The Fräulein looks puzzled, rather than appalled, as if unable to fathom what this word is doing in a polite drawing-room during a polite English teatime conversation. And that, of course, was the heart of the film's appeal. It flirted with the gaminess and reek of sexual promiscuity – of omnisex-uality, as we will see – while at the same time being as cute as a cupcake, about as *fatale* (as Brian says of Sally) as an after-dinner mint.

I heard Lucy laughing beside me. She was clearly loving

it. If she'd been shocked by the talk of sex, it would have been mitigated by the coolness of the Fräulein, who rather reminded me of Lucy. She wasn't as beautiful or elegant as the German model, but she had a lot of natural grace and self-asssurance.

The two women, Sally and Ms Landauer, become emblems of innocence and experience as the film goes on. Fritz asks Sally her advice about how to let the heiress know of his love, and she tells him to pounce on her; that it really is the *only* way. When he finally does, the German beauty reports back to Sally that he has tried to make love to her on (unspeakable sacrilege) her father's library sofa. But also that, even while she was fighting him off and calling him names, 'suddenly there is equal fire, equal passion, in me. Since then, I think only of him. But is it love, or only mere infatuation of the body?'

The ending was a little downbeat, but Lucy and I left the cinema on a colossal high. From the moment when the rich seducer Maximilian's enormous car pulled away, in spectacular long shot, from the beer garden, leaving a hundred hard-faced burghers singing 'Tomorrow Belongs To Me' along with the angelic Nazi youth, I'd decided *Cabaret* was the best film I'd ever seen. So, apparently, had my date.

'It was so fantastically *grown-up*,' she said over our modest Stockpot supper. 'Sally was such a dreamer, even when everything went wrong in real life. God, that scene with all the candles. I'll never forget it. It was the most romantic thing in the world. And even after she had the abortion and they split up, well, even *that* was sort of romantic too, in the end. She loved him but she had to leave him. She just wanted everything to be like life on stage.'

I'd never heard her talk so fluently before, about anything.

'But the stuff on stage,' I said, 'I mean the songs, they weren't romantic at all, were they? They were all about money and politics and, and, er, group sex and so on. Sally was romantic about living a life of decadence.'

'But John, any girl could see that was just a lot of pretence. Even Brian could see that. Sally really wanted to fall in love and get married, to be like Fritz and the rich German girl, you could tell.'

'No, no,' I said. 'She wanted to find a rich bloke who'd buy her furs and things. She was terribly, what's the word, *mercenary* from start to finish.'

'Have we been at the same film?' Lucy asked, a forkful of cheap *coq au vin* halfway to her ruby mouth. 'She was full of dreams of being a nice girl. Remember when she put her hands up to the chandelier in Frau what's-her-name's parlour and said, "Look everybody – positively nuns' hands." Didn't you notice that? She wanted to have her father love her and not ignore her, and to have a nice boyfriend who would treat her properly.'

'She wanted Maximilian,' I insisted, 'because he was a rich smoothie. I don't think a husband and kids were ever in her game plan.'

'God, you're such a cynic,' said Lucy with a hint of crossness. 'I don't think you've got a clue what girls really want.'

'This was a movie, dammit,' I said. 'Not a documentary about the secrets of the female heart.'

A slight *froideur* came between us on the bus-ride home. But we both knew that things had changed because of *Cabaret*. For one thing, we'd turned into a real couple. I'd squired her through the streets, opened doors for her, held her hand up and down staircases, waited for her outside the Ladies' loo, paid for her supper and argued with her, just like you did with girlfriends. And the movie had opened a whole can of worms about the way people wanted to live their lives. I'd loved the film because it was so hard-edged and bittersweet, because the songs were so triumphantly nasty, and because I fancied the dead-eyed Mousie, and

199

suddenly longed for a life of heartless, decadent behaviour. Lucy had loved it because, behind all the grot and sleaze, the ancient gramophones and million-candled sex, she discerned True Love striving for the upper hand. We were both a little staggered by all the talk of screwing and the moments of brutality, but had responded in quite different ways. It had given us both a lot to chew on.

What I most wanted to chew on was Lucy's flesh. I'd never been so turned on by a movie before. And since this was our first proper date, after several weeks of swapping saliva, and having my hands briskly relocated from her lovely body, after all that horizontal frustration, I decided it must be time to take things further. I got her home by midnight, as directed. Her parents were still up. She made coffee for us in the kitchen, while I chatted to them in the drawing-room about the film, and the holidays, and my parents' gripping recent history, but all the time I could think of nothing but Lucy's seventeen-year-old body clad in black pants and a blue sailor top. Memories of the sexy chorus line kept invading my thoughts as I stood in this polite suburban room. I wondered, with a wild surmise, how the girl called Mousie would fit in at Battersea Rise, if I were to bring her back one evening to meet my family.

Out in the kitchen, as I helped Lucy find mugs and sugar, the atmosphere was electric. I could tell she was dying for something to happen. We sat up with her parents, drinking Nescafé ve-ry slow-ly until they went to bed.

'I'll be off in ten minutes,' I told them. 'Just want to play a few records and talk to Lucy about the film.'

They yawned. 'Don't stay up too late, you two,' they said fondly. 'And, John, watch yourself walking back across the Common.'

Yeah, yeah, I said to them, silently. For God's sake, *go*.

Things happened a lot faster than they might have anticipated. Lucy took the coffee mugs out to the kitchen, and washed them up. I went out to join her. She turned from the sink, wiping her hands on a tea-towel. 'That song "Money" keeps running round my head,' she said. 'It was so –'

I grabbed her and kissed her with ferocious urgency. I ran my hands all over her body, heedless of the contract of restraint and decorum and no-go areas that had existed between us. She was mine, now, I'd decided, a sexy possession. All the talking and fencing and coffee-drinking could go to hell. All I wanted was the Mousie in her soul. All I wanted was her dead-eyed acquiescence.

As I ground my teeth into her neck, clutching her breasts with both hands, she pulled away. '*Stop* that, John,' she said. 'Jesus, what's got into you?' Without saying a word, I turned her around and pushed her until she was bent over the sink, and rammed myself brutally against her skinny bottom so that she could feel the tumult in my groin. It was an uncompromising statement of desire. I'd emerged from the cinema convinced that a real woman like Lucy must secretly be longing to explore the joys of hardcore sexual connection, like the girls in the chorus line had been exploring for years. Like Fritz, I was trying the only way I knew to declare my most basic intent. I had *pounced*.

Instead of discovering an answering fire and equal passion burning in her veins, she yelped with horror, as if I'd waved my genitalia in her, or even her parents', face. She was a nice girl. She didn't do that kind of thing (not yet, and certainly not from behind, anyway). She writhed and wriggled, and finally turned around from the sink and smacked me hard across the face.

'Don't you *dare*,' she said. My cheek burned, but not as much as her indignation. 'What, you think taking me to a film and buying some crappy supper means you can maul me around? You *bastard*.' Her voice shook slightly.

'Lucy, I –'

'I *thought* you were getting the point about girls,' she said with terrible evenness. 'I *thought* you understood. But you're just a walking example of everything that's wrong with boys. You chat and you smarm and you buy things, and you pretend to be interested in me, when all you're after is –'

'But Lucy,' I said, 'you know in the movie where—'

'We're not in a bloody movie *now*,' she said. 'It finished at ten-fifteen. This is now. This is Clapham, not Berlin, and I am not some hooker on a stage and you are definitely not some rich bloke who can assume that girls like being bent over and . . . and assaulted like that. What would my parents think if they knew that you were just waiting for them to go to bed so you could *attack* me?'

'I didn't attack you,' I said, genuinely hurt by the suggestion. 'I thought, after all this time, you might want to, you know . . .'

'Well, I *don't*,' she said, in a firm whisper. 'If you want that kind of thing, you can bloody well find it somewhere else. Just go away. Go to Berlin, for all I care.'

I crept out into the rainy midnight, a wretched figure, and mooched home across Clapham Common. If I'd been beaten up along the way by marauding skinheads (who then patrolled the greensward at night, looking for homosexuals and Pakistanis to savage), I'd probably have welcomed it, such was my gloomy degradation.

Despite our desire-shrivelling row, I was still eaten up with lust. My nice-guy Dr Jekyll character had, with bewildering speed, turned into Mr Hyde. I prowled the back streets of Battersea, on the final leg of my journey home, haunted with frustration. I was forever doomed, it seemed, to be dismissed from the warm living-rooms of Proper Girlfriends, in search of a cold-eyed houri in a sailor-suit to muck about with.

Or was that all I was after? One legacy of the film was a new fascination for bisexuality. It was tough being a virgin.

It was a real pain being rejected by girls with whom you seemed, sometimes for whole weeks, in with a chance. For the first time in my life, I started wondering about the erotic possibilities of other men. It was an odd field of speculation. I felt absolutely no desire for any of my male friends. I had never encountered any bloke whom I wanted to kiss, let alone do anything else with (what on earth, I blankly wondered, would be the point?). But I had the example of Michael York to consider – a studenty fellow with a strangely misshapen face (like me, like mine) who had been no good at having sex with girls, but who seemed to take quite naturally to the experience of screwing the sleazy Maximilian, even after he'd finally lost his virginity – at, what? twenty-two? – with Sally Bowles. Perhaps I would have, had I been in his place. Being bisexual, if nothing else, at least seemed to double your chances of getting off with *somebody* in a posh German *schloss* . . .

The character of Brian had been a revelation to me. I'd never seen sexual ambiguity portrayed on screen before. *Cabaret* is saturated with sexual inversion, both explicit and covert. When Sally asked Brian, 'You do sleep with girls, don't you?' it was a startling, unprecedented inquiry. Nobody in a musical – that most conservative of cinematic forms – had ever fielded a direct inquiry about his or her sexuality before. But then, Brian, like me at the time, was so shockable.

There'd been a telling little scene in the Gents of the Kit Kat Club, when Michael York was having a pee and a tall blonde transvestite in a wig came and stood beside him. You couldn't see any peeing going on, you couldn't even register that they were in a Gents, except for the familiar, grunty-male look of concentration on York's face, which turned to the faintest flicker of embarrassment, then intrigue, then alarm at what was going on (what is a blonde Monroe-vamp doing beside me, peeing standing up?) and what might

happen next. In fact, nothing happened to the English innocent. But he was, and I was, startled by the casual ordinariness of the encounter. When Fritz Wenger (Helmut Griem)
first chats to Brian about Nazis and Communism and Sally,
Fritz interrupts their friendly mutual overtures with 'But
you must understand – we do not sleep on each other', and
it's not immediately clear if he's talking about his present
relationship with Sally or his future dealings with Brian.

When Maximilian, the rich adventurer, enters their lives,
it gradually becomes clear that things could go in any direction. Max's gift to Brian of a gold cigarette case was a stonking
sexual metaphor – an invitation in the form of a vessel waiting
to be filled – and when Brian draws it from his pocket in
the *Biergarten* scene, Max responds by touching Brian's hand
(as it holds out an extended flame, whew) with his fingers
in an unambiguous gesture of attraction. The famous scene
when Brian shouts 'Oh, fuck Maximilian!', and Sally pertly
says, 'I do', and Brian trumps her with 'So do I', is notable
for its casualness, as if having a homosexual encounter might
be the result of a whim, a capricious choice one evening
after too much Roederer Cristal champagne. This was mind-
spinning stuff in the early 1970s. The seeds of this interchange had been sown in an earlier scene, a key moment,
for me, in the cinema of the liberating imagination.

It's the drunk scene in the grand baronial hall of Max's
family castle, where Sally and Brian (who have become
lovers) have been invited to spend the weekend. Max is
clearly out to seduce Brian, or at least win the Englishman's
approval. He has persuaded Brian to wear one of his own
blue sweaters ('I was right,' he tells the half-naked Englishman, tossing the wool garment at him, 'Blue *is* your colour')
and they've exchanged meaningful glances all through
dinner. The other glamorous diners long departed, Sally and
Brian and Max are chilling out in the hall – Max lolling
on a sofa, Sally dancing by the huge fireplace in a long

white dress, Brian attempting to walk at least as far as the next bottle of wine.

Anything could happen. That's precisely the point of the dramaturgical separateness of the characters. We have no idea if Sally will pair off with Max or Brian. Then she and Max sway drunkenly, slowly, in a lazy embrace, while Brian prowls through the foliage of the hall, beats his chest like Tarzan behind some jungly potted plant, and is gradually drawn into their slow-dancey embrace. It's not much of a dance, just a triangular ring of swaying togetherness. The camera tracks their faces as they gaze at each other, silently, as the two men, and the woman between them, dip their faces forward and back in a sexy hokey-cokey, until you could not possibly tell who wants to kiss whom.

The music stops but the camera continues its lazy inspection: this is a game of Musical Chairs in which nobody has decided where to sit down. It's the silence that does it, their complicitous, music-less swaying together, the camera closely monitoring (like an intruder, like a fourth presence that is you, the viewer) the faces, the noses and mouths of the threesome, their what-now smiles and flickering looks, the predatory gleam in Max's eyes, the drunken, dazed innocence of Michael York's face, the connoisseur-of-decadence beam with which Sally regards her two handsome *beaux*, sweetly oblivious to the possibility that they might just as easily abandon her and go off and have sex with each other – though *we* recognise that it's a possibility.

We are ahead of the impossibly sophisticated Sally. I was, despite being eighteen and untried in what Samuel Beckett called 'the cloaca of colonic gratification', fascinated by the faces circling in the candlelight. I was aching to enter that magic circle, that troika of sexual possibility, anywhere I might be allowed in. I wouldn't mind what happened. I'd like just to be there, as sloshed as Michael York, willing to try anything that offered itself – whether soft, or hard, to the touch.

Obviously one does not leave the cinema a confirmed bisexual because of a few flickering celluloid shadows. (In fact, that night with Lucy, I left it a determined, but doomed, shag-monster.) But the film left me with a whole gallery of images of transgender attraction: the beauty of the boy who sings 'Tomorrow Belongs to Me' (and the hoydenish plainness of the girls who join in); the ageing, raddled Fräuleins dancing with each other in Frau Spengler's boarding house; Joel Grey turning up *en travestie* in the chorus line, like a bug-eyed Shirley Temple in a curly fright wig; the kissy-kissy mouths of Sally and the gay MC in the 'Money' sequence; Max toasting Brian with a slug of Turk's Blood wine and the words, 'I think it's my duty to corrupt you.'

Homosexuals didn't figure on screen much when I was in my impressionable phase. It was rare to find even a glancing suggestion that any character, male or female, might consider going to bed with someone of their own sex. The word 'homosexual' was never used. In popular English farces, nobody was 'queer'. In the *Carry On* movies, Kenneth Williams and Charles Hawtree were sissies – they were camp and sneery and shocked by the brazenness of female sexuality. But you never got the impression they were dying to Do It with each other, or with anyone else. Sissies were people who ran away from sexual encounters, not towards them. Among the old movies you saw on television, I found myself wondering about ambiguous characters – like Murray Melvin, the hopeless Mod in Tony Richardson's *A Taste of Honey*. Somewhere between the hair stylist, the make-up department and the lighting cameraman, Melvin was made up to look like a haunted medieval monk. His cadaverous face was long and pointy like a crusader's shield, the face of one of those interchangeable knights queueing up to embark on a ship in Italian Renaissance paintings. His hair was black and slicked down like a helmet. His eyes were as alarmed and vulnerable as peeled prawns. Monkish, shielded, not-quite-saintly,

Mr Melvin looked like nothing on earth – a man who shied away from human contact, from looking 'normal' and behaving like ordinary people – but who seemed, in his knowing, haughty way, as if he might hold the key to Something Completely Different.

These things were puzzling to my young mind. *Fellini Satyricon,* which I saw in 1969, was full of beautiful youths rolling around together. It starred the bleached-blond Martin Potter, an Englishman with a decadent streak as wide as the Tiber. But the garlicky tang of foreign celluloid filth, that flavour of willed self-corruption, was a far cry from the dithery British way with bisexual sissies. People in togas licking each other was one thing. Trying to imagine one of your own sort – a student of English literature, say, in a multi-coloured tank-top – getting involved with buggery and nipple-rings was a huge stretch of the imagination, as far from my own experience as Michael York was far from home in 1931 Weimar Berlin.

When I went to Oxford, that October, I was still a virgin, determined to find a mate and have it off with her as soon as possible (it was, surely, going to be a her. Wasn't it?). I loved the fact of just being there. I loved the *idea* of Oxford, as expressed in *Brideshead Revisited*, of a place where you studied just enough to get by, while furthering your social acquaintance at sherry parties, punting down the river, drinking in ancient pubs and finding passionate life-long friendships.

On the second evening of my first term, I was in my ground-floor room in Exeter College just after midnight, writing the words 'Went to Freshers' Fair. Joined Guitar Club. Had 2 pints & ham roll with Kit in Red Lion. Nothing much happening yet,' in my diary when there was a rap at the window.

I pulled the curtains aside, experiencing the old *frisson* of invasion and fright as described in Chapter 2, but the chap outside the glass was neither the Snow Queen nor Peter Wyngarde (although, events would prove, he possessed elements of both).

He was a tall, spectacled chap in a long trench coat, gesturing to me to open the sash. 'Sorry to trouble you,' he said. 'I'm Gerry, I live on Staircase Three and it's too late to get through the Porter's Lodge. Would you mind if I came in through your window? It would be a great favour.'

I'd seen him around. He was a second-year English Literature student, a breed as seraphically remote from us first-year new bugs as a Druid from a sacrificial lamb. 'Of course,' I said, casually. 'Be my guest.' I helped him clamber over the sill. He was freakishly tall and his pebble glasses were owlish, like John Lennon's. We stood awkwardly together on the nasty carpet of my room.

'Well this is, er, nice,' he said, looking at my sparse interior with second-year pity. 'So you like Lichtenstein . . .' (There was a double-poster of the artist's 'Whaaaam!' on the wall, as there was on the walls of 40 per cent of first-year students.)

'Would you like some coffee?' I said. 'Or I've got some port.' God, how sophisticated I was.

No, he didn't want either. But he stuck around for a whole fifteen minutes, and asked how I liked the senior English tutor, Jonathan Wordsworth, and said, 'The thing about Jonathan . . .' and 'What you have to watch with Jonathan . . .' as if they were old mates and I was being granted some rare insights into the inner sanctum.

'If you like Pop Art so much,' he said in the doorway, 'you might consider joining the college Arts Society. We could do with somebody like you.' And he was gone.

I was tremendously excited. A *second-year* had deigned to converse with me for, Christ, *ages*, and chatted about our tutor, and been friendly and, you know, *interested* in what I had to say. He'd even suggested that I join the rarefied atmosphere of the important arty chaps who got to choose which paintings went on display in the Junior Common Room. And when we met again, I could say 'Hi, Gerry' in a cool, insouciant way. My fellow first-years would be so impressed. And, who knows? I might even be invited to join the rectangle of Junior Common Room armchairs where the arty Eng Lit crew paused in their labours over Swift and Dryden to chat about acquiring a Jasper Johns or a Hockney for the college collection.

I'd just had a Brideshead moment – like the one in which Charles Ryder, the hero of *Brideshead Revisited*, first meets Sebastian Flyte, as the latter leans in drunkenly through his open window on a summer evening and pukes elegantly all over his carpet. Out of embarrassment, Flyte invites the callow Ryder to lunch at Christchurch, where he meets the indescribably louche Anthony Blanche. The whole *jeunesse dorée* of Twenties Oxbridge opens up before him, and a lifelong friendship with the doomed Sebastian ensues. Had I just started on a similar trajectory?

In a way, I had. I soon met the arty second-year gang who surrounded Gerry. I was invited for coffee one evening in his room on Staircase Three, after we'd met in the Porter's lodge. His rackety friends drifted in, severally, tapping on his door at intervals of fifteen minutes, drawn there for comfort and solace in the middle of essay crises. They were aloof, difficult, fearsomely well-read and dizzyingly affected. Hector was an ascetic beanpole with curly hair who played the clavicord in his room – a weird instrument, when I finally saw it, in that it didn't seem to make any sound, no matter how intensely he attacked its all-black keys – and collected empty sugar-cube boxes in his cupboards, as if he were a walking advertisement for anal-retentive neurosis. Gilbert wore thick, black-framed glasses, spoke in a hesitant, nervy flow of bitchy put-downs, and had a phobia about cotton wool. Nigel was a geeky classicist with a mad, whinnying laugh, who could be heard weeping down the line to his mother any night of the week in the telephone room beside Staircase Fourteen (he seemed to have issues about manliness and fitting in with his peer group, which only a mother could have listened to). The Anthony Blanche figure was the astonishing Jerome Cash, a gleeful, giggling midget with terrible teeth and a premature pot belly, who dressed in episcopal purple, whose body rocked back and forth as he talked about James Joyce or Cardinal Newman. His eyes shone with wickedness as he rubbed his hands and cackled about the dubious sexual practices of leading Church figures.

After a while, I started inviting Gerry and Jerome back to my room. I had bought some new posters, by Salvador Dali, and thought they might be impressed. They were not impressed. Every fuckwit first-year had bought posters by Dali, and Blu-tacked them to their walls. I played them my new David Bowie record, and they nodded along respectfully, though Hector claimed that he 'never listened to anything later than Monteverdi'. But it was exciting just to have them there. They were riveting company. They talked brilliantly about books I'd never read (Mandeville's *Travels*? The *Confessions of a Justified Sinner*? The poetic works of Ossian?) and French movies and German expressionist cinema. We would play paper games of Consequences, with much hilarity, games that were full of allusions to things I didn't quite understand, like 'cottages' and 'trade' and, indeed, 'intercrural massage'.

One evening I mentioned *Cabaret* and how much it had meant to me – how Joel Grey as the MC had seemed a walking repository of every corrupt impulse that had allowed Nazism to flourish but you couldn't help admire him; how the Michael York character had been so convincingly innocent, so sceptical of Sally's black-fingernailed decadence, yet had so easily welcomed his seduction by the smooth

Maximilian; how the whole film seemed to open up a range of endless possibilities for the sexual drifter.

'I could never have taken my father to see that film,' I told them, drunkenly. 'He thinks homosexuality is a weird English thing. He couldn't imagine any Irish person forgetting his Catholic duties enough to consider having sex with a bloke.'

There was a strange, unclassifiable silence. Moments later, I went off to the cold, draughty loo next door to my tiny room – and returned to find the aesthetes all putting on their coats and making excuses about essays they had to return to – all except Gerry.

'Come with me, John,' he said. 'There's something I must play you, right now.'

'Why's everyone going?' I asked in a slight panic. Had I driven them away with my *avant-garde* views about sexual deviance? 'What's this thing you want to play me? Jesus, Gerry, it's two o'clock in the morning.'

But he insisted. And he *was* a second-year. So I went along with him, across the moonlilt quadrangle, through the stone doorway and up to the top of the endless Staircase Three. In his sparse, Art Deco-furnished room, he sat me down, poured some German wine and talked about his family for a while. Then, with a flourish – a meaningful, this-will-change-your-life gesture – he put on a record. It was Benjamin Britten, a setting of Housman's 'The Welsh Marches', though I didn't know the work of composer or poet. Peter Pears's high sad voice began: 'On Wenlock Edge the wood's in trouble;/His forest fleece the Wrekin heaves;/The gale, it plies the saplings double,/And thick on Severn snow the leaves.'

The voice wailed on. Gerry nodded encouragingly. I tried to talk about my problems getting a girfriend, my skewed relationship with my junior tutor, Simon, who'd been so rude about my essay on Tennyson. Gradually, an abject misery stole over me. It was the God-awful music in the background. I thought Peter Pears's voice was the most wretched, lonesome noise that had ever fallen on the ears of man. Images of my family, back home in London, and the life I'd left behind, my parents and my sister, the garden overlooked by the South Circular Road, the warm fug of my Dad's dinner parties, even the chintzy drawing-room with its ghastly coal-effect fire, stole over me and I felt, suddenly, terribly detached from my real self. Tears filled my eyes. Peter Pears bansheed away, unstoppably.

Gerry's spectacles flashed. He bent forward and took the glass from my hand. 'Look –' he said, thickly.

I couldn't start weeping in front of my new – and crucially second-year – friend. 'I'm terribly sorry,' I said, 'but I must go.' I got up, pissed as an owl, miserable as sin, and looked for my scarf.

Suddenly, Gerry's arms were all over me. He hugged me with a kind of tentative rapture, his six-foot-three frame looming insistently. 'Look,' he said, again, 'I'm terribly fond of you. Will you stay the night?'

The penny dropped, even through a haze of cut-price Piesporter Michelsberg. 'No!' I said. 'No!!' I cried (with increasing certainty) and pushed him away.

I'd never received a homosexual proposition in my life before. Come to think of it, I'd barely received even a heterosexual proposition from anyone, except the gorgeous Lucy. My reaction was entirely instinctive. I knew that, no matter what I'd learned from the movies about sexual behaviour, I couldn't handle whatever was on offer. The very idea of getting into bed with Gerry, with his pebble glasses and his (I imagined all too clearly) voluminous underpants, was too awful to contemplate. I fled into the night.

My first attempts at decadence – at being, as it were, Brian under the thrall of Sally and Maximilian – had crashed ingloriously at the first hurdle.

I managed to work out, through the mortified days that followed, that Gerry's amusing gang of friends were all as gay as bunting, and that all my airy burbling about homosexuality had been taken by them as a kind of small-ad, posted on the college noticeboard alongside the offers to make up a rowing eight, saying that I was, so to speak, available for boarding.

They'd sat in my room that night as I made them coffee, these connoisseurs of rectal speleology, idly wondering if any of them fancied taking on my sorry arse. Even while I was visiting the lavatory, they'd been deciding that Gerry had *droit de seigneur* because he was the one who'd first introduced me to their sophisticated company. That was why they'd all busied themselves to depart when I returned to their company. I had walked into a gay shark pond.

I felt terrible. Such a *naif*. Such an *ingénue* – precisely the right word under the circumstances, an artless young actress. I was revealed as a terrible fake, a camp and shallow pretender to *fatale* misbehaviour when in fact I was as *fatale* as an after-dinner mint.

Bloody hell. I'd turned into Sally Bowles.

It took a while to get over this existential crisis. I threw myself into study, resolving to stop trying to be Ms Bowles, or Brian Roberts or Charles Ryder. As time went on, I found myself going out with Maggie, a nice, plump blonde from the Oxford & County Secretarial College, someone whom you could punt up the Cherwell river on a Sunday evening, alongside half a dozen other boatloads of friends, to the Victoria Arms for hearty pints of Wadsworths ale and helpings of shepherd's pie, before returning for some chaste groping outside her Hall of Residence. The weeks went by and, as if to make up for my tarting around with the seraphic queens of the second-year Arts Club, I became histrionically masculine, noisily macho, scarily priapic. Heedless of courtship proprieties, I bounced Maggie around like an inflatable doll, employing her amazingly pink flesh, her hands and breasts and (especially) her hot young mouth as carelessly as I might use a scrubbing brush. Emboldened by the discovery that you could lie to girls, and promise them impossible things, and shamelessly abuse them, and part them from their underwear, and throw them out when you got bored with their company, I became a nasty piece of work. So much so that she chucked me for a second-year historian (saying, 'I just don't know why you had to be so rude.') just as I was trying, a little nervously, to talk her round to the joys of penetration.

But then I fell in love. She was called Gail, another student at the Ox & Cow (as it was charmingly named) but a funny, clever, sassy young thing who wore Laura Ashley smocks whatever the season, and attracted all the boys with her knowing, bright-eyed empathy and her infectious laugh.

We were inseparable for months. She was my first proper girlfriend. Sometimes, she would stay over at weekends in my college room (when Maria, my Portuguese 'scout' or room-cleaning lady, wasn't going to burst in) and we'd lie blissfully in each other's arms all night, and clasp one another rapturously in the hot, sun-through-the-curtains Sunday mornings, with the sound of church bells donging down Broad Street and the chatter, through the half-opened windows, of walkers *en route* to brunch at the Wimpy bar.

But we never got around to having proper sex.

She was too young. I'd try to persuade her that accommodating my brutal desires would be a register of our true love; but it never worked. She'd made some arrangement with her mother that she would keep herself more or less virginal until her eighteenth birthday, upon which she would be introduced to The Pill and given *carte blanche* to fuck anybody she chose. I was stuck with it. And so I remained technically a virgin through my first year at Oxford. But the legacy of *Cabaret* was hard to shake off – that complicated image-cluster of dead-eyed club dancers, beautiful young men, anything-could-happen encounters in louche mansions, dripping wax and ancient chandeliers, swaying rumps and sailor-suited degeneracy, wind-up gramophones filled with sobbing Weimar elegies to unknown loves, huge chauffered cars, brooding male lovers, the tear-streaked embrace that precipitates Sally and Brian's first venture into bed . . .

It was a *demi-monde* I longed to enter. I loved my sweet, endlessly amusing girlfriend, and all our fiddly, tentative claspings and sunderings. But I knew she wasn't enough. There was something else going on out there, something darker, more abandoned, and the impulse towards it was like a brooding conspirator in my heart. I'd become like a young Victorian bravo, decently brought up, with the prospect of an advantageous marriage in front of him, who longs to visit a brothel, just to see what tableau of unthinkable immorality awaits him behind the plush red curtains.

Time went on, and with it came a stack of freshly confusing images. My first-year tutor, Simon, was a very masculine presence, with his wolfish jaw and his pooh-poohing of my puny attempts to read *Kubla Khan* as an account of Coleridge's first orgasm. Most of the English faculty had a crush on Simon, but it was an intellectual crush – we simply wanted to be near him, to be allowed to stick around in his company.

He was probably used to being hero-worshipped, but was not above a little teasing. When my one-to-one tutorials shifted to the 9 a.m. slot on Mondays, and I found myself struggling up the stone flags of Staircase Ten at 8.45 a.m., it was disconcerting, one morning, to find his disembodied voice floating in from the bedroom off his study.

'Can you put the kettle on and make us some coffee? I'm just having a shave. Be right with you. Actually no, why don't you bring the coffee in here and talk to me?'

A tiny memory of Mrs Robinson in *The Graduate* popped into me head. 'Can you come over here and help me off with my dress?'

Holding two steaming mugs, I found him standing, stripped to the waist, at a mirrored basin, bearded with Palmolive foam, waving a razor. Despite our urgent date with T.S. Eliot's *Four Quartets*, Simon wanted to chat, in his half-serious way, about members of his family.

'Extraordinary, John,' he said without preliminaries, 'how many members of my family are gay. I've just had a letter from my brother, who is shacked up with a man in Plymouth. We both were pretty sure our father was secretly gay, despite having, as it were, had us. And his uncle, who was an Edwardian cleric, was, by all accounts, as gay as a paper hat. I've often wondered,' he confided to the mirror, 'if I must be gay myself.' Saying which, he buried his face in a towel, as if to stop any further disclosures along these lines. 'A terrible thing to find oneself considering, first thing on a Monday morning.' I watched him shrug his big shoulders and long arms into a blue cotton shirt, and stuff the tails into his corduroy trousers. The tutorial finally got under way, but a strange atmosphere of grown-up secrecy hung over our joint elucidation of 'Little Gidding'.

I left his private room feeling baffled, in a way that was now getting to be familiar (*Why* did people talk like this – advancing secret overtures to me when I didn't know how to respond?), but also knowing that I had a tremendous piece of gossip to tell my co-scholars, if I chose. And somewhere under the bafflement and the gossip, a private worry squeaked and gibbered, and I wondered if he'd been . . . you know . . . trying to . . .

No, no. It was impossible. But when he wondered out loud if he was gay, what was I supposed to reply? Should I have said, 'Well, there's only one way to find out –' and begun to massage his naked shoulder? Was he asking if I'd ever wondered about myself? Was that it? Had he, in fact, been seconds away from saying, 'You *do* sleep with girls, don't you?'

Holy shit. My esteemed and brilliant, super-masculine junior English tutor had just turned into Sally Bowles.

This was getting serious.

Cabaret pursued me all through my first university year. I embraced, if not the actual, technical side of wild omni-sexual adventuring, then at least some of its louche para-phernalia. I became a tourist of decadence, bringing home armfuls of souvenirs. I found a shop in Little Clarendon Street called Oriental Crafts which sold a range of exotic bits 'n' pieces. There I bought a florid, ten-branch chan-delier ear-ring and screwed it into my right earlobe. In my college room, I used to cover the lamp-shade with a batik scarf (as Keith of the Rolling Stones used to do on entering any faceless hotel room in any city in the world in the mid-Seventies). I lit Black Vanilla joss sticks and sparked up expensive Sobranie cocktail cigarettes in garish pastel colours; I was especially fond of the pink, purple and crab-apple green ones. I bought scores of candles, churchy beeswax ones, long Satanic black ones, and little red votive-offering lights from the local church repository. I affected a long silk dressing-gown in the style of Noel Coward while writing essays in my room after 10 p.m., heedless of its effect on late-night callers looking for dope or records or emotional counselling. I read Rimbaud and Baudelaire, trying to work out why they might once have shocked readers in the late nineteenth century. I removed my Lichtenstein print and replaced it with Aubrey Beardsley's florid and pompadoured royalty as they toyed with the tiny genitalia of ephebic servants. I bought the *I Ching*, the Chinese text-book of divination, and threw coins up in the air, solemnly expecting to read the future, according to whether they came up heads or tails. If I could have afforded lilies, I'd have arrayed them in bucketfuls round my tiny room on Staircase One.★

I became a fan of the Velvet Underground, especially of their first album. I liked the psychic journey between the first track and the second. 'Sunday Morning' is sweet as a picnic and full of cut-price *Weltschmerz* to luxuriate in, even though I was only just nineteen. ('It's all the wasted years so close behind . . .' sang Lou Reed. Ah yes, I murmured, how true that is, all those wasted years.) It's followed by the accelerating rhythms and screeching discords of 'Heroin', the *ur*-text of Seventies decadence. The combination of sentimentality and ugliness was, I thought, very *Cabaret*.

That summer term coincided with the brief heyday of 'glam rock', when pop bands like Sweet and T Rex and Mud appeared on *Top of the Pops* in baco-foil pants and caked mascara, and huge, beefy, lumberjacky males on bass guitar or drums sat looking self-conscious in spangly tank-tops and silver-glitter eye shadow.

The patron saint of this stuff was David Bowie. He was my hero: so intelligent, so arty, so dramatic, so sensitive, so mocking, so shape-changing – and of course, so fantastically androgynous. I thought I liked him only for his music, but I was kidding myself. I wanted to be mysteriously between-the-sexes like him, having intense and satisfyingly degenerate experiences with both, but never

★ Few of these decadent emblems, of course, actually appear in *Cabaret*. The film's casual amorality is suggested, with admirable economy, in a few key scenes – the huge baronial hall where the three converge drunkenly after dinner, the hundred candles burning on every surface in Sally's apartment; Brian in his hat and cigar, knitted tie hanging over his naked torso . . . But I was surrounding myself with my own talismans of outrage. I was taking whatever was available, from whatever source or generation, surrounding myself with the trappings of loucheness in the hope that it might coax some decadent other-self to make an appearance.

admitting to any one sexual identity. Bowie was the perfect role model for the confused, effete, over-educated male virgin at Oxford in 1973. Rather than have real sex with anyone, you could spend your time dressing up, striking attitudes and confounding people's notions of what or who you were.

During summer term there were Saturday-evening concerts in the Undercroft, the college's student bar, where variably gifted musicians could book themselves a slot to recite, play the piano or sing. One Saturday I was booked to perform a little glam-rock spoof, singing Bowie's 'The Jean Genie' with Jerome Cash on piano, a friend called Roger on bongos, *et moi* on thrash acoustic guitar. I needed a suitably outrageous costume. So Gail, my long-suffering girlfriend, and I spent the afternoon trawling Oxford's strait-laced shopping centres in search of a credibly Bowie-esque outfit. The male outfitters offered cheesecloth shirts, deadly purple loon pants, and little else – a terrible disappointment to the *avant-garde* glam-boy I was trying to become. The afternoon leaked by. Finally, outside Miss Selfridge, Gail paused to look in the metal bargain bins where last-season frocks and nobody-wants-this-stuff fabrics flowed out on to the pavement. Suddenly she scrabbled around with excited hands and drew out a pair of trousers and a tiny top that sparkled in the June sunshine. They were made of some horrible synthetic yellow material, with bits of glitter on the swirly pattern, but they would resemble, at fifty paces, the outfit worn by Bowie on the cover of my favourite album, *The Rise and Fall of Ziggy Stardust and the Spiders from Mars*.

A brief flicker of *déjà vu* ran through me, a tiny frisson from another time – a July evening, a parish hall dance, and a female finger stroking my chest . . .

'John,' Gail said, 'you don't think –' We looked at the clothes in her hand. They were, unquestionably, hideous. The trousers were long, but not long enough for my legs.

The top was a skimpy crossover waistcoat, designed to accentuate a medium-sized female bosom.

'It'll never work,' I said. 'I'd look ridiculous.' But as I touched the material, I knew I was going to do it.

They weren't the kind of clothes a chap could confidently try on in the changing rooms of Miss Selfridge without drawing attention to himself. So I, or rather Gail, bought the outfit anyway, for four pounds. Further down the road, in a Dolcis sale, I bought some knee-length suede boots and an aerosol spray and, in W.H. Smith, purchased some things from the stationery counter. Back in my college room, we discovered the waistband of the trousers was a lissom 24 inches, whereas my own was a strapping 30 inches, so Gail cut the back seam and sewed in a length of straining elastic. The crossover waistcoat looked absurdly corrugated when stretched across my tit-less chest, but it would pass muster provided I remembered not to breathe in. And the boots came up rather well, once I'd sprayed them silver and dotted them with the gold and silver W.H. Smith merit stars, the kind you stick on small children's homework.

After an hour of patient *maquillage*, my eyes were crusted with Ultralush mascara and blue eye-shadow, my hair was an advertisement for Wella conditioner. I took the stage at 9 p.m. to jeers and catcalls from friends in the audience, and howls of execration from the Northern chemists who stolidly played bar-football throughout my electrifying performance.

The 'Jean Genie' is a puzzling song in the Bowie canon. It may or may not be about Jean Genet. It could be a penile metaphor (the genie that lives, trapped, inside the denim lamp of your jeans, waiting for someone to, whew, stroke it and release it). It might have something to do with virginity (the 'small green genie', a simple-minded rube, sneaking off to the city of experience, wanting to be loved, but winding up generally brutalised by waiters and uncaring girls, the 'poor little greenie'), but its compendium of images simply howled decadence to me. 'Talking 'bout Monroe and walking on Snow White / New York's a go-go when everything tastes nice' – I loved it.

I put a lot into it. I scrubbed my guitar, played the simple chord-change from E to A like a serious virtuoso and gnashed my teeth over the lyrics, Jerome played blistering stride piano runs right to the top of the keyboard, and Roger whacked the bongos as if trying to burst them during the climactic bridge into the final chorus. It was all over in four sweaty minutes, not unlike an act of collective self-abuse.

I got off the stage to muted applause, but I was exultant. My first experience on stage, playing a guitar and singing, and I'd knocked them dead. I was a natural. Life *was* a cabaret, after all, old chum . . . Then the MC announced that Jeff Hilditch (a lugubrious public schoolboy with the face of an unusually pissed-off Easter Island statue) would now do a stand-up comic routine based on his experience of drugs, and everybody concentrated on him. Even the Northern chemists relinquished their stooping over the table-football machine and turned to look. I suddenly felt like an exotic fish in a trout farm. There was no dressing-room to return to, no after-show drugs or groupies. I was back in the real world. My best friends Mike and Rob said, 'Well done, John,' and 'Fancy a pint?' as neutrally as possible, as though all the dressing-up, the flamboyance, the Bowie costume, the passion, were of no consequence at all – as if they'd been indulging, not a glam-rock superstar, merely a terrible show-off.

But I did fancy a pint, and had two or three more while the cabaret wound down to a lot of guitar noodling, and I gradually joined in the old rhythm of being a student in a bar, talking about books and records and Junior Common Room politics, and lots of mutual piss-taking.

At one point Gail whispered, 'You *will* take all that slap

off before you go to bed, won't you? Otherwise your poor eyes will feel like shit in the morning.'

I was a bit startled; I'd quite forgotten that I was still wearing my Ultralush mascara and sparkly blue eye-shadow. When it was my round, I went to the bar, as I'd done a hundred times before, helpfully plonking the empty glasses down on the chrome counter. The old barman didn't look at me.

'Sam,' he said shortly, to his young assistant, 'four pints for Widow Twanky 'ere.'

A quartet of boring first-year lawyers burst out laughing. I smiled a knowing smile, which said, Yeah, yeah, but you *know* I'm basically David Bowie inside. But it didn't work. One of them looked over to the table where my friends were sitting.

'Now, which one's Buttons?' he asked.

The idiot lawyers beside him joined in. 'Ooh, Aladdin, I think,' they said in ghastly, mincing voices. 'Jack, you've been a *very naughty* boy . . .' Their stupid jeers accompanied me back to my embarrassed pals.

I should have gone back to my room, dammit. I should have departed straight after the performance, removed the glam costume and reappeared in non-transvestite student mufti. I'd made an elementary blunder, that you can't be an exotic Sally Bowles and a pint-drinking ordinary Brian at the same time. You had to be one or the other.

I went to the Gents, washed my hands and stared in the mirror. A grotesque, raddled old slapper was all I could see, with bits of glitter on her ludicrous cheeks. Soon afterwards, I said goodnight to the company and fled. Gail was too mortified to come with me for a late-night kiss. 'See you tomorrow,' she said, shaking her head sadly. 'I'll bring some cold cream along at lunchtime, shall I, in case you've got some crusty bits stuck in your eyes . . . ?'

A month later, thank God, it was all forgotten. The

glam-rock stuff became quickly *passé*. The first-year exams were looming. People were planning summer holidays. There was an atmosphere of seriousness and work. Gail's birthday was still weeks away, and with it – all being well – the end of virginity. But in my head there was *still* a nagging feeling that having conventional sex with my nice, straightforward, secretarial-college girlfriend wasn't going to be the perfect climax it should be. All the paraphernalia of decadence with which I'd filled my life was, I realised, a substitute for having complicated, transgressive sex with somebody else – and I still didn't know for sure who the somebody was supposed to be.

I admired Susannah, a local beauty who was going out with a second-year student called Tim. Susannah was raven-haired, slender and thrilling, her sharp eyes cleverly matching the razor-sharp hunting knife she wore on the belt of her jeans. How much did I fancy her? And how much (I barely allowed myself to wonder) did I fancy her boyfriend? Tim was small, cool and snarly, his voice a dark-brown, hesitant growl, his small hands always fiddling with liquorice-paper, roll-your-own cigarettes.

I'd watch him moving around the bar in his restless way and note how physically he threw himself at the pinball machine. Tim would approach the winking lights and the cheeping robots of the pinball table like a stealthy enemy. His hands would slide round the table's edges until they found the flipper buttons, which he would finger experimentally, as if in some teasing foreplay. Satisfied, he'd step an inch nearer the machine, ram his groin against the bit where the money goes in, his fingers would agitate away with spidery glee and he would proceed to fuck the long, bleeping *horizontale* for ten whole minutes, until the score whizzed up into the tens of thousands, and the squat metallic roundels dinged and whanged and went thud-thud-thud in ecstasy, and he'd lift the whole palpitating contraption right

y

223

off the floor, its legs dangling, its circuits shorting, until a flashing light showed the word 'TILT' as if it could take no more of this violent rapture. (If a machine could have shouted 'Oh God, Oh *God*!' it would have done.) He would relinquish his masterful grip with a gesture of disgust, and slouch out of the bar, presumably to go and have sex with Susannah.

It was the silhouette that I admired, I think, that image of thrust and mastery and conquest. But whether I admired the priapic Tim as a role model or an object of lust in his own right, I couldn't say. I was still in a state of sexual confusion. I prowled Broad Street and the High, worrying about exams, worrying about what would happen with Gail, worrying about how little I seemed to know myself.

One Friday evening, I was invited to a party in Magdalen College garden by a guy I knew from the English Literature lecture hall. 'Do come along for a bit,' he said. 'There'll be some very genial girls there.'

It was late June. The exams were about to start. Gail had gone home to Guernsey. My drinking buddies were deep in revision crises. I tried to work, but my heart wasn't really in Swift's *The Battle of the Books*. Late sunlight was still poking through my window at 8.30 p.m. Should I go to the party? It was quite a trek to Magdalen College, and I wouldn't know anyone when I got there. Maybe if I really really concentrated on *A Tale of a Tub* . . . But it was no good. By 8.45, I was heading down the High Street in a black T-shirt and white bell-bottoms, my pure new, not-at-all-glam, monochrome look, thinking: 'I'll give it half and hour. A couple of drinks, chat with – what was his name? Andy? – and then I'll go home and read Swift in bed.'

The party was sparsely attended, but the gardens of Magdalen College were, as always, a gorgeous sight, and a long trestle table buckled with chicken legs and party cans of beer and two-litre bottles of Frascati. I drank a bit and ate a bit, and felt OK among the strangers. I even found someone to chat to about Lou Reed and what a travesty of his Velvet Underground days was his new solo record, *Transformer*.

Then someone said, 'Do you know Stephanie? She's at St Hilda's,' and I said 'Hi' to a tall girl in a green dress. She wasn't a great beauty, but her face was full of intelligence, and she had a spectacular chest.

We talked about Andy, registered that neither of us knew him well, and played a little game. It involved us both keeping a conversation going without ever asking predictable questions: 'Which college are you at?' and 'What are you studying?' and 'Do you know Tina Brown?' It was brilliant. We were both rather skilled at this context-free, we-could-be-anybody chat. We talked about music, and hats, and punting, and food, and holiday destinations, and gradually established a kinship. Just one tricky note was sounded.

She said, 'Tell me, but tell me, *without thinking for more than a second*, what's bothering you most at this moment.'

Unhesitatingly I said, 'The fact that I'm about to make a hash of the Honour Mods exams any day now.'

She said, 'Hah! How about the prospect of doing bloody *Finals* next week?'

She was a third-year! Holy mackerel. I'd hardly met any third-years. They were unimaginably grown-up. They mostly lived out of college. I would sometimes see them drifting around the quadrangle lost in thought, identified by awe-struck friends as 'That's Richard Sparks – he's going for a First', exotic as unicorns. And now, to be getting on rather swimmingly with this attractive girl in the bosomy green frock, who must be, by the kindest calculation, two years older than me . . .

It was tremendous. But I kept a lid on my excitement, and we duelled over the chicken legs, and talked more and lit cigarettes in the gloaming, while nobody came near us all evening. Later, we found ourselves beside a tree. Stephanie and I watched the rest of the company chatting and laughing in the dark, their elegant forms flickering past the garden candles that had been lit around 10 p.m. I leaned over to whisper in her ear about the hopelessness of the dumpy girl in the halterneck top who had been flirting with Andy all evening. There was no need to whisper, since we were standing so far from the main action, but. . . .

'Ooh,' she said. 'That was nice. Do that again.'

So I repeated what I'd said, only in a lower, huskier whisper, so the words were blurred and indistinct.

'Ohhhh,' she said.

I curled my tongue, with insane presumption, around her earlobe and, meeting no resistance, ran it inside her ear. The glass dropped from her hand on to the green floor with a muffled tinkle. And at last we were kissing, under the Magdalen tree, and it felt marvellous – literally full of marvels, as if I'd suddenly found myself at the Venice Carnival among masks and jugglers.

It was so unexpected: the girl, the tree, the darkness, the whispering, the coldness of her mouth. The contextless conversation we'd had earlier had turned into a contextless kiss in a dark, wonderful nowhere. And then she broke away and said this fantastic thing, something even more fantastic than hearing a girl say 'Not here . . .' She laid her head against the tree and said, or rather breathed, 'That was the biggest turn-on since "Lay Lady Lay".' Nobody familiar with Bob Dylan's best-ever love song could fail to understand how promising these words were.

Sounds of farewell at the trestle table indicated the party was breaking up. It was time to go home. But Stephanie didn't want to go home. 'So where's your college?' she said, taking a sudden interest in the basic studenty details that we'd so amusingly disdained earlier. I told her it was Exeter, and, with amazing briskness, she stalked off to the trestle table, said 'Cheerio' to Andy (who seemed surprised to see her there at all), swept a long black cloak around her shoulders, linked my arm and set off with determination up the High Street.

I was startled by this turn of events. I'd had a good time, I'd even copped a snog in the moonlight, and with a third-year as well. It was time to return to my room, as planned, congratulate myself (slightly amazed) on my ear-kissing skills and retire to bed with *18th Century Critical Essays*. Instead, I had a 21-year-old grown woman by my side, in a cloak, heading back to my place. An uncomfortable quaking sensation settled around my insides, but we were walking so fast I stopped noticing. Soon we were in Turl Street, before the front gate of my college. The door was shut. 'Goddammit,' I said with (could it be?) relief. 'It's after midnight. There's no way in without ringing the bell for the porter. We'd better say goodnight.'

'Nonsense,' said Stephanie. 'There must be a way in.' As I erred and ummed (behaving, just a touch, like Kenneth Williams or Charles Hawtree in a dozen *Carry On* films when pursued by, say, Joan Sims), she scouted the available windows. 'Up there,' she said. 'I think that one's open a bit on the latch. Give us a bunk-up, will you?' I held her shod foot in my cupped hands as she rose up through the air like the Virgin Mary at the Ascension (curse my Catholic indoctrination), flicked the yielding latch and burrowed her cloaked but substantial body through the narrow opening. A minute later, she'd opened the door and we stood, co-conspirators, in the dark Porter's Lodge.

'Well?' she said with unromantic firmness. 'Where's your room?'

I led her around the quadrangle, where a month earlier I'd ponced about in my Miss Selfridge jumpsuit *en route* to my little display in the bar.

'This is the chapel, here,' I pointed out conversationally.

'It's very old. Fourteenth century, I think. But then the college dates back to –'

'Leave it out, John,' she said. 'I don't need a bloody guide book. What I need right now is a loo.'

We got to Staircase Eleven, Room One. I switched on the light and registered a flicker of twitchy-nosed distaste on Stephanie's face, as she inspected my living quarters. Volumes of Pope and Swift tumbled across the desk. A dark snow of fag-ash stank the place out. The bin was full of twisted Kleenexes. Half a dozen striped mugs bore their reeking cargo of coffee scum. An unfinished Chinese supper told its tragic story of neglect on the occasional table, as did – in its different way – a recent copy of *Mayfair*, featuring Bella the Surbiton Barmaid on the cover.

'I think,' she said, 'you could do something with the lighting in here.'

Damn right I could. I thanked God for my batik scarves, draped one over a lamp, killed the main light, and tried to kick the more repellent supper plates under the bed.

'Care for a glass of port?' I said.

'Port?' she replied. '*Port?* You are a strange person. Yes, I'd love some.'

I hoped it hadn't grown stale, over the course of a year in which nobody – that is, not *one single* male chum – had shown any interest in drinking it. We clinked glasses. The atmosphere softened. She sat down on the bed, with her black cloak around her shoulders. Perhaps she was chilly. Perhaps she was nervous about taking anything off in such a tip.

'OK,' I said. 'Without saying a word about your college, or your tutor, I want you to tell me exactly what you've got on the walls of your room.'

As she did, resuming our earlier game, I thought, *I can handle this*. She's interested in where and how I live, because we have been getting on so well. A couple of glasses of port, a nice kiss and maybe a fondle in the dark, that's all she will expect, this lonesome lady finalist with the determined stride.

Then she stopped describing her college room, looked about and shuddered a little, as if bored. 'Have you got any candles?' she asked.

'Sure,' I said. 'There must be some around here.'

I'd bought about a hundred of the things in my Sobranies-and-Baudelaire days, but could never persuade Gail to reproduce the Sally-and-Brian scene from *Cabaret* with me.

'Jolly good,' she said. 'If you light them, I'll just nip into the loo. Where is it?'

'Just next door,' I said. 'Through that wall.'

'Be right back,' she said. As if mesmerised, I dug out a couple of dozen tiny red churchy votive lights from the cupboard, lit them quickly and arrayed them on every available surface, *à la* Sally Bowles. *Atmosphere*, I thought. Do something with the atmosphere. This is a weird occasion, but I have to get her to relax and take off her cloak. We have the candles. We need music.

I dug out the Velvet Underground LP, with its Warhol-designed banana priapically arrayed on the cover. I heard the door from the lavatory click open, I lowered the needle over the gliding vinyl. Stephanie came through the door, just as Lou Reed was breathing the words 'Sunday morning / brings the dawning . . .'

She shut the door behind her. The black cloak was around her still. But as she surveyed the room, and saw what I'd done, the candles and the flickering light and the wistful music, she said, 'Oh, John . . .' and she put her hands to the dog's head clasp at the neck, and twitched the metal elements asunder and drew the sides of the cloak apart, to reveal that she was stark naked beneath. You didn't need twenty-four candles to appreciate the enormous breasts that poked out from the cloaky folds, nor the long, beautiful landscape of flesh at which I stared, the shadows that pooled around her navel, the slatted *film noir* lines that played across her stomach. She was the most beautiful thing I had ever seen.

We met at the bed, and I kissed her patchouli-scented flesh, amazed to find that it tasted so wickedly foreign, and she finally whispered, 'Are you *ever* going to take your clothes off?'

So I did. I gazed down at my hardened *membrum virile* as if looking at an aghast stranger. 'What in God's name is going on?' it seemed to be saying. 'Who *is* this person? What am I supposed to do now?' I'd never known that sensation of having a part of my body take on a separate existence from me.

Stephanie and I lay down and kissed a bit, and I gorged myself on her astonishing bosom until I could barely breathe.

'Come on,' she said.

Her legs parted.

'*Now*,' she said.

'This'll never work,' I said ignorantly. 'It'll never go in there.'

How could I have been so naïve? But that's the way it is with male virgins. Three minutes later, I wasn't one any longer. I had achieved entry, as the text-books say, but it was an ingloriously brief invasion before I exploded inside her. I went on thrusting away for a while and pretending that it was all going *really well*, but Stephanie had been there before, a few times. She knew the carnival had come and gone. But afterwards, she lay beside me, stroking my hair and cooing about what a nice evening it had been, because she was, despite her tough determination, a kind and sensual woman. She didn't laugh at me, like the lawyers had laughed at my decadent *maquillage*, nor storm out of the room, as Lucy had once stormed out because of my rude presumption.

As for me, despite the speed at which this rite of passage had whizzed by, I was a soul in bliss. It was the most over-whelming single moment of my life – not just because I'd lost my virginity at last, but because I knew that the memory of that whole evening – the kiss beside the tree, the climbing into college, the candles and the music, her black cloak opening – would stay with me for ever as the most perfect memory of decadence. We lay there, she a little bored and frustrated, I spent and emotional, a mismatched pair on my tiny single bed.

Fifteen minutes later, Stephanie retrieved her clothes from the next-door lavatory, dressed with amazing swiftness and left. 'Bye,' she said. 'If you can get over whatever hang-up is bothering you, come and see me at St Hilda's.'

She climbed out through the window, the same window through which Gerry had entered on my second night in college. Back in the days when I was confused. It seemed years ago, the time when I was uncertain about my sexual orientation, when I didn't know shit about myself, or about what I really wanted from other people.

It had been a long trail, but I'd got there at last. Girls were going to be the thing from now on. *Cabaret*, with its seductive, trouble-making questions about the choices you have to make in your life, had been a long-standing ghost. And now I'd laid it, at last.

7

FAR AWAY FROM EVERYTHING

The Enigma of Kaspar Hauser (1974)

The foreign art-house cinema lurked in the background of the Sixties and early Seventies like one of those psychedelic, oily-slithery, lava-lampy, amoebic light-shows that used to writhe away on a wall-screen in the background of wild parties in Sixties movies. The films were indistinct and peculiar and offered little in the way of illumination, but you couldn't take your eyes off them. Prompted by enthusiastic reviews in the *Observer* and the *Sunday Times*, I and my fellow *cinéastes* would high-tail it to the National Film Theatre, or the Academy One and Two in Oxford Street, and try to fathom what was supposed to be so wonderful about the European New Wave.

The films we saw were an education. They made little sense, but their special peculiarity had both a charm and a challenge. They showed you a foreign country that could be, at first sighting, France or Italy or Spain or Greece or Japan, but was always Foreign Film Land.

It was a place that was either fantastically posh or wretchedly poor. I emerged from the unexplained puzzles of *L'Année Dernière à Marienbad* (Alain Resnais, 1961) enchanted by Delphine Seyrig but mystified about what it meant. All I remembered of the 90-odd minutes was the vast garden with its conical cypresses, their geometric perfection, and a sense that the French had a fetish for long loving shots of corridors. Of the relationship between the bloke and the girl, who may have had a sexual connection the previous year, in the hotel or somewhere completely different, not a shred remained in my memory.

Of Fellini's *La Strada* (1954), I remembered only Giulietta Masina's hurt little face in clown make-up, and the off-puttingly poverty-stricken towns into which the circus rolls – perhaps the worst tourist advertisement for southern Italy since the newsreel of wartime Naples. Greece, as represented by the Cretan superman Anthony Quinn in *Zorba the Greek* (Michael Cacoyannis, 1964), seemed to me a hatefully bleak and boring landscape, where you couldn't believe that Alan Bates, playing the stiff British interloper, could be all *that* star-struck by his oafish new friend, no matter how invigoratingly Mr Quinn danced among the rocks with his arms raised in vainglorious ecstasy.

I sat stony-faced through Pasolini's *The Gospel According to St Matthew* (1964), thinking it must take a special kind of genius to represent the miracles of Christ so bleakly, so boringly, so matter-of-factly. A man meets the Redeemer on the road, a man afflicted with some ghastly facial disfigurement. Jesus (Enrique Irazoqui) gives him a piercing monochrome gaze. Cut back to the man again, and we see that he's cured, his face suddenly bland and ordinary. A miracle has just occurred, but represented with all the drama and vividness of a peasant hawking in the gutter. God forgive my philistine soul, but I thought – as our parents used to say about Picasso's late works at the time – a child of five could have done that.

But I persevered with this foreign stuff because something told me that Continental art-house films contained a world of heavy secrets – a freight of hidden meaning that wasn't on offer in the art-by-numbers superficiality of most of the British cinema. It was a time when my teenage intellectual antennae were on red alert for hidden harmonies, cosmic symbols, ghostly indications that art contained more than entertainment: when I read Camus and Sartre, willing them to change my life by dramatising the inner landscapes of emotionally dead people; when I went to gallery exhibitions of Magritte and Matisse and Claes Oldenburg, trusting them to disturb and amaze; when I attended plays by Beckett and Pinter and revelled in their dislocated strangeness. I was never quite sure what I was looking at in these excursions, but I liked their airy contempt for the ordinary, the simple, the easily accessible. It was a time when the sleeve-notes of modern records featured mini-biographies of this or that pop group and promised that 'The Electric Prunes live a semi-existential lifestyle . . .' and I snorted with derision at such reach-me-down posturing, while realising, guiltily, that I hadn't much clue myself what the word 'existential' actually meant.

Occasionally a foreign film would break through my xenophobic bewilderment. Werner Herzog's second film, *The Enigma of Kaspar Hauser*, (the second to be seen by British audiences) knocked me for six – not just because its oddness took me down into dark profundities I'd never encountered before, but because of the figure at its centre, and his instant familiarity inside my head.

The film starts with a man rowing across a lake in 1828. As the boat glides along, a suspicious peasant-woman looks up from her wooden washboard and stares straight at us watching her. She doesn't like the look of the man in the boat. Nor did I, though it was hard to see him clearly. He is rowing to visit his captive who, we learn, has been locked in a cellar from birth, who has never seen a river, a tree or another human being, except his gaoler, in his life. The first of a series of lovingly sustained landscape shots appears, a view of windswept grass, and a calm German voice speaks words that are interpreted by the subtitle, 'Don't you hear that terrible screaming around us that men call silence?' The title sat there on screen, a white line of prose against the dark, agitated grasses, a line flung down like a gauntlet, daring you to enter a world of dislocation. Pretentious, poetic, magnificent, it was a line that would never have appeared in a film made in England.

In the basement where he's been imprisoned all his life, Kaspar Hauser sits in dark shadow – even though we know that, outside, it's bright morning. He appears like one of Count Dracula's 'children of the night' – the wolves that howl in the distance when the Count explains to Van Helsing about his Gothic kingdom. But Kaspar doesn't remind us of a wolf. He is, basically, a pig. He eats his morning meal with feral gruntings, he scratches himself, he peers through the blue darkness the better to wind some old, dirty bandages around a foot covered in sores and streaked with shit. His white nightshirt is unspeakable. Clearly, he has sat here, and slept and eaten and shat here, for years and years. He is presented as a disgusting sub-human apparition, a Caliban on a strange island in Old Europe – but we do not know, as yet, what class of human being we're dealing with.

His gaoler, an indistinct roughneck in a hat and cloak, does a strange thing: he tries to teach him to write. He guides Kaspar's faltering claw around a crayon and tries to make him write letters. 'If you write nice,' he says, as though addressing a child, 'Papa will give you a nice horsey.' Kaspar's hand folds around a toy wooden horse that's on the floor beside him, and agitates it back and forth in a sudden frenzy, and we start to gather that he is just a big, lummoxy teenager, a doltish, mentally backward patient. But today the gaoler seems keen, not just to offer him a basic (and surely a little tardy) lesson in writing skills, but to get him out of the dungeon and into the real world. He rouses Kaspar from a sleep that seems always about to enclose him, dresses him with awkward slowness, forces his unspeakable feet into sturdy boots, and carries him outside.

It's an opening scene of uncompromising bleakness, a scene which guarantees you're in for an upsetting time at the hands of this crackpot German expressionist. But something about Kaspar's stricken passivity held my attention. The guy playing him doesn't seem to be acting. This was not, I felt, an act of impersonation but of documentary realism. The imprisoned man looked as though this doomy slowness of movement, his blank, unyielding characterlessness, came naturally to him – a Beckett figure played, for once, by another Beckett figure.

Outside, we get the first sighting of Kaspar's hideaway: a tall tower wth a conical roof like a witch's hat; a fairytale dwelling. The gaoler carries Kaspar on his back along the brow of a hill, a dark silhouette against the gathering dawn. There was a Biblical quality to the scene, and I thought of the Good Samaritan carrying the mugged victim to safety – not that the Samaritan ever, as far as I knew, had been responsible for the discomfiture of the man he rescued, nor kept him locked up in a dungeon for sixteen years.

When they stop to rest, Kaspar lies on the ground, as moribund as a felled hog. He seems to want to sleep all the time, as if shutting out the world, like a baby refusing to be born. But his tormentor jerks him upright and, holding him fast before him, teaches him to walk, kicking his heels, now the right, then the left, inching him forward along the grassy track. Jerking like a marionette, Kaspar takes the first steps of his life, a Start-Rite Kid projected on to the endless highway of life by a bullying parent.

Between the man's relentless brutality and the youth's

236

uncomplaining compliance, I felt something more than mere pity. It was like looking at *homo sapiens* itself being created by a bullying, God-like overlord, hauled out of a primeval cave and taught to stand, to walk, to write, in a speeded-up parody of evolution. As if to emphasise this process, the screen was filled with wide-screen views of huge fields, forests, blowing grasses, the natural world in a state of Paradisical grace – then a sequence of roofs, brickwork, walls, a clock tower, and the cobbled streets down which Kaspar is pulled into the civilised world, his bare calves eloquently pathetic, like those of a schoolboy taken home after a rough game on the playing fields.

And so he is born at last, as a fully-fledged human. He stands in the market square, as still as a statue, his eyes wide, innocent and wondering, one arm stuck out in supplication, the hand holding a piece of paper that will tell the inhabitants who he is, like a passport to the real world. The man has told him something to say to people he meets, and has repeated it into Kaspar's ear so that he won't forget it: 'I want to be a gallant rider, like my father before me.' Armed with this curious information, he stands in the heart of civilisation, waiting to be discovered, taken in hand and given a life.

The camera regards him in long shot, standing there help-lessly still, looking lost between the big trees in the square. But no crash of excitement greets his arrival on earth. A vast and bothered cow, clearly aching to be milked, regards him suspiciously. A bonneted *hausfrau* inspects him with distaste through her open shutters. Local men, smoking early pipes, stare at him incuriously through their windows, their elbows resting comfortably on cushions. And then the bells ring in the clock tower, the cow ambles painfully off, and the village comes to life. That's the opening of this remark-able movie; what it did, with painterly deliberation and economy, was to bring into my life a big, man-sized baby.

The details of Kaspar's release from the reeking, amniotic nothingness of his prison – how he is carried around, and brutally schooled in walking and talking, along with the imagery of mud, water, fields, roads and town, to the sombrely romantic strains of Albinoni's *Adagio* and Pachelbel's *Canon* – amounted to the gestation of a boy emerging from a man-made womb, and his birth in small-town Nuremberg in 1828.

As the villagers came out to look at him standing in the square, we in the audience were ahead of them. We knew the awfulness of his provenance. We'd seen the cruelty of his upbringing. Kaspar was, in a sense, our boy. We'd started to worry about him, like a cinema-full of four hundred parents. We might not have wished to rush into the screen and rescue him, but we were already wringing our hands on his behalf and hoping nothing bad – nothing even worse than what he's already suffered – would befall him.

The villagers stare at Kaspar, ask him questions and conclude that 'he seems to be not quite right in the head'. The note in his hand explains that his father has had ten children and cannot afford to bring up the boy himself. A soldier interrogates him, a tiny local busybody from the town council takes notes, puffed up with self-importance. Medically minded villagers check out the shocking state of his legs and feet, the evidence of trauma and neglect, the vaccination scars performed with a blunt instrument on his arms. They could be examining the wounds of the cruci-fied Christ. They give him food, but he spits it out. Kaspar cluelessly intones the word 'Horsey', which is all that remains of the baffling sentence dinned into his ear, but cannot stand the yammering of speculation that surrounds him. He stands isolated amid the throng of chatterers, his head leaning against a door like a bewildered horse.

Uncertain what to do with him, the locals put him in the town gaol: 'It's best we keep him in this tower for thieves and vagabonds,' says one, unconsciously voicing the likely fate that, by popular consent, might befall Christ if he strayed, unrecognised, into nineteenth-century Europe. But even without the religious overtones, Kaspar was beginning to get under my skin. He responded to well-meaning gestures with disgust. He looked on with baffled incomprehension as a soldier tried to force a reaction from him by lunging at him, a few dozen times, with his manly sword.

'It's no good,' the thrusting officer tells his audience. 'He doesn't even respond to a feigned *coupé*.' Fancy that. But Kaspar responds to *some* things. He's given his first-ever bath by a kindly village matron, who lathers him with soap and scrubs his portly white flesh, until he cries out, 'Mother, my skin is coming off.' In a significant cluster of images, he is seen as an emblem of both innocence and entrapment. He tries to feed a little bird in a window of the gaol (there were no special effects here – Herzog's camera fixed on the man–bird transaction, waiting until the tiny fledging opened its trusting beak and let him in).

A small boy and his sister visit him in his cell. The boy tries to teach him the German names of parts of the body. His little sister, Agnes, takes over. She is tiny, pig-tailed and sweetly dictatorial, as she demands that their new playmate learn her little rhyme.

Good morning little cat so white –
May I sit down by your side?
Lap lap lap, I like this milk,
Lap lap lap, as smooth as silk.

Kaspar tries his best, and we hear, for the first time, his authentic speaking voice – a charged, grating monotone, an unexpectedly grand, world-statesman kind of voice, as guttural and serious as Henry Kissinger's. But his passionate, knotted attempt to follow the nursery words – 'Guten . . . morgen . . .' – is doomed to failure ('Agnes, that rhyme is too long for him,' says her sensible brother). I found it terribly moving. He was so obviously a man desperate to join in this world of common language and shared feelings, even if it was only 'Good morning little cat so white,' but finding it just too damned difficult.

Minutes later, he discovers fire. Some rowdy youths, who have been playing a game involving a dazed chicken and a white line on the floor, persuade Kaspar to put his finger in the flame of a candle, and he does so, having never seen a flame before. He holds his finger there for what seems a whole minute – then pulls it out in terrible, burnt disarray, and twists his body round, his eyes wide and shocked, like a boy who's just been slapped in the face by someone he trusted.

For the first time, he registers the shock of localised pain, quite distinct from the pain of imprisonment. He sits suddenly aghast. In a movie filled with epiphanies, this is the worst. His face is a picture of bewilderment. Nothing in his life has prepared him for the sensation and shock of burning. This is the new world of excitement and adventure into which he's been liberated, and he's discovering that it's far worse than the dungeon he's escaped from. Moments later, it happens again, as Kaspar stands beside a rocking cradle containing a squalling baby. The baby's mother encourages him to pick up the noisy infant, and he does so, without knowing what this sequence of behaviour can possibly mean. He is a man with no knowledge of comfort or security. He has no idea what the churning of emotions inside him can signify. He looks at the baby's indulgent mama, all nodding reassurance, and holds the querulous bundle of flesh in his arms. 'Mutter,' he says, with tears suddenly coursing down his cheeks, 'I am far away from everything.'

I confess that I wept at this scene along with Kaspar, although its actual thrust is anti-sentimental. This is a man so removed from the ordinary world that he reacts to both a burning flame and a yelling baby as awful things, a trauma to his flesh followed by a trauma to his heart. '*Mutter*, I am far away from everything' expresses just how lost he is in this difficult world that he is trying (and failing) to embrace.

It was a cinematic moment that moved me inordinately, when I knew I'd discovered a film that had taken me beyond the ordinary passive response of a bloke sitting in the audience. In that moment, Kaspar became the little brother I'd never had. I was looking at a 25-year-old man playing a 16-year-old adolescent,* yet I felt a personal connection to him that was so strong I could weep for his discombobulated lostness, as if he were a kid brother in need of help. I suddenly wanted to have him by my side, to look after him, to kick a football with him, and carry him around, and dry his tears and make him laugh, and show him the world was a better place than he thought.

The villagers wonder what to do with the staring-eyed stranger in their midst: he's an escaped British circus performer, they surmise, he's an illegitimate offshoot of the Baden dynasty, he's a notorious swindler who's been terrorising the neighbourhood. They decide he must work for his upkeep by taking part in a freak show: The villagers all turn out to see it, gathering in a field that's shot by Herzog in a muddy, sepia light, like the dim-hued newsreel footage that might have existed, had there been cameras, in the

---

* Played by the wonderful Bruno S., a non-actor as obscure as his unknown surname, plucked by Werner Herzog from his employment as a Berlin lavatory attendant, after he'd spent twenty-two years in medical institutions and prison. He starred in one further Herzog film, *Stroszek* (1977), and thereafter returned to the obscurity from which he came.

1820s. A histrionic ringmaster talks them through (and patro-nises) the freaks on display.

There's a tiny dwarf-king perched on a giant throne; then a catatonic miniature Mozart who has spent his life staring at the ground; then a tribal Indian nose-flautist from the Himalayas. Kaspar is the climax and star of the show, standing *en tableau vivant* just as he was discovered months earlier, his hand outstretched, his eyes wide as the eyes of a horse who has just spotted the knackers' yard ahead. In a brilliant cut-away shot, all four of the freakish exhibits escape and run off across the open meadows of Nuremberg, pursued by the show's ringmaster and his cronies – along with the local antiquary, who chronicles Kaspar's wayward career on a notepad.

Kaspar is discovered hiding in a bee-hut, immobile and appalled among the thousands of threatening hymenoptera buzzing around him, stunned once again by the awfulness of the brave new world into which he's been flung.

Over the next two years, Kaspar moves in with a doctor and his family, learns to eat, to speak and – especially – to gesture like a town bourgeois, waving his right hand for emphasis, with thumb and forefinger clamped together. His every pronouncement is slow and determined and full of *ex cathedra* gravity, as if he's learned to speak like the Nuremberg elders, and he holds his hand up like a lecturer: clearly, he has picked up self-importance from the people around him. But he just can't hack it as a dweller in the modern world. An *avant-garde* young piano player fills him with concern. 'The music feels strong in my heart,' he tells his benefactor. 'I feel so old. Why is everything so hard for me? Why can't I play the piano like I can breathe?' Just as you're assuming he must be happy to be a part of Society at last, he says, 'The people are like wolves to me' (though where did he ever encounter wolves?).

He is disturbed by logical conundra. Looking up at the

little window of the tower where he was imprisoned, he remembers how large his cell had seemed, and concludes that it must be bigger than the whole tower. He looks at the town's *hausfrau* population and wonders, 'What are women good for? Why are they only allowed to cook and knit?' He is becoming a satirical, Gulliverian inspector of the civilised *status quo*. He thinks his disturbing dreams are real – in his dungeon, he never had cause to dream, and his days were spent thinking of nothing. 'I think my coming into the world,' he says sadly, 'was a terrible fall.' The kindly old doctor, who took him in and gave him a home, looks understandably peeved by what seems like terrible ingratitude. Surely Kaspar should thank him for giving him a home, in the best of all possible worlds – namely, human civilisation in the nineteenth century. Instead he has found it unbearable, a place where he can tell that everybody hates him for being an unclassifiable outsider.

Kaspar's is a very Beckettian position, the fully-fledged human who is conscious of never having been properly born, who 'has the inestimable gift of life rammed down my throat' (as Molloy says in the first book of the *Trilogy*), a man who exists in an environment of baffling rules and requirements, discovering language and behaviour patterns which pitch him into a nightmare of misunderstanding.

In a scene that had the philosophy undergraduates, in the Oxford cinema where I saw the film, whooping with joy, a pompous visiting academic arrives for tea to try Kaspar out on logic. He asks him a conundrum. A man comes to a crossroads. One road leads to a village where everyone tells the truth, and the other to a village where everyone tells lies. What one question should he put to a man he encounters at the crossroads that will clarify which route will send him to the Village of Truth? The only answer the logicians will allow is this: 'If I were to ask a man from the *other* village where the Village of Truth is, what would he say?' (And then, whatever the answer, you go in the other direction.) But Kaspar has an alternative answer: 'I would ask him if he was a tree-frog. And if he was from the village where they always tell lies, he will say yes. And if he is from the other village, he will say no. So then you would know which path to take.' The logician is appalled by this display of lateral thinking and dismisses it as methodologically unsound. 'I can't accept that,' he says pompously. 'It's descriptive, rather than deductive.' Kaspar looks disgusted.

Sadly, the dungeon-dwelling *ingénu* is no more beguiled by English sophistication than German provincialism. The village is graced by a visit from an English nobleman, Lord Stanhope, a frightfully camp piece of work with long greasy hair and outrageously constricting tight green pants. He combines the arch delivery of Joel Grey in *Cabaret* with the preciousness of Harold Acton, as he charms the company with his tales of foreign travel: in Greece, 'I loitered, Pindar in hand, 'neath the columns of Corinth – I was forced to wear *peasants' trousers* . . .'

Kaspar is brought out on display, like a prize pig, to meet this drawing-room Baron Suave. He is plonked in front of a piano, to show his educated-noble-savage credentials, but he makes a hash of his performance. Soon after, he is discovered in a side-room, minus his clothes, doing some knitting, in a wholesale rejection of the *haut monde*. Lord Stanhope decides to withdraw his patronage of this awkward *protégé* who will not do what is required of him, and we're left with the memory of their only interchange. 'What was it like in that dark cellar of yours?' inquires his lordship, quivering with nosiness about the conditions of the disgusting underclass. 'Better than on the outside!' says Kaspar, triumphantly.

The movie ends in a welter of inexplicable savagery and apocalyptic visions. Kaspar's old gaoler and tormentor inexplicably returns – we watch him creeping up on the stricken

Kaspar, while he's peeping through the chinks of an outdoor privy, where he has gone, boyishly, to suck eggs in private – and thumps him around the head for no obvious reason. Kaspar retires to bed and turns inside himself. The camera lingers on one more landscape of windswept fields, the innocent Elysian Fields that were all (we must infer) he thought about while in his dungeon. But now they've been eclipsed by another dream, of a mountainside up which people are climbing, a mountain at whose summit is Death.

Kaspar recovers, but he is now a broken man, looking at his reflection in a garden pond and breaking the water to shatter the fragile image therein. He never quite manages to play the piano. Soon after, he is stabbed, mortally, by an unknown assailant. He is found lying in a heap, with a bloody wound on his coat, and is led to safety by the doctor, barely aware of what's happening to him. On his last-ever journey through the garden, he walks with a stricken, sideways gait, his arms held up before him as though to fight off some terrible indignity, his whole demeanour bewildered and fussy and appalled – an elder statesman with the widened eyes of a terrified child.

He is put to bed, attended by local church elders, and there he has a final vision, of a caravan moving through a desert. The screen takes on a grainy, flickery texture, full of looming, slow-motion camels and shrouded mystic Arabians on their way along a Silk Route to salvation – a caravan that is led by an old Berber tribesman who is blind. The blind leader picks up some sand and tastes it, dubiously, as if to say this whole thing may be fake – these are not real mountains, they're only bits of your imagination.

'What happens after they reach the northern city,' says Kaspar, 'I don't know.' He tells the baffled townies around the bed that he's tired, and then he dies.

His departed life is celebrated in two ways. One is a bleak shot of a mortuary note tied with string to one big toe to remind attendants who he is. The other is a post-mortem examination of his brain, which is sliced up before us and discloses an abnormally enlarged cerebellum, which – the busybody little notary gleefully concludes – explains everything about all his strange, counter-intuitive perspectives on the human community.

The film ends with this ignorant little man walking importantly through the town, concluding his report on Kaspar Hauser and why he behaved so oddly, leaving us modern sophisticates, in 1975, to reflect upon how poorly nineteenth-century logic could understand this essentially modern, indeed modernist, hero, his skewed insights and his ferocious rejection of the tight moralities of civilised living.

Kaspar Hauser is the perfect embodiment of a character that recurs through many of my favourite films – the Tragic Kid Brother. I seemed to be a sucker for celluloid siblings. Kaspar is a classic character in the cinema of pathos – the innocent outsider, pitched into a world he dimly understands, but which, in all important respects, he *sees through*. But he turns up all over the place in film history, and his influence is vitally important in the breeding of sympathy in twentieth-century hearts.

The Little Brother is sometimes a genuine little brother, or a hopelessly innocent kid-in-trouble, in dozens of movies that stuck in my mind like a spectral infants' class. He is the gaunt-faced John Howard Davis asking – no, whispering – for more in David Lean's *Oliver Twist*; the hero-worshipping, blond-haired Brandon de Wilde in the Alan Ladd Western *Shane*; the plucky young shaver pursued, along with his kid sister, by Robert Mitchum's psychopathic hellfire preacher in Charles Laughton's *Night of the Hunter*; the pathetic, school-blazered Lucian John, lost in the Australian outback in Nicolas Roeg's *Walkabout*; the tiny, flaxen-haired Martin Amis, dying picturesquely in Sandy Mackendrick's *A High Wind in Jamaica*; David Bowie's hunchbacked kid brother, whose bullying at school haunts the eponymous hero in *Merry Christmas, Mr Lawrence.*

But he's also the young servant-boy whom Peter O'Toole ushers into the officers' mess in Cairo after walking out of the desert in *Lawrence of Arabia.* And his spirit is there in the middle of the action, being annoying, attention-seeking and self-destructive, in Horst Buchholz as the tag-along kid in *The Magnificent Seven*; in Robert de Niro's friend, the headband-wearing, Russian roulette-fixated Christopher Walken in *The Deer Hunter .* He is also, of course, the sweet, doomed, passionate, appropriately-named Angel (Jaime Sanchez), forty years younger than his grizzled associates, who does for them all at the end of *The Wild Bunch.*

And Billy (Dennis Hopper) in *Easy Rider* is a classic Little Brother, helpless and in need of constant reassurance. When the two bikers stop at a gas station, Billy worries that their hitch-hiker will somehow discover the money stashed away in the petrol tank. 'Don't worry, Billy,' says Peter Fonda, 'everything's all right.' 'Well – I don't know . . .' says Billy. 'I do,' says Fonda, the man who is so obviously his more capable sibling.

The moment when Kaspar puts his hand into a flame, and reacts with a combination of outrage and bafflement, reminds us of Frankenstein – the original 1931 *Frankenstein,* directed by James Whale, not the Hammer Studios stooge – in which the monster was a big, bewildered baby, unable to fathom what was going on around him. He discovers fire for the first time in the hermit's cottage, and reacts, like Kaspar, with frenzied disarray. When the hermit puffs cigar smoke in his face, he fails to appreciate the classy pong of a fancy Corona (and what, pray, is a hermit doing with one of those?) and kills the luxuriating recluse, like a terminally effective smoke alarm. He also meets a little girl playing a childish game, pulling the heads off daisies and tossing them into the river, and imitates her actions until he runs out of daisies, at which point he reaches out for the only other thing in the vicinity which has a head on it, namely the little girl . . . But it's his innocence we respond to, not his homicidal logic. He is a lumbering kid out of control, his actions driven by an endlessly-thwarted desire to fit in.

Kaspar's ghostly avatar appeared later in Spielberg's *ET: the Extra Terrestrial* (1982), another classic outsider, grotesque at first, gradually becoming lovable and familiar, a lost soul who is smuggled into Elliott's family, who prowls into the bedrooms and kitchens and toy cupboards of a modern family in Los Angeles, and is socialised to a degree, like Kaspar, without ever becoming attuned to the rhythm of ordinariness. Like Kaspar, ET never fits in with his modern surroundings, and yearns for a home somewhere else. In ET's case, it's a home in the sky. In Kaspar's case, it's a home in the desolate wilds of his imagination.

He's also present in *The Elephant Man* (1980), one of my favourite later films, whose central character, John Merrick, is a repellent, bulbous-browed, twisted-faced, stunted refugee from a Victorian freak-show, who is given a home in a London hospital by a kindly doctor, and – despite weirding-out the nursing staff who have to deal with him – becomes a minor celebrity in Victorian society. David Lynch, the director, seems to have borrowed, or at least echoed, some of Herzog's filmic effects when he fills the screen with slow-motion visions of rampaging elephants and visions of Merrick's mother's beautiful face; and Merrick shares Kaspar's tragic inability to assimilate into a society in which he will always be a curiosity, a bizarre outsider.*

I wept buckets over Kaspar, as I'd seldom wept in a

---

* Even when Merrick preens himself, conceitedly, in his fancy clothes, and talks in gracious condescension to unseen admirers in his hospital room – a scene oddly reminiscent of both Peter O'Toole in *Lawrence of Arabia*, pirouetting in the desert in his new,

cinema before, and by the end I was wrung out. This was a blast of romantic-intellectual European movie-making that I'd never encountered before, emotionally miles removed from the sterile Marienbads, the bleakly reductive Pasolini Biblicals, the pretentious Antonioni weirdnesses and the camp Fellini grotesqueries. This one made you cry. It offered you strange, out-of-focus visions (those rough 16-mm shots of the Caucasus, the camel trains and mountain-scrambling pilgrims) that pierced your heart because they were symbolic journeys to the core of some gigantic mystery. They gave you glimpses of the sublime in a way that no British or American movie would dream of doing. And the film gave me, most of all, a figure to adopt like a child in my secret heart, and keep there for ever.

I sometimes wonder what Bruno S. is doing these days. His chunky body and his square face, book-ended by massive, Dundreary side-whiskers, recurred in my dreams for years. He was a unique combination of peasant and lordling, village idiot and *idiot-savant*, innocent and sophisticate. But it was his face, his eyes, and his walk, and his clenched, held-in, flinching refusal to compromise with the wolves of the new world that really got to me. The scene where he sits chewing bread, as unconcerned as a cow ruminating with a mouthful of grass, while a soldier in full uniform thrusts and parries and lunges at him with his regimental sword, trying to elicit some response. The moments when he suddenly opens up to his surroundings: feeding the tiny fledging bird on the window of his prison cell, dancing with a puzzled cat; noisily, ill-manneredly devouring a plate of soup while chatting to Katy, the amiably bovine housekeeper. All these intimate, domestic Kaspar moments

---

Arab-warlord robes, and Robert De Niro striking 'You-talking-to-me?' attitudes in front of a mirror in *Taxi Driver*.

recurred in my heart like a series of little shocks. *You must take on the outside world with belligerent innocence.* That was the last cinematic lesson I learned before going off to join the real world in 1975, just as Kaspar had left his reeking prison to encounter the modern Nuremberg in 1828. I was twenty-one when I was pitched into a world of grown-ups, having to leave university, get a job, find a flat in London, and get serious.

It was time to find a career. I was living back home with my parents in Battersea, with a bright, shiny, useless Oxford English degree in my pocket and no obvious future. I wrote to twenty London publishers explaining, in perhaps too languid a manner, that I was a newly fledged literary genius, and that I might be available to work for them, commissioning books and editing manuscripts with flair and insouciance. A dead, heart-shrinking, soul-withering silence followed these bumptious overtures. I got two rejection letters from the least impressive of the publishing houses, and nothing from the rest. Were my applications for employment, I wondered, being handed round the offices of Jonathan Cape and Heinemann, Macmillan and Collins to be read by sneering publishing types in tweed jackets with leather elbow-patches, who guffawed and wept and punched each other on the arm at my callow presumption?

I read Margaret Drabble's first novel, *A Summer Bird-cage*, about a smart young Oxford graduate called Sarah, returning from Paris to her family home and finding a job with the BBC just like that ('It seemed better than nothing,' she coolly remarks, the smug bitch, on page 65), so I applied to the Corporation as well. Inexplicably, no urgent summons, insisting that I attend an immediate interview with the Director General, fell through the letter-box.

Over pints in the White Horse in Fulham, a kind friend pointed out that *every single* English graduate from *every single* university in the country had probably written the same letters to the same publishers and the BBC the same week that I'd written mine ('though slightly less floridly presumptuous than yours, John, I dare say'), and that I couldn't expect to bang on the doors of high-rolling employers, and expect to be admitted, just like that. He himself was going to his second interview with the British Council, so he was all right. He counselled me against trying the same employment route, on the grounds that I knew nothing about the political set-up in Honduras or Nicaragua, which were the only places you could currently expect to be sent on a British Council ticket, and I took his advice. He was obviously afraid I might be a frighteningly brilliant rival. In my dreams.

I thought about journalism, which had been my career fantasy from schooldays, but it seemed a closed shop. Nobody, they told me, could expect to get near Fleet Street until they'd spent ten years of apprenticeship in the provinces, writing tiny stories about garden fêtes and coach parties trapped in unseasonal snowdrifts for the *Moreton-on-the-Marsh Gazette*. I made a journey one day to check out the offices of the *South London Star*, thinking I might start at the bottom, as teaboy and cub reporter, just as Keith Waterhouse had once done, or like young Jimmy Olsen in the *Superman* comics; but their offices looked like the premises of a mini-cab company. A vestigial Oxford snobbery told me I must be destined for better things, and I stalked home, nose in the air.

I was, however, getting desperate. I went to morning seminars held by companies in need of salesmen, in draughty rooms off Piccadilly, where my co-hopefuls were mostly anxious foreigners in cheap suits, learning rudimentary English. I signed on the dole and was propositioned by an Australian bisexual in the queue, who promised me a lucrative couple of years in the office-cleaning racket, supplemented by weekends of sexual frolics with his mates. 'And we often get a few girlies from the pub to join in too,' he assured me, appetisingly. The post-Oxford autumn rolled by.

None of my (increasingly pleading, decreasingly conceited) letters elicited any response. I spent endless mornings under the feet of my mother's cleaning lady in a kitchen full of the scorched smell of ironing and my mother's try-out recipes for Chicken in Aubergine Pickle Sauce.

Then my father suggested a way out. One of his patients worked at Wandsworth Borough Libraries. A junior position had recently fallen vacant. 'It's a job, it's full of books, and it'll tide you over till Christmas, and you'll earn some money to buy a few presents. And you won't be under Mrs Geogehan's feet in the kitchen all feckin' day.'

This was a poser. Could I work in a library? Of course I could. Would they pay me anything? About £150 a week. Was it a career I had anticipated? Can you be serious? I, the living embodiment of W.B. Yeats and Oscar Wilde, reduced at the onset of his professional life to working among shelves and trolleys and signs saying 'Silence'?

But Philip Larkin had worked all his life in a library, and so had John Lewis, the hero of Kingsley Amis's second novel *That Uncertain Feeling*, and Trollope had worked for the Post Office in Ireland, and T.S. Eliot had had a lowly job in Lloyds Bank, and Joyce had taught English as a foreign language in Trieste, so in theory (I reasoned) a literary supernova could start his salaried life just about anywhere.

I went along, and was interviewed by a grey-bearded, defeated-looking man called Mr Palmer. He scrutinised my minimal *curriculum vitae*.

'It says here your interests are music, films and creative writing,' he said. 'I'm afraid there won't be many opportunities for any of those while you're working here.'

'I realise that,' I said. 'I wasn't thinking of spending my time composing a masterpiece of social satire under the desk, while waiting for people to come up to have their books stamped.'

He looked at me.

'*A-ha*-ha-ha,' I laughed.

Damn. I'd fallen at the first fence. My chronic affliction of saying out loud what I was thinking – since I *was* expecting to write just such a book, in precisely those circumstances – had made me vocalise my cunning plan. But perhaps I had got away with it, by my self-deprecating laughter.

'Excuse me a minute, would you?' he said, and disappeared. I looked around at this dismal municipal office. Across the desk lay a letter whose bold, slashing handwriting I instantly recognised. Recklessly, I twisted it through 180 degrees, and gazed at a letter from my senior tutor, Jonathan, who had been one of my referees for this puny job. 'You'll like John Walsh,' it began. 'He's full of enthusiasm and charm, although I have to say . . .' But I heard Mr Palmer coming back, so I never discovered the true burden of my tutor's withering analysis. Mr Palmer sat down heavily, took off his glasses and wiped them.

'Have you any experience of lending out books?'

'Not really,' I said.

'Have you any experience of dealing with the general public?'

'Not as such,' I said, 'though I'm sure I could get on with, you know, people.'

'Have you ever taken on any management responsibilities of any kind?'

'Not specifically,' I said, 'though I ran the chess club at my school.'

'Have you a working knowledge of the Dewey Decimal System?'

'Well I – no.'

He sighed.

'Would you know how to deal with a lady who wanted to borrow a nursing romance but couldn't remember any titles or the name of any authors?'

'Well, I suppose I'd suggest she reads, er . . .' I waved

my hands and floundered for a while, then had a brain-wave. 'I'd suggest she reads *The Voyage Out* by Virginia Woolf. It's got a marvellous long scene about the heroine, Rachel, becoming consumptive or something, and there's this beautiful passage about a giant hand coming and turning her over at the bottom of the sea. It's very evoc—'

'Have you ever had occasion to remove a down-and-out or a drunkard from a public place?'

'Well, no,' I admitted, 'but I've seen it done.' I didn't like to add that I'd seen it done *to me*, after one too many light-and-bitters at the Fox and Grapes on Wimbledon Common. He passed a weary hand across his middle-aged, librarian's brow.

'You're obviously completely over-qualified for this rather menial job,' he said, 'and quite unsuited in every practical way. But I'm prepared to take you on because, frankly, Wandsworth Borough Libraries could do with an injection of young blood. So can you start next Tuesday?'

I was exultant. A job at last! I duly appeared at 8.45 a.m. the following Tuesday, hair-washed, clean-jeaned, white-shirted and resplendent in a perhaps ill-advised combination of corduroy jacket and psychedelic tie (the only one I owned), to meet my fate in my first-ever place of employment. I stood at the front desk of the library in a passable simulacrum of Kaspar Hauser's arrival at the door of civilisation, the unseen letter from my tutor standing in for Kaspar's bit of recommendatory paper, my scrubbed and shining face aglow, wondering what the world of work would be like, and confidently casting myself in the role of the *idiot-savant*, who would take on the system, ask strangely knowing questions, and beguile everyone with my innocent, instinctive wisdom . . .

The library staff began to arrive, and surreptitiously inspected the Infant Phenomenon in their midst. A thin, rather pretty woman called Phoebe showed me the communal room, the loos, the snack machines and the back stairs, like a kindly teacher showing a nervous first year his desk and his coat-peg at a class of mixed infants. She had a charming smile, but a vague manner, which left her smile still switched on when she'd lost interest in what you were saying. She was one of the library bosses.

In the staff room – which was exactly like the prefects' study at school – I met Janet, a bulky, older dame in a beige skirt and Guernsey jumper, who was stirring a mug of Nescafé. She regarded me coldly.

'So – where have you come from?' asked Janet.

'Well, I live in Battersea,' I began.

'No, I mean – where were you before?'

'I was at university,' I said. 'In Oxford.'

'But which library were you at before this one?'

'I wasn't at any library.'

'But you must have come from *some*where,' said Janet crossly. She was a woman whose every syllable breathed hostility.

'No, really,' I said. 'I used to take books out of Battersea Library on Lavender Hill, but that wasn't really work. I haven't done this kind of thing before.'

'But you must know how the system works, don't you?'

'No, not really. I was hoping someone could show me.'

Janet let out a small noise, like gas escaping from a pressure cooker. 'You mean this is your first job in libraries, with your fancy degree and all?'

'Yes, and I'd be really grateful if you could show me what to do,' I said with an attempt at charm.

'Well. *really*,' said Janet. 'Some people think they can just walk into jobs with no experience, no CV, no background, nothing.'

'Sorry,' I said. 'Mr Palmer offered me the job last week and said I should turn up this morning.' I shrugged hopelessly, as if in the hands of some municipal Fate.

Janet turned to the indefatigably smiling Phoebe. 'He doesn't know what to do,' she said shortly.

'John is the new assistant,' said Phoebe brightly. 'They've decided we need some new blood here, *ay voyla*.'

Ay voyla? What was she talking about?

'I suppose you want me to show him around?' asked Janet, tersely.

'If you wouldn't mind, Janet,' said Phoebe, sleekly. 'Just get him started on the desk this morning, tell him about Ticketing and Fines and Shelving and so forth, that would be a real help. I'd do it myself, but I have an important meeting with Gordon and June.'

I looked from one face to the other. Neither was over-brimming with enthusiasm.

'So it falls on *me*, does it, the training of juniors?' asked Janet. Phoebe seemed oblivious to her subordinate's distaste.

Perhaps, I thought, she sees me as a dangerous rival to her position, a brilliant young intruder in a world of dim-wits, a threat to her settled bourgeois existence, like Kaspar, arriving from nowhere in the town centre . . .

I looked at her face.

. . . but then again, I thought, perhaps not.

So Janet was my first guide to the world of work. She showed me the desk where returned books were ushered on to trolleys, and how you checked the date stamped into the form on the flyleaf, and computed how latecomers were to be fined and coldly upbraided for their fecklessness. I learned the Masonic ritual of the checkout region, where you flicked out the docket from the cardboard envelope glued into the early pages of an outgoing volume, and deposited it in a long metal file, how you stamped the date on to the paper with a satisfying, metallic *ker-chunk* noise.

With my new Oxford degree tucked in a desk some-where at home as official proof that I had a brain, I felt I had reverted sixteen years to the days of cutting things out and sticking things down, playing with glue and cardboard, putting bits of paper into other bits of paper, identifying simple shapes, getting quickly hardening glue all over my hands. Soon we would be moving on to finger-painting. Like Kaspar learning to walk and write at sixteen, I was receiving a basic education at twenty-one.

Working the library shelves became a form of playtime. I soon perfected a rapid-fire alphabeticisation of all the newly returned books on the Fiction trolley, so that, as I swanned with it across the brown vinyl flooring, I learned to slot the homecoming volumes into their spaces on the shelves in a fluent ballet – glide-and-slide, check the Fs and the Gs because their section is coming up two yards ahead, glide-and-slide, and *off* you went again to the long stretch of the H section. In the H section, I noted with sorrow that the names with which I was most familiar – Hartley, Hawthorne, Heller, Hemingway, Hesse – seemed to be stuck immovably in their positions on the shelf, as if nobody was ever going to take them out and read them *ever*. They sat there like statues, the cold, marmoreal guardians of Western culture, wholly failing to interest the idle, grunting readers of south London.

By the late afternoon, I'd become familiar with the Dewey Decimal System – the subtle, numerical calibration of non-fiction books into subjects and tiny sub-genres, each with its own special number like a complicated mathematical identity, so that a work of literary criticism could be found at 821.337, but a work of humorous literary parody would be sternly consigned to the more frivolous regions of 854.309.

O, my America, my new found land. I'd used the local library in Battersea since high-school days, but I'd never dreamed that there existed a section devoted to newspapers and journalism, nor social histories of fashion and eating, nor the tiny speak-easy sub-sections, where lurked appealingly po-faced studies of sexual deviance and forensic medicine.

It was brilliant. The world where people worked was evidently a marvellously logical place. I can do this, I thought, I can familiarise myself with every book in this library, I can become a polymathic bore on a hundred subjects while stamping books out with a flourish and greeting them back with infinite condescension ('Did you enjoy it? I'm *so* glad. It's one of my favourites too.'). My first sight of the working environment, where men and women were paid for processing information and entertainment, seemed like a vinyl-floored, air-freshener-scented Paradise – even though I had Janet growling beside me all morning, pooh-poohing my cry of rapture on finding that a biography of my hero David Bowie existed in the Biography section (920 BOW) on a shelf between Balzac and Brahms.

At lunchtime, I went for a walk in the Balham streets, bought a sandwich and ate it with a bottle of Fanta on a bench in the sunshine, like Kaspar trying bean soup for the first time in the local doctor's household. So this was what a working lunch was like! I sat happily masticating egg mayonnaise while I worked out what to do with my first pay packet.

A hundred pounds! At University, where I'd lived on a government grant supplemented by an allowance from my father, I'd got by on living expenses of £10 a week. It went mostly on drink and books, and taking girls on cheap dates to the Berni Inn for steak and chips with button mushrooms. Now I was a grown-up, I could practically fling money around. I could stroll down the King's Road, Chelsea on a Saturday, and kit myself out in loon pants and platform-soled shoes until I was the trendiest, most *au courant* geezer in town. I could even pay my parents a small, condescending honorarium for my temporary stay in their tragic bourgeois home, with the Irish-mutton cooking smells at one end and the clinical pong of surgical spirit at the other. I could even, I reflected, afford to buy my mama a little present. I took a swig of Fanta, allowed myself a discreet belch, and wondered what it might be: a new teapot from Peter Jones? A cultured-pearl brooch from Liberty? I screwed up the remains of my sandwich and chucked it in the bin. Everything was going to be so simple. Was this (I asked myself) how simple the real world really was? Piece of cake.

But it all started to go wrong when I realised that evening something that had passed me by. The next day you had to go back and do it all again.

I turned up on the second day, in the same corduroy jacket but a different shirt and, recklessly, no tie (I had only the one). I said 'Hi' to Phoebe and Janet, made coffee for myself, put books on the fiction shelves, and greeted the old-lady borrowers who arrived at 9 a.m. sharp as though their lives depended on their early perusal of the works of Catherine Cookson.

By 10 a.m., I was wretchedly bored. Wasn't something else supposed to happen beyond waiting for people to appear, waiting to sign out their books or to accept them back? I'd enjoyed the tour of the library the day before, but what did it mean to me on the second day? It meant nothing. I was just the chap on the desk, metal date-stamper in his hand, about as vital to the local community of South London society as an Australian rancher branding a ewe on a Brisbane sheep farm.

When things were quiet, mid-morning, I prowled the fiction shelves, seeing what I could find by writers I admired: *The History Man* by Malcolm Bradbury, *The Clockwork Testament* by Anthony Burgess, *The Infernal Desire Machines of Doctor Hoffman* by Angela Carter, *Dead Babies* by Martin Amis. They were all there, magically intact, unborrowed, virginally unsullied by the local literati. In an act of sulky complicity, I took them all off the shelves and stamped them all out on my own ticket. If nobody else wants you, I said severely, I'll adopt the lot of you for the next two weeks.

Phoebe, the perma-smiling boss lady, was more steely on my second day. 'You're taking too long over the shelving, John,' she said, sweetly. 'I'm sure you'll learn to speed up in time. Just remember, you're here to work, not to sample the merchandise.'

So I was becoming a marked man, the guy who worked in a library and was discovered being interested in the books . . .

'Sorry,' I said. 'Just familiarising myself with the stock.'

'You'll find there's no need to familiarise yourself with the fiction shelves,' she said, with the same sweet smile her ancestors would once have used on a gardener trying to improve himself with a copy of *Self-Help* in the potting shed. 'If it's not on the shelves or in the catalogue, we just haven't got it. Try to remember that. It saves a lot of time-wasting.'

Mid-morning, a woman came up to the desk. 'Have you got anything by Genet?' she said.

I looked at Phoebe.

'Jenny?' said Phoebe with a bright smile. 'Jenny whom?'

My boss clearly had a slight problem with French pronunciation.

'Not Jenny,' said the woman. 'Genn-ayy. You know, the French guy.'

'Oh *Genet*,' said Phoebe with a tinkling laugh. 'Do you mean the, er, educationalist?'

'No,' said the woman. 'I mean Jean Genet. You know – the French criminal, admired by Cocteau and Sartre. He was locked up in prison for years.'

'Oh, of course,' said Phoebe with breezy confidence. 'You can find him in the social welfare section, along with the other prison books, in Aisle Three.'

'One moment,' I said. 'Are you looking for *The Thief's Journal*? Or *Our Lady of the Flowers*?'

'I think it's the first one you said,' said the woman. 'The thief book.'

I pointed with my left arm. 'You see the corner of that bookcase, over there at the end of the yellow wall? Second shelf down, grey spine, the Penguin Modern Classic? That's *The Thief's Journal*.'

'Oh, OK,' said the woman and scuttled off to find it.

I was proud of myself. I had spotted the Genet stuff while prowling among the Gs and Hs, wondering why nobody borrowed the works of Hesse any more, and now I'd steered a customer like a bullet towards the book she wanted. I was a natural at this stuff. Pretty soon I'd acquire a reputation in library circles as The Man Who Knows Every Book in the Fiction Department . . .

Instead of praise, though, there was a strained silence.

'There's no need to show off,' said Phoebe in a hurt voice. 'I don't think it's a terribly nice way to behave. You'll have to learn there's more to life than being a smart arse.'

The staff from the music library and the junior library came round to inspect the new stranger in town, to find out what he was doing there and whether he posed some kind of threat. The music library was run by an oily, middle-aged man called Gordon. He moved in a cloud of Aramis after-shave, and behaved more like a snooty business mogul visiting one of his lesser manufactories than a paid-up executive of Wandsworth Borough Council. Standing at the music-books desk, he was smooth and charming and lent out boxed sets of Wagner and Richard Strauss with fantastic insouciance, as if his evening job was to conduct the London Symphony Orchestra, and he was, for personal reasons, slumming it by day in a mere lending library.

Gordon was friendly but odd. He could be confiding and larky one moment, then aloof and distant the next. He was fastidious and fussy with borrowers, but rude and gossipy about them once they'd left. He could be astonishingly physical. One morning he reached over and prodded my cock through the crotch of my jeans. 'What have you got there?' he asked. 'A tube of fruit pastilles?' I was too astonished to reply. He would sit in the staff room, eating his lunchtime pasta salad, and nod along with Janet's droning complaints about her lack of a decent job in a university library (where she knew she secretly belonged); then rubbish her, once we were back among the sheet music and the vocal scores of Gilbert and Sullivan. 'Poor sad old cow,' he'd say. 'So convinced she's going to find a don or a Fellow of History one day to shack up with.'

'But if she wants to get married,' I said, baffled, 'why doesn't she try some dating agency or something?'

Gordon looked at me in a funny way. 'I'm not quite sure you've got the, ah, measure of dear Janet quite yet, have you, old thing?'

He was full of such gnomic pronouncements. One thing I liked Gordon for was his attitude to the local Afro-Caribbeans. You didn't get many black borrowers in the place. The seats in the reference library were crammed with Asian scholars, busily working away at text books of aerodynamics and law, a community of South London's clever-but-poor immigrants trying to better themselves with the nearest thing to a university education they could afford in the mid-Seventies. In the main library, huge racks of novels in Urdu and Gujarati testified to the literary passions of local Muslim and Hindu population. Of the immigrant blacks, however, there was generally no sign. They just didn't do libraries. But when Gordon was around in the music library, large black men, their hair done in spectacular braids and corn-rows, would gather and mill about him, and he would make them laugh in huge baritone guffaws with his twinkly verbal sallies. As an outsider, I watched it all with interest and approval. How nice of him, I thought, how disinterested and non-judgemental of him, to look after the needs of the local community, to suck them into this temple of learning by his infectious enthusiasm.

His assistant, Brian, was a pale, balding 25-year-old vegetarian with a music degree and a craven manner, like someone crushed too often for voicing an opinion, or ridiculed too many times for resembling a failed monk. He was conversationally maladroit to a striking degree, and retreated every lunchtime behind a novel and a raw carrot, which he would nibble down to its ferny green root over twenty minutes. I once recommended *Watership Down* as a tremendous read, just so I could savour the sight of Brian nibbling his carrot while tackling the popular rabbit saga – but the moment never came.

The junior section was run by a sweet-faced ex-primary teacher called June. She was about twenty-eight, single, thin and emotionally on edge. The junior library suited her virginal demeanour. She was clearly happier steering small children through the Bettelheimian forest of witches and goblins, and the wizardy epics of Tolkien and C.S. Lewis, than engaging too closely with the hot breath of grown-up imaginations. I developed an instant crush on her, for her wide blue eyes, her tiny rosebud mouth and her hair-trigger vulnerability.

Once I found her weeping in the staff room.

'What's wrong, June?'

'It's nothing,' she said in a tiny voice. 'I'm just being incredibly silly.'

'About what?' I asked, putting my hand on her skinny, cardiganed arm. 'Tell me.'

'I'm just being pathetic. Don't worry about me.'

'No really, tell me,' I said, all manly solicitude. 'I'm sure I can help, whatever it is.'

She was silent for a time. 'I do *like* children,' she said, simply. 'I became a children's librarian to steer their hopeless young steps into the best imaginative writing. You know those Blake poems about Innocence and Experience? I wanted to be the bridge that would take them from one into the other. But if one more little beast comes up and says to me' – she adopted a simpering tone – ' "Please, miss, can I have a picture of a shark biting a lady's leg off?", I will really scream. It's all because of that bloody film, isn't it?'

I was shocked too. I had no experience of horrible children. I thought they were mostly charming midgets who drew rudimentary paintings of houses and suns and boats and their mummies. June, weeping about a nasty little boy's pictorial requirements, reminded me of Kaspar weeping over the first yelling baby he'd ever held in his arms. Her tears had been prompted by the little sod's identification with a movie poster, one that could be seen on every advertisement hoarding in the summer of 1975. What was it? *Jaws*.

Prowling the back rooms of my new home, I discovered a windowless vestibule where about a hundred books were shelved in a kind of detention, away from the scrutiny of human eyes. Books like *The Joy of Sex*, and a collection, entitled *Née de la Vague*, of arty naked photographs of female breasts, each pair spotted with foamy droplets of sea water. There was also a copy of Hubert Selby's *Last Exit to Brooklyn*, which had been the subject of an exciting obscenity trial when I was at school in the Sixties, and J.P. Donleavy's *The Ginger Man*. They were all vaguely sexy, but by no stretch of the imagination pornographic. Some of them had once been the subject of elderly scandals, but there wasn't one that couldn't have been purchased in any decent bookshop. What were they doing in this limbo? I decided, unilaterally, to rescue them, and spent a pleasant half-hour slotting them all out on the main shelves again.

In the staff room, at tea-time, I told Phoebe and Janet

what I'd done. There was consternation. How could I even *dream*, they shouted, of taking books from the Banned Room and introducing them back to polite society?

'For Christ's sake,' I said, '*The Ginger Man* was published in 1955. It's fantastically tame by today's standards. You can buy it in W.H. Smith's. Why should it be kept off the shelves in 1975?'

'You just cannot go around . . . *changing* things,' said Janet. 'It has to go before a committee.' And within the hour she had reported me for naïve (and smutty) insubordination.

'I'm disappointed in you, John,' said Phoebe.

Shelving some novels the next day, I found, inside the final endpapers of one pastel-covered love story, a line of initialled pencil marks in a dozen childish hands, ranged down the page like a miniature shopping-list. Such vandalism! It was terrible. I found a schoolkid's eraser and rubbed out the offending marks. I found a score of others, at the back of titles like *Moonlight Over Cordoba* and *Flames Over Zanzibar*, and erased all the little markings in those too. I was a crusader for purity.

'Someone's been defacing the Mills & Boon romances,' I told Phoebe later. 'I think that's shocking. We must find out who's been doing it and ban them from the library.'

'No, John,' said Janet. 'You don't understand. Lots of women read these books, but there are so many of them, and they're all so similar, borrowers get confused sometimes, and can't remember if they've read this or that one before. So they put their initials in the back to warn themselves not to take it out again.'

'But they're still graffiti,' I protested.

'No, John, they're not. They're just ayd memoyers.'

'But I've spent the afternoon rubbing out the pencil marks.'

She stared at me. 'You bloody fool. You've gone and upset a lot of old ladies. They won't know which ones they've read now. We're perfectly happy about the pencil marks. The people who make them are our most consistent regular borrowers. And then you have to come along with your great galumphing ideas and ruin everything.'

'Jesus, Phoebe, I –'

'*Why* do you have to interfere?' she said cruelly. '*Why* do you have to poke your nose in where it's not wanted?'

Oh, marvellous. I'd discovered a flagrant piece of book defacement, and now I was being told off for doing something about it.

I spent an hour on the Mills & Boon trolley, wondering how to make amends. Now that I knew that these books weren't to be put on the fiction shelves – too time-consuming, since they'd be borrowed by other romance enthusiasts within the hour – I decided to arrange them in colour co-ordination, starting with the violet-spined ones, moving through the indigo-blue shades to the green, yellow, orange and red ones. By the time I'd finished, the romance trolley was a perfect rainbow of pastel hues, a gorgeous symphony of graduated shades, a work of art.

It was disastrous.

None of the lady borrowers came near this Dulux-swatch colour scheme all that day, or the next, or the next or the next. Eventually, some kind soul came along and muddled them all up again, and the Mills & Boon devotees gradually returned, like shy, elderly wildebeest rediscovering a favourite waterhole that had briefly become a polychromatic theme park, and started taking them out again and leaving their tiny spoor of initials on the virgin greensward of the back page.

And so I gradually became a loose cannon, an unwelcome outsider, regarded with suspicion and loathing. I was sent off to the purdah of the music library, where I punched tickets and checked out long-playing records and noted, as benignly as possible, that Gordon's large black friends seemed regularly to arrive returning eight or nine Isaac Hayes or Jimmy Ruffin LPs, when, according to library rules, borrowers were allowed only two at a time. In the children's library, June finally put a *Jaws* poster up on the wall to satisfy the blood-lust of local seven-year-olds.

I took June out for a pint and a curry once or twice. We talked about work, and her previous job at a publishing company, and about the possible fulfilment that might await her at the Allfarthing Library in Earlsfield, should she ever make it to that head-spinning Elysium of library management.

She never asked me anything about myself. Neither our conversation nor June's body language ever turned in any sexual direction, but I still idly wondered if I might one day slide my hands beneath one of her dozens of Marks & Spencer's cardigans; nothing about our desultory conversation ever seemed to suggest we'd get to such a stage.

In the staff room, a slight *froideur* would settle on the company whenever I walked in. I would sit reading my book, while my fellow librarians munched their sandwiches and talked about things they'd seen on TV the night before. Occasionally I'd try to amuse the company with some gossip.

'I hear that Gordon is giving singing lessons to the children of Mr Ogakpe,' I'd say brightly. 'You know, that large Nigerian guy who's always in the record library. I didn't know Gordon could sing. Has anyone ever heard Gordon sing?'

This was met by a strange, mortified silence. Once, when June was eating her take-away Russian salad, I cheekily alluded to our recent evening at the movies (it was Fellini's *Amarcord* at the NFT) and reminded her of the hilarious scene with the store-keeper's wife who gets turned on by the pubescent boy's attempts to lift her up, and fishes an enormous breast out of her –

June fled the room in tears. I looked around at my co-workers in amazement.

'You *bastard*,' said Janet.

The others – Phoebe, Brian and a work-experience teenager called Jill – glared at me, then settled back into the publishing small-ads at the back of *The Bookseller*. '*What?*' I asked. What had I done now?

The following day sealed my fate. I spent the morning where I was happiest, at the main desk, taking in returned books, whizzing around the shelves, looking forward to reading David Lodge's new novel *Changing Places* in the cavernous pub around the corner at lunchtime. But I had a terrible falling-out with Phoebe. She'd looked at a request form filled out by a local housewife, asking to be first to read a new biography of Albert Camus when it came in.

'That should be no problem,' Phoebe told her breezily. 'I don't think there's likely to be much of a queue for Mr Came-uss.'

'I think, Phoebe,' I said, 'it's actually pronounced "Cam-*ou*", you know.'

Something inside her finally snapped. 'I've just about had enough of your clever-dick ways,' she said. 'You come in here, throwing your weight around, telling people they're not saying things right, putting smutty books on the shelves without a by-your-leave, you upset our lady borrowers by ruining the Romance section, you're so bloody tactless about Janet and June when they're trying to make a go of a very *difficult* relationship, not to mention the things you keep implying about Gordon. You think you're so high-and-mighty because you've got some lah-di-dah degree and it means you can take over this library, ahead of people who've slaved here for *years*, hoping to become a manager one day. I mean, who the *hell* do you think you are? Who in God's name would give *you* the time of day in any library circles I've ever come across I just don't know, when all you do is swan about causing trouble and telling people, "Oh *no*, oh *dear*, you've got that slightly wrong, it's Cam*ooooo* actually," because you're so frightfully educated and everyone else in the world has got to be so impressed because you think you know how to pronounce things properly. Well you can just – sorry?'

Her spectacular rant ended abruptly. A peaky-looking member of the public was standing before us in a donkey jacket.

'Have you got any books by David Attenborough?' he asked. 'I love his thing on telly where he talks to the gorillas. There must be a book out from the BBC. Is it out yet?'

'Let me look for you,' said Phoebe, as smoothly as though we'd just been singing a duet together. 'John, you can take care of the desk for a while, I'm sure.' And she disappeared towards the Natural History section, leaving me feeling like someone recently mugged by their adoptive parent.

I was upset. I went to the local pub and tried to read David Lodge, but the paragraphs swam in front of my eyes, and the smoke from the assembled lunchtime darts players made my eyes smart until a stupid, literal-minded person might have sworn I was crying. I didn't want to go back to work. I knew a rumour of my huge row with Phoebe would have spread like a virus. I didn't want to go near the library again. I didn't want to go back where the people were like wolves to me.

But I had to go back. By 2.30 p.m., I was feeling a pressure in my head I'd never known before. It was my first experience of the Protestant work-ethic, the thing that challenges your instinct to flee the awfulness of your employment, the boredom and suffering of work, and says: 'Get back in there. This is what you were born for . . .'

In the afternoon, I stood behind the desk of the music library, thinking, Nothing must go wrong here. I was fantastically nice to the music borrowers, even the man who kept asking for 'the sheep music'. I directed him to the library of sheet music, and he kept coming back with the same

269

idiotic enquiry. 'Nah, I mean the sheep music. Little lamb, right? Walking about, all wobbly, music in the background, lamb gets bigger, turns into bloody great ram, music in the background goes round and round in circles. Know what I mean?'

It turned out to be Pachelbel's *Canon*, the music that accompanied the current TV advertisement for Pure New Wool – and had, coincidentally, accompanied Kaspar's boat drifting across the German river, past the oblivious swans. As I watched the man leave with his *Masterpieces of the Baroque* LP tucked under his arm, I felt a small throb of nostalgia for the old days, when I was a university student with no knowledge of the world of responsibility, when I was a free agent, when I had the liberty to go anywhere I pleased in the sunlit mornings or rainy afternoons, when I could watch films about strange, innocent intruders into human society without feeling myself turning into one and having a whole library-village ranged against me in bafflement and loathing.

I busied myself. I rearranged the ticketing system, I re-collated the opera-score files. I went round the stacks, tut-tutting like a nurse about the torn plastic envelopes that encased the LP records. I was pretending to be a punctilious junior librarian, longing to be accepted, to be a model citizen of this unruly place, my first sighting of civilised employment, where I had proved so amazingly easy to dislike. From now on I wanted to fit in, to stop suggesting how people should do things better, since that just seemed to lead to trouble. I had entered a world whose actual procedures were simple, clear and filled with a kind of logical beauty. The only drawback was the people. Like Kaspar, I got on fine with the outside world, but the people in it were a nightmare. This town, to the extent that I conceived the library to be a town, was full of furious, miserable or slightly cracked citizens who responded to the young stranger in their midst by inspecting him with suspicion for days on end, treating his innocence with hostility and regarding his naïve questions about the *status quo* as implied criticism; they were clearly plotting his destruction.

A large West Indian guy, in a long black leather coat straight from the recent *Shaft* movie, breezed in and plonked a plastic Tesco carrier bag full of records on the counter.

'I'm returnin' most of these,' he said in a deep rumble. 'But I wanna keep the Jimmy Cliff and the Stax box set for another couple of weeks.'

I looked at the ten records on the counter. You were only allowed to take out two at a time. It was Rule Number One of the music library.

'How long have you had these?' I asked.

''Bout a fortnight,' said the man.

'I assume you're a friend of Mr Ross's, then,' I said, as neutrally as possible.

'What?' He jerked upright and glared at me.

'I mean, I'm assuming that you have some private arrangement with Mr Ross, the Music Library head?'

'What do you *mean*, exactly?' asked the man in suddenly furious tones. 'What're you trying to *say*?'

Bloody hell. I seemed to have touched another raw nerve. I was becoming remarkably adept at finding the raw nerves of colleagues and complete strangers.

'I'm not saying there's anything wrong,' I hastily reassured him. 'It's just some people might think it a little unorthodox . . .'

'WHAT ARE YOU SAYING TO ME HERE?' he bellowed. 'You accusing me of some kind of deviant behaviour? Shit. I walk in off the street to a goddam *library* to hand back some goddam records and I have to *justify* myself to some damn *kid* . . .'

'Nononono,' I pleaded. 'Look, it's no concern of mine what you and Mr Ross –'

'WHATTT?'

'All I'm saying,' I said, with a firmness that came from God-knows-where, 'is simply this. People who borrow from this library are allowed only two records out at any one time. It's a rule. If you have *not* got some private lending arrangement with Mr Ross, then I need to know what you're doing with ten records. If, on the other hand, you have a Special Borrower Understanding, then of course that's quite all right. There's no need to get upset about it.'

He looked at me closely. Yes, I silently told him, you *are* dealing with a half-witted junior here, and certainly not somebody who has been implying for the last five minutes that you are the object of Mr Ross's homosexual lust and therefore have been able to borrow hundreds of pounds' worth of records every week against the understanding that you will, one day, let him have his predatory way with you.

It was a strained moment. I tried to make myself look as innocent as possible. I think I may even have essayed a shy little smile.

'A Special Borrower Understanding?'

'Exactly. It's a privilege extended to a few friends of the library who are trusted associates, academics, special music enthusiasts. Like yourself.'

He seemed mollified.

'OK, then. But you had me going there for a bit. You have a strange way of putting things.'

'I'm new,' I said, showing him my fetching dimple. 'I haven't been here long. I do things by the rule book.'

'OK, we'll say no more about it. Mr Ross not here?'

'He's downstairs in a meeting,' I said, alarmed that he was going to report our conversation anyway. 'Probably be ages. Did you want to take anything *else* out?'

'No, I think I'll just wait.'

And he did. He went and saw my gay boss and told him, not that I'd been making insinuations about their relationship, but that I'd been obstreperous and rude, and most of all that I'd been drinking. I had the smell of two pints of Courage Best on my breath, from my lunchtime pub visit after my row with Phoebe.

It was enough to finish me off. Gordon had been in a meeting, as I'd assumed. It was a meeting to discuss what to do with me. How I'd upset everybody, male and female, gay and straight, staff and borrowers, how I'd never fitted in, how I must be pursuing some private, hidden agenda, as the only person in the library with a degree, how I was bent on a local-council version of world domination.

A week later, I was called by the droopy Mr Palmer, informed that my work 'while on probation' hadn't been up to scratch, and that I was, in consequence, out on my ear. I'd known that I was in trouble, but it was still a shock, getting fired from my first job.

I felt like I'd been murdered. The image of Kaspar Hauser, walking to his death, full of doomed and helpless importance, through his patron's garden, where he'd come to learn the mysteries of what it was like to be *really* human, staggering in his pathetic, sidelong hobble through the garden with a fatal bloody gash in his heart and a look of terrible surprise on his face, came back to me from the cinema in Oxford a year before and wrapped itself round me. Instead of Kaspar being the little brother I never had, he'd turned out to be me all the time. I'd been the *naif* tortured by the locals, the dim visionary who thought he knew it all but misunderstood everything, the suspicious-looking fool who asked awkward questions, and I had to go.

In the movie, Kaspar has his final vision of the great camel-train ambling through the desert. I had a vision of sorts myself, in the dog-days that followed my sacking. It was also of a hot place with sand and trudging people, but it was an optimistic vision that said: You will get the hell out of England for a while and do something that is *not* working in an office and *not* about planning a career struc-ture, with life insurance and pension plans and mortgages. It was a vision about having a good time instead, on the Italian Riviera or in the South China Seas, a place to escape from my dismal embrace of working life for a while, away from preening London grandees, away from people who were always monitoring your progress, like the little notary in the film with his constantly updated report (he was, I realised, a less pretty version of Phoebe), away from the whole ghastly crew that made up office life.

I thought of the sign that had sat on the library's front desk for the two months I was there, symbolising every-thing that was wrong and boring about the serious world of work. SILENCE, it had read.

'What is that terrible screaming around us,' I said to myself, 'that men call SILENCE?'

8

AFTER THE RED RAINCOAT

'Don't Look Now' (1973)

Clairvoyance – the faculty of seeing clearly in the mind what is hidden from view – is one of those subjects for which the cinema was invented. What, after all, are we doing in the dark auditorium but trying to see clearly both what is being shown on screen and what is being half-concealed? For every shot and every camera angle, there are a thousand shots and angles that would show us a different, perhaps a clearer, perspective. When Lieutenant Arbogast, the detective who goes ill-advisedly snooping around the Bates Motel in *Psycho*, walks up the fatal stairs to encounter Mrs Bates's swooping carving knife, we see her murderous attack only from above, as if we, the audience, were dangling from the rafters. We have to imagine for ourselves the face that we would see, coming towards Arbogast, at ground level.

In the right director's hands, the camera becomes an unreliable narrator, a dodgy witness. It is never on oath. It is not to be trusted. It will show you things that aren't really there. It will terrify you by hints and warnings that what *is* there is full of menace. And it's especially good at showing you things that don't exist at all in the ordinary visual world

– memories, sexual fantasies and dreams, things which play in our heads like small movies on a flat screen. The cinema can show you pictures that exist only in a character's mind, and make them as real to you as the ice-cream salesgirl in the Odeon Haymarket. It is the supreme deception of the art form.

Movies about second sight (the business partner of clairvoyance) are meat and drink to any director who likes to play with reality and the imagination. Second sight, as it's generally conceived, is about having pictures in your head, but pictures which are obscurely connected to the real world of events. The pictures usually frighten the person who possesses the clairvoyant gift, because they're premonitions of horrible future events. But I can think of only a handful of movies which deal in such potent material.

A sensitive kid, I was frightened to death (at 11) by *Night Has a Thousand Eyes*, a 1948 black-and-white movie in which Edward G. Robinson plays a bogus clairvoyant in a vaudeville show, pretending to tell people's fortunes, until the night when things go all fuzzy in his head and he suddenly yells, 'Lady in the hat! Yeah, you in the fourth row! Go on home, your house is on fire and your kid's sleeping!' I'd heard about, but never seen, an ancient 1934 movie called *The Clairvoyant*, starring Claude Rains, of *Casablanca* fame, and King Kong's dream girl Fay Wray, from which the *Thousand Eyes* movie had pinched its plot, but I could never track it down. Brian Forbes's *Seance On a Wet Afternoon* (1964) was a glum two-hour depressant about a fake medium (Kim Stanley) who persuades her husband to kidnap a child so that she can discover its whereabouts by her 'gift' and become famous. And that was about it.*

---

* David Cronenberg's *The Dead Zone* (1983), featuring a haunted-looking Christopher Walken as a teacher who wakes from a five-year

Falsity, fakeness, gloom, depression, panic, suffering – according to the movies, it's no fun being blessed with second sight. You wake up one day, and discover you've got it, like a rash, and from then onwards you can't shake it off. How awful, I used to nod, what a ghastly affliction to have, the ability to see what's going to happen in the future.

And then I woke up one day and found myself afflicted – not quite with clairvoyance, but with something close. But it wasn't a random virus-from-nowhere that did it. It was a film. It was Nicolas Roeg's 1973 psychic chiller, 'Don't Look Now'. Watching it was like watching snatches from my own life – both past and future – teasingly, hauntingly laid out before me.

It's one of the few films whose title sits inside inverted commas, as reported speech. It was originally Daphne Du Maurier's short story, with which Alan Scott and Chris Bryant, the co-scriptwriters, took several liberties. In the story, the title-line is spoken by John Baxter to his wife Laura in a Venice restaurant: 'Don't look now,' he tells her, 'but we're being stared at' – stared at by the two English sisters at a nearby table, one of whom has seen a ghost sitting between them, the ghost of their five-year-old daughter, a blonde angelic creature called Christine, who died a few weeks earlier. In the book her death is caused by meningitis, and is nobody's fault; in the film, she drowns in the family pond, and blame lies with her father, John Baxter,

---

coma after a car smash, to find he is stuck wth visions of the future, and Sam Raimi's The Gift (2000) with Cate Blanchett as a cabin-dwelling psychic in Arizona, who listlessly tells her neighbours' boring fortunes, but finds her head spinning with visions of death after she meets the local headmaster's new girlfriend, lay in the future, but my own premonitory powers couldn't anticipate them in 1973.

who assured his wife the children would come to no harm. The whole film is an expiation of guilt, a refusal to accept the nearness of tragedy, a clinging to ordinary life in the face of a hundred signs that life has something bloody awful in store for you.

I saw the film in 1973, shortly after it came out. The reviews were unanimously positive. Critics praised its high style, its enigmatic sophistication and the intense poetry of its central love scene. I knew the director's name – Nicolas Roeg, the man who'd made *Performance,* starring Mick Jagger and James Fox, and had all my generation of sensation-hungry adolescents turning somersaults of glee at its cool violence and druggy psychedelic amorality. So I went to see *'Don't Look Now'* with high expectations, at a cinema in Oxford with a girl called Juliet, a black-haired beauty from the local high school, full of English-rose rationalism and a dislike of any airy-fairy nonsense about the para-normal. At the end, she came out shuddering with the fright she'd just experienced, but was soon restored to normality by a half of lager. I came out changed for ever, unrestor-able by any magic potion.

The film starts with the death of the little girl. Over the credits, the rain beats down bleakly on the family pond where she will drown in the first five minutes. The camera zooms in, menacingly, on the boring grey water, and shifts to an image of sun-piercing shutters. Only later did I realise it was the view through the shuttered window of John and Laura's hotel room in Venice, where the sparkle of sunlight seemed to promise a glowing future beyond the impris-oning windows of the present.

But this is to race on ahead of the immediate narra-tive, which is something the film does all the time (and so shall I).

Christine and her older brother Johnny are playing in the field outside their parents' house in the country. A white horse canters by in the background. It's an idyllic setting, underscored by a childish piano theme that walks five notes up the scale and tries, and finally manages, to tip over the edge of an interrupted cadence in C major.

Just after lunch, in their fire-lit living-room, John (played by Donald Sutherland) is examining slides of the church he is scheduled to restore in Venice. One in particular holds his attention: a shot of the altar, with a stained-glass window in the background, and a pulpit on the right. John frowns and the camera tracks over to see what he's looking at. We become aware of a figure in red, a neutral back-view of someone in a red cowl, like a flamboyant monk who had oddly decided, one day, to pursue his devotions in the pulpit. John looks puzzled. We wonder (like him) what we're looking at.

The red cowl becomes, in a sudden inter-cut, the red hood of the raincoat worn by Christine, as she plays with her Action Man toy, which barks tinny orders in a woman's voice, things like 'Hold your fire!' and 'Mortar attack!' and – alarmingly, when the child goes near the pond – 'Fall in!' Then she throws a ball that lands in the pond . . .

Back in the house, John throws a pack of cigarettes to Laura (Julie Christie) on the sofa, where she is reading encyclopaedias and scientific books, looking for a solution to Christine's sweet-kid enquiry: 'If the world is round, how come a frozen pond is flat?' She comes up with an answer – Lake Ontario curves three degrees from east to west when frozen – and John says, offhandedly (but portentously), 'Nothing is what it seems.'

1971: I bought my first proper camera, a single-lens-reflex 35mm Olympus with a telephoto lens, and took it with me on walks on Clapham Common. I wasn't sure what to photograph – perhaps some moody shots of trees reflected in the water of the pond where hobby-loving men raced their home-made, petrol-driven model boats; perhaps the behaviour of amusing dogs, perhaps (shades of

Blow-Up) a pair of lovers furtively canoodling by the hedgerow. Beside the swings, I took some pictures of children mucking about in the afternoon sunshine. One of them was a sweet blonde girl, about eight, in a blue dress. I took some pictures of her through the telephoto lens, as she ran about, laughing, with her siblings. In the long lens, she was a perfect subject — innocence, gaiety, guileless joy, blue-eyed beauty. When I developed them in a friend's dark room, they were the best photos of the afternoon session, and I kept them, discarding the others. The dogs and trees and racing boats were just stuff on the Common: they meant nothing. But the studies of the little blonde girl were different. They were like blueprints of some family portraits I might take in the future.

Suddenly John Baxter knocks over a glass of water, and cuts himself. The camera flits back to Johnny riding his bike over broken glass and getting a puncture, Christine's feet are seen running over a puddle, like someone walking on water . . .

Back in the house, the first signs of alarm are signalled by a crashing cello note. We see that, on the slide with the puzzling church, a trickle of John's crimson blood has spread from the red-cowled figure in the pulpit and is stealing across the transparency. John's face is wide-eyed and stricken. He knows something is wrong. He gets up and moves to the door in a trance.

'What's the matter?' asks Laura. 'Nothing,' he says, but he — and we — know something is terribly wrong.

The camera cuts, with shocking abruptness, to Christine disappearing, face white, eyes closed, under the surface of the pond. Johnny, her brother, is running towards the house, hair flying. His father, somehow knowing the tragedy that's happening right in front of him, runs down the long garden, wades into the pond, gasps, and stands ineffectually, out of his element, for a whole minute before plunging under the water to find his little girl.

Back in the house, on the wrecked colour slide, the stream of blood has bulged and grown across the whole church interior until it explodes into a washy, pink, prawn-shaped foetus. The cello notes come crashing in again, a full orchestra in *Dies Irae* mode . . .

Even if you're watching this upsetting scene through latticed fingers, you cannot look away. Roeg slows the action down as John emerges with the red PVC coat in his arms – emerges one, two, three, four times in agonised, this-isn't-happening slow-motion – and opens his mouth to wail, a ghastly, primal, keening noise that unseats the hair on your head. On the bank, he tries to revive Christine, but he, and we, know that she's dead.

Johnny, the older child, stands anxiously by the bank, twisting a piece of broken glass in his fingers until they bleed. His father, stumbling in the mud, carries his tragic red cargo towards the house, where Laura, knowing nothing of what's happened, is coming out to look for him. The camera moves in – determinedly, like a policeman – on Ms Christie's matchless profile. Laura moves forward to the doorway, before she turns and sees the most terrible sight . . .

Her face seems to shatter as she screams. Inside, we scream with her. The memory of countless productions of *King Lear*, when the king enters with the dead Cordelia in his arms, crying 'Howl! howl, howl, howl! Are you men of stones?', cannot eclipse the image of Donald Sutherland's muddy despair as he carries the dead, blonde-haired, PVC-clad, tiny burden of his sweet, dead daughter back to the house where things were so cosily normal only minutes before.

I dwell on this opening scene at length because the whole film evolves through its extraordinary mosaic of images: of water and blood and broken glass, of the colour red, of alarming churches and the deceptive safety of home, of peering to see what's there without realising its significance, of asking questions which have no real reply, of Christine running upside-down and the upside-down world of reflections and the paranormal, of Laura's face turned away, of connection and bafflement and rejection between two people intimately conjoined; of falling, of pushing away horrible things, of the dead rising up from the grey waters of England and Venice . . . and of a filmic world in which everything is connected.

1963: The Walsh family is on holiday in Italy. Mum, Dad, my sister Madelyn and I. We come here every summer, to the Hotel San Georgio in Bellagio, near the tourist Mecca of Lake Como. The owners beam at us children and invite our parents – their regular, reliable, middle-class, nearly-English visitors – to take vermouth with them in the drawing room. There my father practises his Berlitz-guide, Italian-English charm: 'Si si, Io sono dottore di Londra, but er, originalamente, de Irlandese, capisco?' In the afternoons, we explore the surrounding towns, with their absurdly similar, joke-Italian names: Menaggio, Pelagio. In one village, our parents take us on a hike through the Stations of the Cross on an overgrown hillside. The fourteen tableaux of Christ's journey to Calvary are encased in plaster pill-boxes at intervals of 200 yards. Catholic visitors can peep through a grille in each one, to gaze at the Scourging of Jesus, the Crowning with Thorns, the Weeping Women, the three falls of the Saviour beneath his weighty Cross, and all the gory details of the final Crucifixion. It's an unusual way to spend a holiday afternoon, but there will be a tutti-frutti ice cream at the end, so Mad and I do not complain.

One afternoon, down by the lake, I go paddling. An uncertain swimmer at nine, I stick to the shallows, venturing out only until the cold Como waters creep up to my waist. Suddenly, a couple of local rowdies start a water fight. They and their friends splash each other with thuggish abandon, scooping surges of lakewater over their pals' teenage heads. I find myself caught up in it, an innocent foreign bystander, and back away from the fight. But I'm facing the shore, trying to see where my family has got to, and I'm stupidly backing into the deeper waters of Lake Como. My feet lose their footing as the lake shelves suddenly down, and I disappear beneath the water. Lake Como has no tides or treacherous currents, but it has secret angles and declivities, and I have stumbled into one. I come up, mouth full of water, lungs fighting for air, only to encounter the Italian roughnecks redoubling their attack. Someone's elbow knocks me back under the lake again, deeper this time. My eyes are closed in a sudden pressure of concentration, then open again — and I know I'm in trouble. Down here in the slumberous green, everything is foggy, occluded, terribly, terminally quiet. It occurs to me that I may have to stay down here — in this horrible, green-shaded, lung-bursting nowhere — for ever. My arms lash out as I break the surface again and I try to yell, but I'm too weak and too desperate to make an effective noise. Any second now, I will be going down for the third time . . .

Then a large masculine arm scoops down and hoicks me out of the watery grave. Some Italian parent, used to seeing boys in trouble, has yanked me up, one hand under my right armpit, in the most casual life-saving manoeuvre. 'Hey,' he says, 'You occay?' I cannot speak because my lungs are full of lake. Instead, I goggle at him, as he walks me up through the shallows to the beach where my mother is standing, scanning the breakers. I fall down beside her, heaving with relief, making pathetic choking noises. Later on, perhaps out of guilt, my mother tells the story to the Hotel San Georgio owners. 'I saw that he was in trouble,' she confides, 'so I waded in and carried him out in my arms.' The whopping lie comes between us for days. I nearly drowned, while she was standing around in her Irish-matron swimsuit, and I will find it damn-bloody hard (I'm not used to swearing) to forgive her.

Only a heart of stone could not be moved by the nightmare of the opening scene of '*Don't Look Now*'. And only a moribund intellect could not be intrigued by the interlacing, flickering images which will recur, tantalisingly, for the next

100 minutes. John and Laura go to Venice, he to work on the restoration of an ancient church, she to try to recover from her loss. When we next see them, he is a professional man in a three-piece suit and serious blue overcoat, arguing in halting Italian with local artisans about the placing of statues – and later, about the matching of mosaic shards that will restore a crumbled Renaissance saint's head on the church's mural. Laura is full of brave resilience, playing a supportive wife with too little to do except write letters to her son (at boarding school back in England) and meet her husband's business connections. But that's when they meet the two sisters in a *trattoria*.

The weird sisters, hand in hand – we seem to have strayed into *Macbeth* – are heading into the Gents lavatory when Laura goes to help them. One is blind but psychic, the other sighted, but temporarily blinded by a speck of dust (a nod to *Brief Encounter,* perhaps) when a gust of dirty wind blows through the French window into the restaurant. Laura helps them find the Ladies, and that's where her life changes again. The blind woman Heather (Hilary Mason), her thrillingly mad face with its opaque, shuttered cataracts reflected in three mirrors, tells Laura not to be sad because she has seen Christine sitting between her parents, laughing and happy, but trying to communicate with them.

Laura is appalled but fascinated; her troubled face in the bathroom mirror is full of anxiety mingled with hope, appalled at hearing about her dead child but desperate to believe the woman. A high, whining violin note accompanies Laura back to her table where she faints in cataclysmic slow-motion, bringing food, furniture, cloths, plates, menus and wine carafe crashing to the floor, as John will, in due course, bring a dangling cradle crashing a hundred feet from the church's upper balcony.

In the recovery ward for fainting wives (actually a children's hospital), she tells her husband that Christine is still with them, happy and contented on the Other Side, and keen to bring a message – some kind of warning – to them. John, one of nature's sceptics, is appalled by this mumbo-jumbo, but has to admit his wife's condition is wonderfully improved. 'Seeing is believing,' he says – a throwaway line that's significantly different from his 'Nothing is what it seems' in the opening scene.

This is John Baxter's problem. He doesn't *want* to see, doesn't want to believe and doesn't even know what he *is* seeing. The imagery of blindness turns up everywhere in *'Don't Look Now'*. From the title onwards, looking and seeing, inspecting and turning away, eyes that are blind or oblivious, eyes (or the camera lens) straining to make out an image or a vision, are vital, repeated effects. John and Laura's central, disabling problem is about second sight, and whether there may be something to it. Laura is entranced to think the blind woman can see Christine, even though Laura is herself blind to her daughter's presence. She longs to see into this other world. John, rational and apparently clear-sighted, refuses to have anything to do with it. He is blind to its appeal. But he is spookily gifted with premonitions of disaster. He is stuck with visions of everything going wrong . . .

1967: The Walsh family are back in Italy, on another holiday. This time we're in Florence, of which I remember nothing of the artworks, the gorgeous churches, the Duomo or the Piazza, but I sure as hell remember the dog. I was thirteen, I was fond of animals, but the only pets we were allowed at home were tortoises and an Indian Hill mynah bird called Nicky. My cousins in Ireland had a huge wolfhound called Ushna, which I longed to kidnap. Deprived of a dog of my own, I petted any stray mongrel that came my way, fondled any small yappy terriers I found tied to metal lamp-posts outside supermarkets, paused to pass the time of day with any lolloping hounds that went by my home on Battersea Rise.

In Florence, dogs nearly did for me. My parents and sister were wandering down one of the sunlit streets that were full of shops selling tourist geegaws. At thirteen, I didn't need to hold any grown-up's hand any more, and halfway down the street I left my sister's side because I'd spotted a sweet dachshund in an alleyway, gnawing a rubber ball. I went over to pat it.

The dog had no interest in anything except its ball. So I picked up the ball and bounced it a few times, and the dog responded. The ball bounced off the cobblestones and disappeared down the dingy alleyway — and the dog followed it. I followed the dog, thoughtlessly, and tried to find its ball in the shady gloom of a courtyard, set about with red geraniums in earthenware pots. 'Here boy,' I called. 'Where have you gone?'

Whereupon, something horrible happened. A different dog, a snarling mastiff four times the size of my sausage-dog, appeared from nowhere like a belligerent security man (I'd evidently strayed into private property), bared its teeth and growled a warning. All empathy with the canine breed disappeared from my heart. Down a side-alley in Florence, I'd encountered Cerberus. I turned my back, and it started to bark, its muzzle jutting upwards like a miniature Mussolini. I ran. It ran behind me, snapping at my heels. I ran as if the hounds of Hell were after me. I had no thought except to get away from this enraged, murderous bouncer. I ran back down the alley, out into the harsh sunlight of the Florentine shopping street I'd strayed from — and ran straight into the road.

There was a squealing of brakes as I ran into the path of a procession of Fiats and Vespa motorcycles. The car closest to me slammed on its brakes and slewed sideways, and I cannoned into its front wing. As I rested there in shock, another local car slammed into the back of it, and the impact lifted me clean off the bonnet, banging my chin and bouncing me into the gutter. Unseen cars honked and hooted. The Fiat's owner rolled down his window and shouted something along the lines of, 'Will you for fuck's sake look where you're going?'

I had a small collapse, a juvenile swoon, there in the roadway. I was surrounded by Italians, seizing my shoulders, scolding me for jaywalking ('Whaddayou, crazy or something?'). I tried to explain that I'd been running from the most frightening dog in the world. They shook their heads, and smote their brows theatrically. I'd nearly died.

Jesus Christ, I'd nearly died twice, once down a back street, once in the main road. The world was suddenly full of awful back streets. And when you ran away from the sudden fright of what you found there, you nearly died anyway . . .

Back in the film, a marvellous scene is played out in St Mark's church. Laura has come to say a prayer for Christine. Laura is, we infer from her husband's joshing surprise, only an occasional believer. She has suddenly got religion because of her brush with the after-life. She shuts her eyes in prayer, then gets up and lights six candles in memory of Christine. As John waits for her to finish her casual devotions, he glances around the church – and sees the more dumpy of the old sisters at the end of a procession of tourists. Reluctant to meet either of the barmy old ladies, he turns and drops to his knees, eyes shut in fake prayer. He is like a kid, shutting his eyes and refusing to admit there's anyone there.

Ahead of him, a ghastly vision appears – the smiling, rapturous face of the blind woman, Heather, as she passes in front of his unseeing eyes, trailing one hand along the iron grille. You can imagine, for a moment, that, though blind, she sees him. But maybe she's just a mad old soul in ecstasy, gliding along the bars in the grip of religious dementia, like my parents' co-religionists back in Clapham Common on Saturday evenings.

In the original screenplay, John kneels and pretends to pray because he sees Heather's face appearing before him. In the film, he has no idea she's there – we, the audience, are the ones who shiver and recoil from her crazy, knowing smile and nodding head. We do not allow ourselves the luxury of shutting our eyes and turning our faces away. We want to engage with whatever lies behind those creepy, milky cataracts.

We aren't just seeing things from his point of view; we're seeing *more* than him, because we're not rejecting the truth of experience as John does. When he meets Laura, and realises they're late for an appointment with the bishop who has commissioned the church restoration, they run out of the church. A gust of wind, caused by their departure, blows out one of the six candles Laura has lit. The smoke inscribes a contemptuous squiggle in the air. We know suddenly that there's no hope of salvation after all. We're ahead of the action. We know someone is doomed.

The fantastic love scene in *'Don't Look Now'* shocked me in 1973. I'd never seen anything so explicit, so startlingly athletic, so frankly interlocked and (not to put too fine a point on it) so triumphantly focused on Julie Christie's bony spine and phenomenal bottom. It was so real, many cinema-goers assumed for years (wrongly) that it was a real-life fuck rather than a bit of intense acting. To me, it went beyond acting, beyond the world of studio make-believe and the stylised clinches that I was used to seeing. It was the real thing, made the more real by the fact that the love-making proceeded in tiny flickering glimpses of sweating bodies, spreading limbs and lazy, voluptuous rollings-about, intercut with tiny flashes of John and Laura getting dressed after-wards, before going out to dinner.

The bravura intercutting seemed, to some people at the time, more a device for escaping the shears of the British Board of Film Censors than a legitimate piece of artistry, but things became clearer in hindsight. In a film of a million interconnections, Nicolas Roeg had to show, to the most *verité* limits, the interconnectedness of the central couple. When they're about to be fatally driven apart through a dispute that's about things of the mind – the unconscious, the belief-oriented, the metaphysical – he had to indicate the intimate physicality, the urgent need, that bound the couple together. And to show the amazing vulnerability of flesh without a protective armour on it.

It's a life-enhancing few minutes in a movie that otherwise takes a distressingly entropic view of human life. It restores John and Laura to their sexual identities. When it's over, Laura preens and titivates herself in the mirror and pulls at a single curl around her temple, transformed from the gaunt, flinching face in the mirror of the *trattoria* where she listened to the blind woman talking about her daughter's ghost. You realise it's the first time they've made love since the tragedy. John, waiting for her to finish getting ready, reclines on the bed, sips a pre-prandial whisky and bares his teeth in a wolfish grimace – a long way from the nervy, uncertain figure who knocked a glass of water over the mystifying slide in the first scene and realised too late that his daughter was drowning.

After being the Bereaved Couple, then the Professional Restorer looking after the Neurotic Dreamer, after being awkwardly cast as Hospital Patient and Primary Carer, they are now back being man and woman.

1983: I went to Venice for the first time, with my girlfriend, Carolyn. We were young, we were in love. We rented a hotel room near the Academia, a first-floor room of monastic simplicity, with a bed, a wardrobe, a basin, and a balcony that overlooked a leafy square. The balcony had two white plastic chairs on which you could sit in post-coital silence with slugs of duty-free Scotch at 1 a.m., listening to the sound of a drunken saxophone player leaning against one of the trees, out of sight, playing 'Somewhere Over the Rainbow' and gettting the middle passage all wrong. By day we walked everywhere and looked at the Tintorettos, the Rialto Bridge, the stone lions, the horses of San Marco, the gondola impresarios murmuring 'gondolagondolagondola' in their lascivious, liquid monotone. Three days into the holiday, we came out of a trattoria at midnight one evening, and decided to walk along the bank of the Giudecca, the wider and less romantic of Venice's two main canals. The wall on our left was covered with boards and scaffolding, but we persevered. To the right, across the wide plopping water, huge alien cabin-cruisers from Greece and Turkey lined the far shore, their expensive lights winking feebly in the dark night. On our left, the wall opened from time to time to reveal the obscure lineaments of a vast white mass – the Santa Maria della Salute church that looms its pristine magnificence over the Grand Canal – before returning to its scaffolded nothingness. Carolyn was keen to go back. This walk was leading us into a builder's backyard of grot and puddles and obscure hostility. But I knew there must be something at the end.

And there was. In one of those perfect moments, like the climax of some romantic movie, the wall fell away, we walked round a concrete headland – and suddenly there was the whole of Venice stretched out before us. 'Come over here,' I said. 'I've found the real world.'

We'd discovered, serendipitously, the point where the Giudecca and the Grand Canal converge and Venice is arrayed before you – St Mark's Piazza and the Doge's Palace rearing up on the left, the Lido in the distance, and on the right, the tip of the Giudecca island. It was a heart-stopping panorama of Venice as Byron might have seen it the day he impetuously leapt into the Grand Canal. And there was this perfect thing before us, the last thing I expected to see: a simple park bench that could accommodate two lovers, with a single street-lamp looming over it, in an unconscious echo of the lobby-advertisement for Woody Allen's Manhattan – two figures on a dark bench, with the lit-up Brooklyn Bridge rearing magnificently behind them. Carolyn and I took our seats on the bench and gazed at the most amazing view we'd ever seen. It was just a bench, a night and a view, but it seemed like an affirmation of love.

In the days that followed, we walked and talked from morning to night, and I wondered if we should get married. We wandered through the back streets on the Rialto, got lost in dismal alleyways, and let the strange, harsh spirit of Venice guide our steps. The more we walked, the more Venice became a city full of alarm. Windows would bang shut as we drifted through the back streets. Haunted, stony faces glared through metal grilles like the faces of prisoners. A freak storm on the main piazza left the surface outside Florian's café gleaming with inches of water — the famous aqua alta that's an attractive feature of Venice in winter but is a sloshy pain in midsummer. And once, an apparition came and went in front of me.

We'd walked on to a bridge over one of the back canals, one of a dozen minor bridges that ran, like rungs on a ladder, across the trail of dazzling water. We stood in the middle and contemplated the washing lines and window-boxes of geraniums on the far wall.

Then I saw a man stride on to the next bridge but one, a tall, striking chap in a long black coat and a tall hat. He was alone, but he walked with an awful, sacerdotal gravity. He gained the middle of the bridge, stopped, turned and looked at me. Though he was fifty yards away, I got the impression that he was displeased to see me there, a noncey tourist in my summer T-shirt and jeans. He stood very still, black-draped and looming like a six-foot-six crow, and he stared right at me. A shiver ran down my spine. I looked at Carolyn.

'Don't look now,' I said, 'but there's a modern-day doge eyeballing me.'

She looked round. 'Where?'

'Just over —'

But the man had gone. He had vanished across the bridge. He must have covered twenty yards in three seconds. I looked at the empty bridge, and beyond it to the next bridge, where tourists were posing for photographs.

'He was just there, for God's sake,' I said. 'I saw him clear

291

as day. He was standing just there, unmoving, glaring at me.'

'You're paranoid,' said Carolyn. 'It's some kind of religious guilt thing, from going into all these churches.' And we moved on. But I looked back at the one bridge among the twelve that was empty of strollers, and all I saw was a man-shaped absence in the dazzling sunny morning, and I shivered again, like someone who'd been given a warning.

The film deepens in texture, as the location shots of out-of-season Venice suggest a place of random mystery and infinite hostility, where windows slam shut, or alarming householders in sweaty vests watch blankly as John and Laura walk by. Pigeons fly up in small, avian explosions. Dark canals harbour swimming rats. A stroll home from a restaurant pitches the couple into a circular, Dantesque world where every canal and bridge conspires to pretend that this must be the way to your hotel. Venice becomes a place of mad shadows and Stygian gloom where John glimpses, for a half-second, a flash of red coat along the back-water canals. Your eyes can't adjust to the light and dark quickly enough for you to know what you're seeing, but you peer and strain into whatever darkness the camera allows you, anxious about what you *might* see. The camera pulls slowly towards something – and, when a flash of light from the reflected water illuminates the dark corner of the screen, you see a little red figure. It seems to be jumping, like our memory of Christine playing in the garden, but it's jumping in and out of boats moored in a backwater canal, and fleeing from a terrible noise that sounds like someone being murdered. Is it trying to get away? Is it Christine, back from the dead to warn them?

John finds the street that will lead to the hotel. He calls out to his wife, 'It's OK – I've found the real world.' But sadly, for him, there is no 'real world' any more that doesn't include the back streets world, the dark waters and the cataracted eyes of Heather and the flash of red in the threatening gloom.

It's part of his world now. And because we have become absorbed in the looking-to-see-what's-there, we are stuck with it too. There's a Venice of eye-piercing sunlight and gliding gondolas, and another Venice where suspicious men ask what you're doing snooping around, and bodies are pulled out of the canal, a Venice of peeling terracotta and sickly, caramel-coloured walls where nothing is safe or secure, even the city itself (John and Laura walk past 'Venice in Peril' signs), where the furniture at their hotel is covered in dustsheets like funeral shrouds, the lift door says 'Closed' and the manager seems to be always telling them, as politely as possible, to leave.

It becomes a place of personal threat. Laura attends a séance and learns that Christine is trying to warn them to leave Venice as soon as possible. She and John have a blazing row. Then they're rung up in the middle of the night to hear that their son, Johnny, has been concussed in an accident. Laura leaves for England at 5 a.m., leaving her husband in the city that's suddenly become a hostile, dangerous land.

The trouble is that John Baxter is a man trying to do the impossible. He is trying to hold back Fate. His job as a conservor of churches means he is always trying to reverse the processes of time and decay, to halt the inevitable, to stop the clocks that are busily ticking away the stability of Venice and the survival of the flesh and the ageing of children and the death of us all. While the old sisters realise that he has 'the gift' of second sight and can foresee the future, he refuses to buy any of it. 'Our child is *dead*, Laura,' he cries to his distraught wife. 'Dead, dead, dead, dead, dead! She does not come peeping with messages from beyond the fucking *grave*.' But the more he pushes away the fateful, the suggestive and the minatory, the more it comes back and attacks him – like the horrible gargoyle he tries to maneouvre into position outside St Nicholas's church, that seems to lean upon him with baleful weight as if trying to crush or unbalance him.

Most alarming is the scaffolding scene, when John visits the church and climbs a swaying ladder to hang precariously in a rickety wooden cradle, while comparing mosaic fragments with the decaying mosaics on the church wall. It's a dizzying climb; it seems like a drop of two or three hundred feet. Our point of view moves from above to below, so we watch John climbing up like a pirate in the rigging, then watch his ascent from below. Beside him on a rickety, glass-topped cradle, a Venetian workman discusses whether the mosaics match. All he has to do is hold the new pieces up against the decayed jigsaw of the original.

We (and the bishop) watch him anxiously from below. There's no spooky music on the soundtrack, no sound except the creaking of pulley ropes and straining wood. The camera comes up above him, again, looking down benignly as he works away matching mosaics, trying to make things better. And then he comes crashing down, hanging on for dear life, as the dangling cradle disintegrates in a violent cascade of ceramic bits, pots and pans, tool-kit stuff, wood, rope and building paraphernalia. But *why* does everything come crashing down? John Baxter himself has no idea. The other workers would write it off as an industrial accident. But we in the audience know why it's happened. We watched it happen. It was a single plank, teetering on the edge of some higher-up scaffolding, that suddenly dipped downwards and fell like a wooden missile through the glass screen of Baxter's cradle, bringing the whole rickety structure plunging down.

I've watched the film umpteen times, and still can't work out *why* it happened. A malevolent plank? A sudden freak pull of gravity? In the film it's incontrovertibly, *visually* true that the lump of wood suddenly has a life of its own and is the occasion of his near-death. You have to conclude that, in filmic terms, almost anything would have done. When you're looking for a symbol of Fate working its relentless way with a man's life, any random detail (plank, child's ball, photographic slide) will suffice. All Nicolas Roeg did was demonstrate, quite casually, that when a character has *had* it, he might as well not leave home to walk down the street, because a flowerpot will blow off a roof and land on his head. No matter how ingeniously you make your life perfect and unassailable, no matter what ramshackle construction you put together, of secular hope and religious belief and socially-ordained moral system, all in the service of persuading yourself that you will live a good life and not die – none of it matters when Destiny comes a-calling. You think it's going to be easy, saving the mosaic (and the church, and Venice, and the world) but it isn't. For no particular reason, down will come baby, cradle and all.

August, 1987: Carolyn is about to give birth. Our first-born. Her waters break at six in the morning and she emerges from the bathroom with the stylish understatement, 'I think something's happening,' as amniotic fluid courses down her legs. She is so calm. I am full of nameless forebodings. We flee outside. The Fiat has developed a flat tyre overnight. We summon a taxi, and spread a copy of the Independent *over the back seat. It proves surprisingly absorbent. At the hospital, we're told labour could take hours, and we should all relax. Carolyn is hooked up to a huge machine covered in winking lights. Electrodes and random, spaghetti-like loops of wiring twist in and out of her body. We pass a whole day of inconsequential tests in the gloomy Victorian pile of the West London Hospital. Conversation between us hits a* Waiting For Godot-*like antiphon of reassurance and satire. At 7 p.m., I am sent away to have dinner with Carolyn's Aunt Robin, a large, bibulous Australian grandmother who feeds me dry martinis and a salad liberally garnished with her own-brand, reeking vinaigrette.*

At 8.30, I realise the baby could have been born while I've been sitting here regaling myself. I guiltily rush back to hospital. In the ward, the expectant mother is grumpy and bored and alarmed by what seems a commotion in her bowels. 'I get this feeling that I'm about to have a massive attack of diarrhoea,' she says. 'It comes and goes, every few minutes . . .' We suddenly realise these are contractions, that the baby is due any minute.

We call the nurse. Carolyn is told that the cervix isn't dilating as it should, and everything goes on hold once again. But how can the baby not be emerging? The waters that have buoyed up the growing homunculus for nine months have gone. What is the kid waiting for? Christmas? The nurses are mystified. So are we. Nothing is as it should be.

At 11 p.m., befuddled by Aunt Robin's vodka bracers, I am told to hit the sack in an adjoining room. It's been the longest day I can remember. But everything's OK, isn't it? The nurses have seen it all a thousand times. The atmosphere of joshing encouragement will see us all through . . .

At 5 a.m. I'm roughly awakened from a dream of Hell's Angels roaring towards me on tiny infant motorcycles. There is a crisis. The baby inside Carolyn has gone into distress. It's running out of oxygen. It is aching to be born, but cannot engage its head between Carolyn's slender thighs. There will have to be an emergency Caesarean. 'You must sign this document, saying you agree to this course of action,' says a businesslike theatre technician, 'no matter what the consequences.' Do I have a choice? The atmosphere surrounding the birth, which was once so larky and carefree, has become charged with alarm and danger. This is now about life and death. I am told to put on a green theatre gown, paper hat, plastic clogs and gangster mask and come into the operating theatre. No thanks, I reply, I'd rather not. This isn't birth-canal, sing-a-long-a-delivery stuff any more. This is a major operation.

'No no,' they cry. 'It's just a small lateral incision across the abdomen. You will sit at one end, reassuring your wife, while we bring the baby out at the other.'

There is no getting out of it. At the back of my mind, a terrible fear is sounding chords in my heart, that neither Carolyn nor the non-emerging child is going to get out of this alive.

Twenty minutes later, twenty minutes of dream-time, like watching a movie where you don't understand the dialogue and you've lost the narrative logic, Sophie Matilda Rose was born. She was hoicked up out of a morass of blood and guts, and brandished before me, yelling and fantastically pissed-off. As I looked at my first-born, through a sudden film of tears, I noticed she was covered in a white grease, like someone who'd just tried to swim the English Channel. Like a child just rescued from drowning.

Two-thirds of the way through the film, I was hooked into the screen in a way I couldn't remember being hooked before. It was uncomfortable, but oddly bracing, like looking at a disaster taking place in a high wind that blows your hair back and flays your cheeks, but only makes you widen your eyes and refuse to blink.

The film becomes a headlong race to destruction. John, in a *vaporetto*, sees the extraordinary sight of his wife standing on a funeral launch with the two eldritch sisters. She is supposed to be in England, looking after Johnny. He thinks Laura must still be in Venice, abducted by the witchy women. He asks the hotel manager if she's returned. *Non.* He goes to the police, and gets no help. The cop in charge doodles on the (fantastically inept) Identikit pictures of the old women, as if their actual appearance were of no consequence anyway. He asks, 'What ees eet you fear, Mister Baster?', a question loaded with hostility and portentousness. He behaves as if John is responsible for Laura's disappearance, and fears being found out, and he sends a cop to trail him. John fears that Laura has been done in by the strange old women.

What about us in the audience? What ees eet that we fear?

We are becoming afraid on his behalf. We can see, behind the reassuring physical solidity of Donald Sutherland, in his long blue coat and sensible, red-orange muffler, a glimpse of somebody starting to panic. The omnicompetent church-restorer and statue-wrestler, the sexual athlete and geometry-of-space thinker, has started to fall apart. We learned from Laura that, because he had reassured his wife that the children would be safe playing in the garden by the pond, he's responsible for Christine's death. While trying to manhandle the statue into place, nose to nose, he looked like a man being mugged by a gargoyle. When he sat for hours at a bar, waiting for Laura to emerge from the *séance*, he drank enough to make himself sick ('I haven't thrown up in ten years,' he groaned). Now he is in a maelstrom of uncertainty, struggling to cope with the all-too-real image of the funeral gondola, unable to rationalise its terrible portent.

1989: I am bathing Sophie at home in South Wimbledon. She is two-and-a-bit, getting longer every day. She hates having her hair washed, but it has to be done. I tell her to calm down, that she will smell and feel gorgeous and clean and pure and re-born afterwards in her pyjamas, and that, if she doesn't make a fuss, we will read about the scandalously subversive Little Rabbit Foo-Foo in bed afterwards, and will act out all the parts – the goblins, the earthworms, the Good Fairy, the whole dramatis personae. She decides to be good, and lets me lather up her blonde mane without complaint, even when my fingers scratch away at her tiny cerebellum. Then she leans back in the water, resting on her arms for the first time. Without being told to, she leans her soapy head back into the bathwater and shakes it, so gently, so slowly in the clouding wave, you could swear she had decided to enjoy being immersed in the first-ever element of life on earth. My right hand reaches down to support her head and massage her hair, teasing out all the soapy penumbra, turning the water into a Cleopatran milk bath. As I lean over, a brief film of water glides over her eyes and mouth. She shakes them away and, half-submerged, opens her eyes as if to make sure she is not drowning. But she knows she's safe and her eyes close again — then they open and look straight at me, as if to say, 'Who are you? Why are you doing this?' Her eyes are unfrightened, calm, indulgent. She has suddenly discovered, aged two, that having someone wash your hair is an experience based on trust. I look down at her, and at the watery film that is flooding away from her face like liquid fingers caressing her cheeks, and I gaze into her open eyes and suddenly realise that hers is the most beautiful face I've ever looked down on in my whole life.

John goes in search of the women, who are duly arrested by the police, but realises they are innocent as Easter lambs. He gets a phone call from the school in England: Johnny is restored to health and no longer stricken with concussion (unlike, you might say, his father). And in a classic directorial tease, Roeg plays with our concerns about what has happened to Laura.

The headmaster's hockey-sticksy-voiced wife, Mandy Babbage (a Penelope Keith name to go with a Penelope Keith role), is all calm reassurance, but the camera pulls back like a conjuror when she says, 'But I expect . . . I expect you'd like to have a word with your wife, Mr Baxter.' We see Julie Christie on the phone, and hear her loving, everything's-all-right-darling voice, but the scene is shrouded in foggy obscurity. As John tells her about the vision on the funeral barge, and she cuts across his voice to talk about airline timetables, the camera closes in on her mouth speaking into the phone. Suddenly, she could be anywhere. Something is not right. Behind John, a long dark shadow is looming, a shadow that seems to keep switching sides every time we see his face. Absurdly, he asks, 'Laura — where *are* you now?' (she's obviously in England, at the school) and we see her sliced in two by the camera, with only the left side of her face visible. It's very unsettling. 'Nothing is what is seems' – John's offhand remark from the first scene – comes winging back to us. We are as confused as John Baxter about what he is hearing, but we have at least the advantage of being able to see Laura; that image, again, of his lack of clear-sightedness at a crucial moment.

1996: Our son's school rings the newspaper where Carolyn and I work, to say: 'I'm terribly sorry, but Max has had an accident.' We are not at home, in the middle of the night, like the Baxters, but the shock still jars, coming in the hours of sunlight, with all the ordinary things of the work environment buzzing about us.

I grip the telephone. 'What kind of an accident?'

'He was in the gym, where the children were jumping over a wooden horse, and they were told to do a starfish jump, with their arms spread out. I'm afraid your little boy didn't break his fall in time, and we think he's fractured his elbow. But the doctor's here, and he's sure it will be perfectly easy to fix, and he'll be as right as rain . . .'

We left work, headed for the school and took the stricken Max (aged five) to the hospital in Dulwich. He was a little concussed and enfeebled, and had to endure several hours in the Casualty section surrounded by bleeding GBH victims and detoxing junkies. And when he emerged from the operation to re-set his elbow, his arm was on the wrong way round. If he flexed it, his elbow stuck out upside down, like a freak-show performer. It was a shock, to see my gorgeous, golden-haired son with a back-to-front limb. For years afterwards he has brandished his funny arm with pride, enjoying the discomfiture of strangers.

The music, meanwhile (by Pino Donaggio), has developed into a character of its own. The early scenes were full of the simplicity of childhood: that haunting little piano figure of five consecutive notes – dah-dah-datta-dah – to evoke the figure of Christine in the garden. A long thin violin note played behind Laura's realisation that she might be reunited with her dead daughter. After the film's halfway mark, a grander, more operatic score pushed its way into my consciousness: threatening Wagnerian cello strains accompanied the retrieval of murdered bodies from the Grand Canal, a lush sub-*Love Story* theme carried the funeral barge before John's horrified eyes. And in the final reel, bleak, wintry strings *à la* Sibelius give way to terrible noises, booming echoes, howling feral growls, throaty gurglings and crashing piano discords, as John wanders around a Venice that's increasingly empty and unwelcoming. There's something fugue-like, too, about the way the colour red invades the dirty ochres and faded purples of the Venetian cityscape. The red of the Bishop's night-light, the red woolly hats of people in the crowd as they witness another dead body, Christine's red PVC coat as her image is summoned up again and again. Whatever is happening to John, the production designer and the musical arranger have it in for him as well . . .

And so we are pulled inexorably towards the frightful ending. Laura is returning to Venice on the 11 p.m. flight. John is with the ugly sisters when Heather, the blind clairvoyant, starts to hyperventilate and to scream warnings. He leaves – just as Laura is making her way from the airport to the sisters' hotel – and sees the little red-coated figure reflected in the canal. At last, he is going to confront this tantalising will o' the wisp. He sets off in pursuit. Laura, meanwhile, meets the sisters, and hears that he has plunged off into the night. 'Fetch him back,' pleads the blind but staring Heather, at her most frightening. 'Make him *not go*.' And Laura runs off into this final, tripartite chase. Through alleys, canal-ways, huge iron gates and dim, smoky courtyards, the little figure scurries ahead, followed by John's long strides and Laura's panicky footsteps. Even at this late stage, mysteries pile up. Why does John, having followed the red coat through the enormous gates, turn round and lock them? And why, when Laura reaches the gates and stretches her arms out in frustration through the bars, does she scream 'Darlings!' in the plural, when (as far as we know) she is only chasing her husband?

1999: On holiday in Italy, I take my youngest child, Clementine, aged four, into the swimming pool in our Tuscan retreat near Florence. She cannot swim. But she is in my arms, and is therefore safe. We glide about in the shallow end. Her arms are about my neck. On the surrounding bank, Sophie (now twelve) lolls on a sun-bed, reading an unsuitably grown-up chick-lit novel, Max (now almost eight) blows up a li-lo and shows off his peculiar arm to our holidaying friends. In the pool, my tiny daughter kicks and splashes in my manly grasp.

Suddenly, I take a step that sends us over the pool's steeply angled floor. We are falling over, Clementine and I, and because she is clutched tightly around me, I can't strike my arms out, to swim us out of trouble. I cannot stop myself from falling and bringing my baby girl with me. Her arms are trapping my arms. My legs are kicking frantically, trying to balance us, but it's no good – we are both falling sideways, under the water.

In a sudden impulse to save the child while righting myself, I grab her under the armpits and fling her through the air into the shallow end – but the shallow end is still deep enough to drown her. Clementine disappears beneath the water, her first total immersion in nothingness, her first experience of being out of her depth, unable to swim, her mouth full of chlorinated water. On the bank I can hear Carolyn shouting, 'Get her out of there.'

Sophie has slid into the swimming pool and is standing smiling as if to say, 'Dad – he's so incorrigible. Ducking the baby who can't swim . . .'

Seconds pass by like hours. I yell, 'Sophie, get her out of the water!' And she plucks Clementine to safety. Her eyes are not (thank God) shut like Christine Baxter's as she disappeared under

the pond. Clementine's eyes are open and full of outrage and she
yells at her father with an expression I will never forget – a look
of furious pain at being flung away and abandoned in the water.

Minutes later, she was all right again. I was full of apologies
and explanations and what-could-I-do excuses. My four-year-old
sweetheart was OK; luckily she'd been surrounded by her mother
and sister. But something terrible had passed between us. I had
abandoned her (or so it must have seemed) to her fate. I had liter-
ally thrown her away. And I knew that, somewhere deep in her
heart, she would never forgive me.

So we move into the final confrontation – the pursuit,
through hellish smoke and infernal gloom, of the little figure
in red who comes to rest in a ruined church, with a high
choir loft – perhaps the one John Baxter was looking at in
the colour slide right back in the opening scenes. At close
quarters at last, John moves slowly to confront it. What is
he expecting? What are we expecting? If it *isn't* his daughter
– a ghostly revenant – who or what the hell is it? 'It's all
right,' he tells it (in English, significantly). 'I'm a friend. I
won't hurt you . . .'

And then the figure turns – and even before it's fully
turned round, John's face has frozen in horror, as he realises
he has walked into a trap, and is meeting the murderer on
the loose whose victims have been fished out of the canals
throughout the movie.

Apart from the apparition of Quint in *The Innocents*, it
was the biggest celluloid shock I ever experienced – the
face of Adelina Poerio, a hideous female dwarf with an
expression of pure, terminal malevolence, smiling with an
awful, knowing, sidelong rictus. She walks forward with a
jerky, lopsided roll, and smiles some more while shaking
her head, just slightly, from side to side, as if she's saying,
'No, no, no, no, you silly man, you shouldn't have come
here, you should have left things alone, you should have

read the signs, you didn't want to meet me, you didn't *have* to meet me, and now that you have, I'm afraid I'm going to have to kill you.' Whereupon, with awful deliberateness, she draws a long knife from her coat pocket. Roeg boldly takes the camera round the side of the action, so what happens is seen from our point of view, and we watch, like horrified spectators, the awful simplicity with which she reaches up and draws the long knife across Baxter's throat. He offers no resistance, as if frozen with the realisation that he had it coming all along. As if he's powerless to stop an inevitable sequence reach its grisly, inevitable end.

The music, instead of going into horror-spasm, hits a high point of romantic lushness, as though in mock celebration of a life that's pointlessly over. There begins a sequence of flashbacks that's a calm, stately editing of John Baxter's life through key seconds of the movie you've just seen: the colour-slide of the church, with its trickle of John's blood that resolves into a prawny foetus, the broken glass under Johnny's bike, the stained glass in the church, John's and Laura's bodies sexually intertwined, the battle with the looming gargoyle, the sea of blood that now floods the floor behind John's head, John hanging from a collapsed cradle, Christine's sweet, eternally-lost face, the dying man's kicking foot, the cops on the canal balcony looking for clues, the embracing gargoyle, the blind cataracts of Heather, rain on the family pond, the extinguishing of the church candles, the Bishop waking with a start at 1 a.m. and seeing his red night-light glowing with menace, the dwarf turning round, the disaffected detective, the sparkling light on the lido, the sight of John's funeral procession, the raising of the corpse from the lagoon . . . until we're back in the present, staring at John's kicking-foot death agonies, gradually slowing to nothing as his blood trickles down a blank and dirty Venetian wall . . .

So we understand, at last, that the image of his own death

had been waiting for him all through the film, buried in clues and hints and nasty secrets. Everything that was going to happen was prefigured in these images, from the moment he looked into the slides of St Nicholas's church and felt something was wrong with his daughter. Everything that was to come – bereavement, Venice, the sisters, the church, the statues and mosaics, the falling cradle, the chase after the red raincoat – had been staring him in the face all the time, along with the awful truth that everything might have been avoided if only he'd heeded the warnings of a blind woman in a ladies' loo, and got out of Venice while he had the chance.

John has spent the film uncertainly pitched between memories of the past and bewildering echoes from the future. And now, when it has all come together at last, it is too late for him to do anything but marvel, as his blood drips down the wooden church screen, at how beautifully interlinked his life had been.

The film closes with the funeral procession, the one he foresaw from the *vaporetto*, the one he didn't believe in because nobody can foresee their own death. And as I watched it, overwhelmed with feelings of *déjà vu*, I wondered about the significance of John's 'gift' of second sight. It's not strictly relevant to the plot – he could have seen the little flashes of red raincoat in Venice without any gift of clairvoyance, he could have decided to chase it at the end from simple curiosity. And you also wonder if it's all been a punishment that he half-imagined and half-dreaded. Everything we see, in this cat's cradle of images, happened since his daughter drowned – and, as we have inferred from something Laura said, he was indirectly responsible for her drowning. Since her death, his imagination has played tricks with him. But is his supine acceptance at the moment of death connected with his guilt about his daughter? Is the hideous dwarf in some sense the figure of his dead daughter, returning to revenge herself on him, for his failing to prevent her life from ending?

2000: Clementine is in trouble again. One morning she asks her father if she can go to play at her friend Alexandra's house. Why, of course she can. At 4.30 p.m., the call comes: there's been an accident. Clementine has fallen over, and crashed into a low wall in Alexandra's parents' conservatory. She is not seriously hurt, but the impact has left her mouth a bloodied mess, and her teeth have come through her upper lip . . . Carolyn rushes home. I have an article to finish at my newspaper and must stick around. We talk on the phone, once Carolyn has surveyed the damage and returned from the hospital. I learn that my daughter is OK, but weepy and swollen and in need of a dentist to see if her teeth are going to survive the blow. Reassured, I meet a couple of friends for a drink and am home by 9 p.m. I expect to see a kid with a bruise and a cut lip. Instead, I stand in the hallway, aghast, while a frightful apparition comes down the stairs, trying to smile, shaking its head from left to right with awful menace. The whole of her five-year-old-face has changed. Her beautiful Bambi features have bolted like a cauliflower. Her perfect mouth, with its Jeanne Moreau pout, is swollen as if bicycle-pumped into a gross, porcine snout. She is unrecognisable as my baby daughter. She suddenly looks old, wrecked, grotesque, full of terrible experience. Instinctively, I cry out in alarm and she starts to weep because she knows – even at five – that her beauty has (temporarily) gone. I put my arms around her and coo in her ear that everything will be all right in a day or so, even while my heart is breaking that it may not be true. I look at her traumatised little face and wonder if it's all my fault, that I should never have let her go round to her friend's house to play, that I should have come home immediately to comfort her, that I should never ever let her out of my sight into a world where terrible things are lying in wait for her. And as I look at her smashed-up jaw, her exploded upper lip and blackened teeth, the dwarf from 'Don't Look Now' comes disoblig-ingly into my head, and I wonder if the way she looks now, and *the trauma in my heart, isn't some kind of fateful retribution for many moments of fatherly neglect in her short life . . .**

Pauline Kael, the great American movie critic, didn't like 'Don't Look Now'. She thought it was trash because all its high style was wasted on a subject as trite and silly as second sight. But as Neil Sinyard points out, in a fascinating book on Roeg's films, that all depends on whether you think second sight is an idiotic subject or something that can be made vividly real and alive in the cinema. It depends, he says, on 'whether you think it is part of the essence, and indeed greatness of cinema, that it can endow you, through montage, with the gift yourself'.

I emerged from the cinema bowled over by what I'd seen. I was so moved, I could barely speak. My date, Juliet, was shocked but not moved – shocked that such an intelligent film could have such a Grand Guignol ending. 'It's basically just an enormously protracted Hammer horror film with some clever editing,' she said. 'Isn't it?' I didn't agree. It was a great deal more than that.

---

* I once interviewed Nicolas Roeg, and asked him if he'd ever had any terrible shock about someone close to him when he was young. Yes, he said, there was the business of his father, who came back from the Second World War with a disfiguring injury to the side of his face. Roeg, who was seventeen when the war ended, had accepted it as just his dad's face. He had gone off to war when Nicolas was eleven, and the boy hardly remembered what his old man looked like before. But one afternoon a schoolfriend came to tea at the Roeg family home and later said, 'So how long has your father looked like that?' 'Like what?' asked Roeg. 'You know,' said his friend, tactlessly, 'all horribly disfigured.' They had tea *en famille*, and Nicolas sneaked a look at his father's face. 'And I registered for the first time that my father looked hideous, monstrous.' Hence the theme, in many Roeg films, of a love object – think of David Bowie in *The Man Who Fell to Earth* – turning out to be either hideous or mad, or an alien; or all three.

I told my pooh-poohing, intellectually brilliant friend Glyn how much I'd loved it, and went on about its 'implications' without knowing what I was talking about. He'd seen the film. 'Explain to me,' he said, 'what "implications" it could possibly have, except those of an averagely spooky adventure yarn.' I said, 'It makes you believe in Fate.'

I would say that today. The film presents its audience with a dazzling enigma of scenes from past, present and future that are finally resolved in its own filmic terms. When Baxter is dying, the scenes that flash before his eyes are not memories of his own life (we never learn John and Laura's circumstances before the death of their child, nor what John was doing for the forty-odd years he lived before it happened), but memories of where the camera has chosen to take us, to direct our gaze and channel our vision. They offer us a jigsaw of filmic seconds and moments, and dare us not to find them all interlinked. And in doing so, these scenes offer the unsettling suggestion that our lives too might, if examined from the outside, be full of similar random seconds and moments that add up to a similar frightening movement towards a destruction that is staring us in the face.

My whole life, when run on the flickering screen of the editing-room that lurks in the back of my head, is full of fearful images that correspond, with spooky fidelity, to the iconography of 'Don't Look Now': images of drowning at nine, images of fearful pursuit and near-death on Italian streets, images of religion, of children in the park, images of children in distress, one rescued from death at the point of birth, one falling through the air and crashing to earth, another flung into a watery doom by the father she trusts, and surfacing later in another random accident, disfigured and howling that it's all been *your fault*, Daddy, for not taking better care of me . . . It's as though I was given, at nineteen, a series of images of my future, of the joys of love and the fear of love, its very existence a challenge to my own fecklessness, my latent inadequacies, my capacity for neglect.

No wonder I was so bothered by the bloody movie. I *was* Donald Sutherland back then, vouchsafed a glimpse into a future that I wasn't equipped to handle.

No other film resonated both backwards and forwards in this way. 'Don't Look Now' has stayed in my head for years because it awoke echoes of danger and threat from my past, and hinted at epiphanies of danger and threat in the future, when I would have a partner, and difficult relationships, and children, and responsibility and that chronic 4 a.m. trauma, familiar to all family men, where you lie staring at the ceiling, worrying about money, work, the hole in the roof and the imminent plane flight, convinced that everything is tending towards tragedy.

Perhaps I had unresolved 'issues' back in 1973, about giving up the Catholic religion and having nothing to put in its place. But into the gap of belief came a new, secular obsession about the interconnectedness of things. I began to believe in signs and portents, clocking small events that seemed to conspire together to make a terrible mess of my life. Years later, I still believe in it. I watch in amazement as completely disparate events start to converge. A long-planned family holiday, say, is imminent. So is the deadline for an important article I'm writing for an American magazine. Unopened letters from the Inland Revenue have been piling up on the hall table for weeks. A strange grumbling sensation in the bowel region has been bothering me, intermittently. My credit card is nearing its limit. . . . And suddenly a high, thin violin note starts whining away at the back of your head and telling you something terrible is about to happen, although you could have guessed what it is because so many clues have been staring you in the face. Something called Fate has been gathering the strands of your life behind your back, silently braiding them together, and soon the master-plan behind it all will be revealed. The tax bailiff will appear on your doorstep demanding ten thousand pounds, just as the family are trying to finish packing and you are nearing the final American deadline, the bank rings to say some unknown person has been abusing your credit card, the bailiff takes your car, the holiday is in ruins, the children weep, and the grumbling bowel condition decides that *now* would be a good time to make itself apparent at last . . .

Rational people might write it off as a bizarre pile-up of coincidences. But you know in your secret heart that life has been storing up all this stuff, patiently, until the time when Fate can work its most spectacular mischief on you for not believing in it for so long.

'Don't Look Now' is the film that ends this book, not just because it's the film that affected me most profoundly in those dozen years of movie-going that began with the first visit to the Odeon, Leicester Square as an eight-year-old to see *Mutiny on the Bounty*. It's a climax of sorts because it shows how a film's influence can continue on into the future, working its alarming alchemy year after year, shadowing your life like a strange, un-shake-off-able *döppelganger*. Its correspondences with my life predated my seeing it. And when I did see it, I couldn't fathom why it moved me so much, because it hit me somewhere between the memory and the mind's apprehension of the future, and it has gone on since then, mirroring my own experience, far into the distance, long after the final credits rolled in the summer of 1973.

I don't believe in second sight, or in the afterlife. But 'Don't Look Now' portrayed the workings of Fate with such diligence that I lost more than a few wretched tears, and the last vestiges of religious faith, at nineteen. I lost the illusion that life is under your control. Nicolas Roeg, weaving his brilliant web of interconnections, succeeded, all those years ago, in making me believe my life was not in my own hands.

That's what the special movies of your youth can do. They offer you images of a counterlife that you might, but probably won't ever, live – dazzling, moonstruck, transformed and blissful. Or they show you something about your own life, pulling back the camera to reveal the bigger picture, displaying the way you live – hunted, querulous, endangered and doomed – as if your own life were itself a movie, with you in the bittersweet role of the struggling adventurer, the would-be swashbucker, the occasional hero who doesn't quite understand what's going on, the bourgeois dreamer who unfortunately dies in the last reel.

They reveal that your own life is a movie. You do not yet know who has written the script, or who is directing it or what the climax will be. But you would give anything to find out.

FURTHER READING

Sixties British Cinema by Robert Murphy (BFI Publishing, 1992)

English Gothic: A Century of Horror Cinema by Jonathan Rigby (Reynolds & Hearn, 2000)

The Crowded Prairie: American National Identity in the Hollywood Western by Michael Coyne (I.B. Tauris, 1997)

Easy Riders, Raging Bulls by Peter Biskind (Bloomsbury, 1997)

The Star-Spangled Screen: The American World War II Film by Bernard F. Dick (University Press of Kentucky, 1985)

Your Face Here: British Cult Movies Since the Sixties by Ali Catterall and Simon Wells (Fourth Estate, 2001)

Flickers: An Illustrated Celebration of 100 Years of Cinema by Gilbert Adair (Faber & Faber, 1995)

Illuminating Shadows: The Mythic Power of Film by Geoffrey Hill (Shambhala Publications, 1992)

All Pals Together: The Story of Children's Cinema by Terry Staples (Edinburgh University Press, 1997)

The Rough Guide to Cult Movies, edited by Paul Simpson (Rough Guides, 2001)

P.S.

Ideas,
interviews
& features...

Interview with John Walsh

By Rachel Holmes

'I KNEW I WANTED to be a journalist when I was sixteen.' John Walsh surveys the teatime cakes on offer in the Hay Festival hospitality tent, and opts for an impressive Victoria sponge. 'We had a class exercise to produce a piece of journalism in any style we liked. I wrote a film review of *2001: A Space Odyssey*. That was the start of it.' His shimmering blue Italian designer jacket is twinned wittily with striped bell-bottomed jeans, and his favourite skull ring. 'I interviewed my childhood hero Keith Richards. I used to do my homework listening to the Stones on a transistor radio. The part of me that was still a blithering fan just had to ask, "Keith, where do you get your rings?" After the interview I went to Crazy Pig Designs to buy my silver skull.'

Among a host of other events at Hay, John is here 'to talk bollocks about apostrophes' with Lynne Truss in the Channel Four tent. Eleven hundred tickets have been sold to an audience keen to hear Truss and Walsh debate grammar. This is reality TV for literary boffins. Does the celluloid guru watch reality TV? 'Out of the corner of my eye, over the shoulders of my kids. I just can't get over how unimaginative is this cult of Instant Fame. People are convinced they're wonderful and heroic just because *they turn up*. But then again . . . ,' he bites into a strawberry-topped piece of Victoria sponge, 'I am entranced by *Heat* magazine – it's full of things that are disgraceful at every level, and thus completely irresistible. So yes, I think there are better uses for public broadcast money than reality TV, but, who am I kidding, I'm a hypocrite.'

The reflexive undercut that pulls back from polemical judgement is typical Walsh. Central to his ingrained journalistic instinct, it also reveals one of the key seductions of his writing: its quality of inveterately humorous self-scrutiny. *The Falling Angels* and *Are You Talking to Me?* bring together the aching yearning for self-discovery with a life-embracing capacity for the comic. Walsh is always the target of his own satire, and the fall-guy in the general idiocy and hilarity of life. His work explores the ways in which, in the individual drama of our own consciousness, we imaginatively project ourselves as tragic-comic heroes. In often exquisite prose, Walsh teases at the constant ambivalence as to whether or not life should be taken seriously.

Walsh is not a natural joiner, and would probably scoff at being seen as belonging to something as conformist as a literary movement. Nevertheless he is one of the key writers of the new generation of memoirs published during the past decade. He offers homage to a pioneer: 'We are all in the debt of Blake Morrison. He did it first. Without him, none of us would ever have written books that are just about ourselves, our families and ordinary lives, rather than about famous ▶

> 6 Walsh is always the target of his own satire, and the fall-guy in the general idiocy and hilarity of life. 9

LIFE AT A GLANCE

BORN

24 October 1953 in
London, to Irish parents
Martin and Anne

EDUCATED

Wimbledon College;
Exeter College, Oxford;
University College, Dublin

MARRIED

No, though partnered
with Carolyn Hart and
three children, Sophie,
Max and Clementine

Interview with John Walsh *(continued)*

◄ people with extraordinary lives. People
read memoirs because of the quality of the
writing, and the value of the insights. Blake
Morrison freed all of us to do this.' In *The
Falling Angels* Walsh explains how his return
to Ireland to be with his dying mother
prompted his quest to write a book about his
dual cultural identity, and about his
relationship to the homeland of his parents
and ancestors. Walsh does not write about
belonging, but mines that rich seam of the
permanent state of in-between-ness, the
sense of constant alienation from a projected
true self, always just out of reach. It's the
element of alienation essential to genuinely
funny comedy, and it completely explains
how he came to write his second memoir,
Are You Talking to Me?, through the lens of
inspirational movies with which he grew up.

Are You Talking to Me? includes the
episode in which John launches his career as
an employee of Wandsworth Borough
Council. His English degree from Oxford
tucked into his back pocket, his first full-time
job was as a junior librarian at Wandsworth
Library. A series of deliciously comic mis-
understandings led to a swift sacking, and
John was back home on his uppers. His father
suggested postgraduate study at the
University of Dublin: 'You've been a fake
Irishman in England for long enough, now
go over there and be a fake Englishman in
Ireland.' Back in London with a first in (of
course) Anglo-Irish studies, John landed a
job with Victor Gollancz the publisher in
newly restored Covent Garden. He recalls
Angela Carter's visits: 'She was passionate

and marvellous, and had this gorgeous, sarcastic drawl. I hid behind the door in terrified adoration.' From Covent Garden publishing Bohemia he went to pillared, upholstered and posh offices in Pall Mall, where he wrote for *The Director*, in-house magazine of the Institute of Directors. Fate was waiting to ambush him, however, innocently cloaked in an apparently anodyne feature on the uses of graphology for corporate management evaluation. John playfully dropped a sample of his own handwriting into the examples sent for analysis. The profile came back, 'Number 6 appears to be an irascible middle manager of absolutely no ambition.' Is it true? he asked his boss. 'Well,' she said, 'apart from wanting to win the Nobel Prize for Literature, *do* you have any practical ambitions?' 'I was twenty-six. She sent me for a walk in St James's Park to think it over. I came back resolved. "When I am thirty-five I will be literary editor of the *Sunday Times*."' In fact, he got the editorship one month before his thirty-fifth birthday.

Four years down the line Walsh was feeling restless: 'Literary editing is much to do with Jiffy bags. Cascades of books arrive, in Jiffy bags. A sweaty urchin, always called Jerry, opens the Jiffy bags. Then you, the editor, knowledgeably select which books will be put back in Jiffy bags and sent out to reviewers (who also get a lot of Jiffy bags). Twice a year the media come to ask you who will win the Booker or a Nobel, and in between you do a great deal of air-kissing at literary events. After a while it seemed a bit limited. I wanted to write about other ▶

Top Ten Favourite Films

1. **Don't Look Now**
   Nicolas Roeg

2. **Cabaret**
   Bob Fosse

3. **The 39 Steps**
   Alfred Hitchcock

4. **Bonnie and Clyde**
   Arthur Penn

5. **Brief Encounter**
   David Lean

6. **City of God**
   Fernando Meireilles

7. **The Enigma of Kaspar Hauser**
   Werner Herzog

8. **The Piano**
   Jane Campion

9. **The Wild Bunch**
   Sam Peckinpah

10. **This is Spinal Tap**
    Rob Reiner

Interview with John Walsh (continued)

◀ things – movies, music, fashion, travel, everything – as well as books.' Key roles as features editor of the *Evening Standard*, editor of the *Independent Magazine*, and now assistant editor of the *Independent*, fulfilled this ambition to expand his range.

The cinematic leads with whom the young Walsh identifies in *Are You Talking to Me?* are all figures of male heroism. Are there any female figures for him now? 'Sigourney Weaver in *Alien*, stripped down to her knickers in the space pod.' (I'm unclear at this point whether he identifies with Sigourney Weaver, or the alien fortunate enough to find itself in her pod.) 'She's one of the most admirable figures from the eighties' cinema, a great image of human heroism and human compassion.' Were Armageddon imminent, the three films he would choose to watch for the last time would be the Marx Brothers' *Duck Soup*, Hitchcock's *Foreign Correspondent* (the journalist-hero movie is a favourite genre) and Jane Campion's *The Piano*: 'It's absolutely beautiful. Perfect. Mind you,' he pauses, 'you'd think Baines could have given her something better than a *metal* prosthetic finger, he's meant to be bloody inventive for chrissake.' But, changing register in a characteristic move from humour to pathos, his conclusion is elegiac: 'I am transfixed by that moment when the piano and Ada (Holly Hunter) go over the side of the boat, and those lines from the Thomas Hood poem, "There is a silence where hath been no sound/There is a silence where no sound may be . . ."'

Walsh's cultural in-between-ness is the

grit in his literary oyster. To his pleasure and surprise, his children have recently shown signs of allegiance to their Celtic heritage, knowing instinctively the difference made by having 'another string to their bow of identity'. In some ways John Walsh is as English as Victoria sponge at teatime. His books lure you with the uncanny to be found in the comfortably familiar. But the polyphonic melody of his writing, and the critical underside of the Victoria sponge, come from the double vision of his Anglo-Irish inheritance. The relentless twinkle in his eye, and the brightness of his writing, are part fantastic humour, part the reflection of Celtic twilight. ■

Top Ten Favourite Books

1. **Ulysses**
   James Joyce

2. **Catch-22**
   Joseph Heller

3. **Confessions of a Justified Sinner**
   James Hogg

4. **Our Mutual Friend**
   Charles Dickens

5. **Germinal**
   Emile Zola

6. **The Grapes of Wrath**
   John Steinbeck

7. **The Pursuit of Love**
   Nancy Mitford

8. **Molloy/Malone Dies/The Unnameable**
   Samuel Beckett

9. **Enemies of Promise**
   Cyril Connolly

10. **The Age of Illusion**
    Ronald Blythe

I Found It at the Movies: Silver-Screen Epiphanies

By John Walsh

I'VE ALWAYS BEEN fascinated by the curious things that influence a generation – the songs, the catchphrases, the pungent ephemera, the airborne virus of rebellion that crossed oceans and continents in the 1960s, the cultural flotsam that bobs around us for far longer than it should when we're growing up – and one day I decided to write a book about it. It seemed obvious to me that the films we see when we're at our most impressionable – from the age of about seven to about twenty-one – give us images and scenes and close-up faces that imprint themselves on the back of our consciousness and give us a particular, perhaps a skewed, perspective on the world that lasts, that goes on and on. When I started writing this book, in May 2002, I talked to several people about the films they saw, when they were young, which bothered them or puzzled them or stayed with them in some way. The replies were very interesting.

Ian Jack, the editor of *Granta*, told me he grew up with a chronic terror of the IRA – not because of the Troubles after 1969, but because they were the bad guys in a 1937 Will Hay movie called *Oh Mr Porter*, set on a single-branch railway line in Ireland. Francine Stock, from Radio 4's *Front Row*, told me that, at her girls' boarding school, on rainy afternoons when they couldn't play netball or lacrosse, the girls were allowed to stay in and watch a film. But the only film the school seemed to possess was *Throne of*

Blood, Kurosawa's savage reworking of
Macbeth. So for years she associated carefree
girlish recreation with deranged Japanese
faces, with woodland witchcraft and blood-
boltered mayhem.

John Boorman, the British director of
Point Blank, *Deliverance* and *The Tailor of
Panama*, told me that he (and perhaps his
generation) had picked up the first germs of
post-war anti-authoritarianism, the first
stirrings of social revolution, in Powell and
Pressburger's *The Life and Death of Colonel
Blimp*. The great Robert Altman, director of
MASH, *A Wedding* and *Gosford Park* and the
cinema's most consistently brilliant *épateur de
genres*, told me that his big defining moment
in the cinema wasn't watching some
subversive tract. It was *Brief Encounter*. He
used to go to the movies, he said, in order to
get off with girls. One day, uncharacteristically
by himself, he'd wandered into an art-house to
watch the only thing playing, 'and when I came
out,' he said, 'completely in love with this plain
and nagging-voiced Englishwoman who
wasn't like anyone I'd ever met, I realized the
power of what cinema can do, and resolved to
be a part of it.'

We know, of course, that movies give us a
view of the world that may be idealized,
sanitized, melodramatized or tragified, but
will always be more vivid than reality. It gives
us a procession of human types, heroic
archetypes, character stereotypes rather than
real people. And it gives us a whole series of ▶

‘ The great
Robert Altman
used to go to the
movies, he said,
in order to get off
with girls. ’

I Found It at the Movies...
(continued)

◄ repeated filmic tropes, movie-shorthand situations and hackneyed effects that recur from film to film, as if the world portrayed on celluloid had a number of rules all its own. You know the kind of thing I mean:

- Anyone who shares a night of passion with Sharon Stone or Glenn Close always has the foresight to pull their underpants back on before sleep overwhelms them, so they can get out of bed without embarrassment in the morning.
- In any cop thriller, no investigating officer will ever defeat the villain until he has been officially taken off the case by an exasperated senior detective.
- Asking directions to Castle Dracula in any Transylvanian pub, no matter how quietly you pitch your voice, will always silence the rowdiest clientele of inbred hairy yokels.
- Any proposal of marriage in a modern American romantic comedy is considered more effective if made in front of hordes of people in a bar, a restaurant or a train station.
- If anyone goes shopping for groceries in a Hollywood movie, they always buy a baguette, so it can be seen sticking out their shopping bag when they get home. Otherwise they might run the risk of looking like a Bag Person.
- If anyone in a room switches off the bedside light, the room will not go dark. It will look exactly the same, only blue.

> Movies give us a view of the world that may be idealized, sanitized, melodramatized or tragified, but will always be more vivid than reality.

These are the sillier lessons you learn from the movies. But there are more important things you learn from them – like outrage. Nobody could emerge from watching, say, Kubrick's *Paths of Glory* or Joseph Losey's *King and Country* without feeling a personal indignation about the courts martial and the executions. Of course you could be moved to tears by other anti-war art-forms – by the poems of Owen and Sassoon, by *Birdsong* and *Catch-22* – but without, I think, experiencing the same intense ninety-minute empathy with the screen deserters, the look on their faces, the pathos of their inevitable end.

In the courtroom drama *Twelve Angry Men* Henry Fonda is at the wrong end of an 11–1 jury split and has to convince his fuming co-jurors, in a stifling courtroom during a heatwave, that words like justice and truth and understanding are more than just platitudes. Crucial to the film's effect on us was that it offered a rare dramatization of logic – Fonda's bit-by-bit examination of the evidence – and showed that rational argument, if followed sufficiently scrupulously, could win over ignorant prejudice and lazy assumptions, even if the opposition is ranged 11–1 against you.

Logic didn't, of course, always carry the day in the cinema of influence. Sometimes it was hidden or abandoned altogether. My generation of aspirant hippies was collectively traumatized by the end of *Easy Rider*, when the two bikers, Peter Fonda and Dennis Hopper, get shot dead by a couple of ▶

> ❝My generation of aspirant hippies was collectively traumatized by the end of *Easy Rider*❞

I Found It at the Movies ...
(continued)

◄ passing rednecks. It was, in hindsight, a completely arbitrary finale – the equivalent of a novel ending 'Then a volley of shots rang out and they all fell dead. The End' – but we all sat there, outraged and appalled that such a thing could happen, and instinctively blaming the American military-industrial complex, or whatever we assumed must be responsible. The only person responsible was, of course, the writer/director Hopper, but we were too lost in sympathy for poor, dead, idiotic Billy to register that. Behind the hair, moustache, hat and fringed jacket, Billy was an innocent, a fretful, stoned, giggling kid who looked to Captain America to look after him. He was just one of literally hundreds of little-brother figures the movies offer you.

After outrage, sympathy is what the cinema most vividly teaches you – sympathy with innocents-in-danger, even though they come in a hundred shapes and sizes. The kids in Charles Laughton's *Night of the Hunter*, on the run from Robert Mitchum's frightening homicidal preacher, are obvious examples, as are the Dickens children in David Lean's *Oliver Twist* and *Great Expectations*. Less obvious are the young cowboys, Horst Bucholst in *The Magnificent Seven*, whiningly tagging along with the six grown-ups and trying to join in their games, and Angel in Peckinpah's *The Wild Bunch*, pinching a few of the Generalissimo's guns to help out his struggling peasant community, but becoming the agent of all the gang's deaths by the end.

> ❝After outrage, sympathy is what the cinema most vividly teaches you❞

It doesn't take a genius to see that ET is a kid brother, or perhaps a baby brother, grotesque and unwelcome at first, but becoming more charming as he is gradually socialized. So is the Elephant Man, from whom we shrink at first (understandably) but for whom we weep real tears as he finds a home at the hospital and learns to be gracious, vain and stage-struck. If you press me, I would maintain that both King Kong and Frankenstein tug at our kind-sibling heartstrings and dare us not to find them sweet, misunderstood and far from home, out of step with a world that finds them horrifying, rather than just confused and a bit peculiar-looking.

Third, the movies taught us about beauty in a close-up, dropped-jaw, intensely personal way, as no novel, no stage drama, no TV show ever could. I mean beauty caught in tiny moments, like the first appearance of Grace Kelly in *Rear Window*, when she kisses the slumbering James Stewart, and Hitchcock films the kiss in slow motion, as if he simply *cannot believe* how beautiful Ms Kelly is. Or the face of Julie Christie in *Billy Liar*, her third film but her début as perfect Sixties girl – the ideal woman as a freewheeling dreamboat, forever on the move, her huge wide mouth and artlessly crinkly smile expressing indulgence and sympathy and love, but also her tiny *tristesse*: she'd love to stick around and save your life but she has to be moving right along now . . .

My book is about a number of personal epiphanies connected with moviegoing ▶

> I would maintain that both King Kong and Frankenstein tug at our kind-sibling heartstrings

13

I Found It at the Movies...
(continued)

◄ when you're young and foolish and hot to try out new things, new personalities. It's about how some movies – whatever shifting moralities they may inculcate – can make you do weird stuff. I wouldn't want to make excessive claims for the cinema's role in world affairs, but it is interesting to learn that Adolf Hitler was a big fan of *Gone With the Wind*, presumably more for its heroine's obsession with land than for the appeal of her swishy crinolines; interesting that Josef Goebbels admired Hitchcock's *Foreign Correspondent* as a masterpiece of propaganda; interesting that, in North Korea, Kim Jong-Il hired a film director, gave him some money and told him to make 'good films', like his own favourites. Which were? It seems he especially favoured the Rambo films starring Sylvester Stallone, the many *Friday the Thirteenth* slasher pictures, and middle-period James Bond movies, starring Roger Moore. How extraordinary to think that the North Korean dictator wasn't content just to be a Beloved Leader. Clearly what he secretly wanted was to drive a customized Aston Martin, shag Britt Ekland and talk to his associates (and enemies) in a succession of suave innuendoes.

It was riveting to discover, from the journalist Adel Darwish, that he had met Saddam Hussein in the mid-1970s, when Saddam was a humble deputy in the ruling party, and that they'd talked for two hours. What had been the subject? Oil? Arab unity? American imperialism? No – according to Darwish, he'd just gone on and on about the brilliance of *The Godfather*. Watching

> ❝It is interesting to learn that Adolf Hitler was a big fan of *Gone With the Wind*❞

George Bush, a year ago, arriving in an aircraft carrier to address troops in the Gulf, sporting a USAF uniform complete with wings (to which of course he is not entitled), I couldn't help but think: Here is a man who watched *The Longest Day* when he was – what? 16? – and has ever since wanted to be Robert Mitchum or John Wayne leading the Normandy landings. You look at Donald Rumsfeld and see a man whose main attribute for the job of Secretary of State is that he looks (but not quite sounds) like a four-star general from Central Casting. You can't help wondering if, when they initiated the war in Iraq last year, they were confident of victory because that's how it works out in Hollywood movies when you send off bombing missions. Nobody on the big screen worries that you may be destabilizing the Middle East for ever.

Movies redefine reality for us. They show us the world through a thousand new perspectives. They offer us versions of ourselves to which we may aspire, they tease and taunt us with a counter-life that could be ours if only we were bolder or better people. We must, however, learn to resist the promise of filmland, that we can alter our lives by clinging faithfully to the idealism (or the heady corruption) of celluloid. You start off pursuing girls just because they look like Natalie Wood or Julie Christie. Next thing you know, you'll be invading neutral countries, declaring a thousand-year Reich and muttering under your breath: 'Look, Ma! Made it! Top of the world!' ∎

> ❝Nobody on the big screen worries that you may be destabilizing the Middle East for ever. ❞

Have You Read?

The Falling Angels (Flamingo)
The story of a London-Irish boy who has two identities and feels at home in neither. John Walsh found the Irishness of his parents' Battersea home stiflingly warm and puzzlingly foreign. Spellbound equally by Mick Jagger and images of Irish martyrdom, he discovered at the age of sixteen an extended family he had never known existed. In the hidden life of Galway was a revelation that begged a crucial question: how do we know where our true nature lies? By his mother's bedside in a Galway hospital, thirty years later, he starts to unpick the past, looking for clues to his identity.

'The reader should be warned that this is a book that makes you laugh out loud in public. A magnificent entertainment.'
Bernard O'Donoghue, *Independent*